Indigenous Language Media, Language Politics and Democracy in Africa

Indigenous Language Media, Language Politics and Democracy in Africa

Edited by

Abiodun Salawu
North-West University, South Africa

and

Monica B. Chibita
Uganda Christian University, Uganda

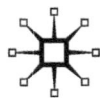

First published 2016 by
PALGRAVE MACMILLAN

Palgrave Macmillan in the UK is an imprint of Macmillan Publishers Limited, registered in England, company number 785998, of Houndmills, Basingstoke, Hampshire RG21 6XS.

Palgrave Macmillan in the US is a division of St Martin's Press LLC, 175 Fifth Avenue, New York, NY 10010.

Palgrave Macmillan is the global academic imprint of the above companies and has companies and representatives throughout the world.

Palgrave® and Macmillan® are registered trademarks in the United States, the United Kingdom, Europe and other countries.

ISBN 978–1–137–54729–3

This book is printed on paper suitable for recycling and made from fully managed and sustained forest sources. Logging, pulping and manufacturing processes are expected to conform to the environmental regulations of the country of origin.

A catalogue record for this book is available from the British Library.

Library of Congress Cataloging-in-Publication Data
Indigenous language media, language politics and democracy in Africa / Abiodun Salawu, North-West University, South Africa ; Monica B. Chibita, Uganda Christian University, Uganda, [editors].
pages cm
Includes bibliographical references.
ISBN 978–1–137–54729–3
1. Mass media and language—Africa, Sub-Saharan.   2. Mass media—Africa, Sub-Saharan—History—20th century.   3. Local mass media—Africa, Sub-Saharan—History—20th century.   4. Mass media—Political aspects—Africa, Sub-Saharan.   5. Indigenous peoples—Africa, Sub-Saharan—Communication.   I. Chibita, Monica Balya, editor.   II. Salawu, Abiodun, editor.   III. Title.
P96.L342A35749 2015
306.44'967—dc23   2015023415

Typeset by MPS Limited, Chennai, India.

Contents

**Part III   The Indigenous Language Media in
Political and Cultural Expression in Africa**

List of Figures and Tables

Figures

Tables

Foreword

This volume on indigenous language media, language politics and democracy is an invaluable contribution to the growing literature on African media and critical media studies as a field of inquiry in Africa. Indigenous language media and the dynamics of the role of the media in democratization have been largely neglected in studies of the media in Africa, which has had a bias towards studying privately owned print media and the emergence of privately owned FM radio stations that coincided with the 'democratization era' of the late 1980s and 1990s.

In this phase the focus was on how privately owned media and the FM radio stations that emerged from the 'liberalization of the airwaves' provided voices for a range of democratic actors, from opposition movements preaching a gospel of multi-party democracy to civil society organizations focused on human and women's rights, the youth and economic actors wanting free-market policies that had been shut out of state-owned and/or controlled media. Mediation of opposition discourses was the focus if not the obsession. Analysis of language was ignored and by default the language(s) of mediation were assumed to be English or European languages like French. Mainstream print and broadcast media were also the mediums receiving the most analytical attention.

What this volume does is to shine a critical analytical focus on indigenous languages, which are the languages spoken by most people even if they might not be used by most of the mainstream media in those genres that explicitly deal with issues of democratic politics. Ironically, indigenous languages often reach the largest audiences in broadcast space.

The volume is rich because it covers different mediums – from print media through different forms of radio to emergent online media – as well as a range of African countries including those with large populations, like Nigeria, Kenya and South Africa, and small countries like Malawi; it also covers community media and not just the mainstream media. In this regard, the book demonstrates that even though Africa is a continent with over 50 countries, there is merit in producing a volume that investigates trends, patterns and developments that are comparable.

The book is invaluable because it does not romanticize or shy away from the complexities and dynamics of the use of indigenous languages across different mediums, which can both promote democratic discourses and also mediate discourses that promote genocide (as happened in Rwanda in the early 1990s or inter-ethnic conflict in the case of Kenya). The focus on appropriation of indigenous languages in the commercial media domain and discourses is an interesting departure from an approach that can tie indigenous languages to a burden of maintaining ethnic identities and reminiscing about an African past, into an exploration of the dynamism of languages and their deployment in ever-changing political, commercial and technological environments as well identities that are in a state of flux in Africa.

This volume will contribute to the ongoing creation of a distinct tradition of African media studies and the de-Westernization of media studies globally.

Professor Tawana Kupe,
University of Witwatersrand, South Africa

Acknowledgements

We are grateful to the contributors and thank them for their confidence in us. We also thank them for their patience, since this project started in 2012.

We thank all the organisations whose platforms we used to make the Call for Chapters. These include the South African Communication Association, the International Association for Media and Communication Research and the Nigeria Chapter of the African Council for Communication Education. We also thank every colleague who assisted us in reviewing the papers we received in response to our call.

We acknowledge Tawana Kupe, Associate Professor of Media Studies and currently Deputy Vice-Chancellor (Advancement, HR and Transformation) at the University of the Witwatersrand, South Africa, who wrote the Foreword. We also thank our friends Felicity Plester and Sneha Kamat Bhavnani at Palgrave Macmillan and Geetha Williams at MPS Limited for their support in the course of publishing the book.

The National Research Foundation (of South Africa) is acknowledged for providing Abiodun with a Knowledge, Interchange and Collaboration (KIC) grant for Africa Interaction. This enabled him to visit the Uganda Christian University in Mukono in 2014 in furtherance of the collaboration between him and Monica on the project.

There are many other people we are indebted to, who are closely or remotely connected to this project. We are grateful for being able to forge a partnership with all of you that has resulted in this volume. Thank you all.

Abiodun, Mafikeng, South Africa
Monica, Mukono, Uganda

Notes on Contributors

Ufuoma Akpojivi is a lecturer in the Media Studies Department, School of Literature, Language and Media, University of the Witwatersrand, South Africa. His research interests are in the areas of citizenship, new media and political participation, media policy, journalism ethics and practices in Africa, media and democratization processes in emerging democracies, amongst others.

Thabisile Buthelezi is an associate professor at the University of KwaZulu-Natal in the Language and Arts Cluster of the School of Education. She is a qualified teacher, nurse and practitioner in adult basic education and training. She has vast experience in teacher education. She teaches at both undergraduate and postgraduate levels and supervises postgraduate research at all levels. She is a recognised scholar and a researcher rated by the South African National Research Foundation. Her research interests are in the areas of African languages, language education, curriculum studies, sexuality education, HIV and AIDS in curricula and indigenous knowledge systems.

Monica B. Chibita is Associate Professor and Head of the Department of Mass Communication at Uganda Christian University. She has also taught at Makerere University. She is a member of the editorial/advisory board of several refereed academic journals. Her research and publications have been in the areas of media and democracy with a focus on broadcast media regulation, indigenous language media and media curriculum and training.

Modestus Fosu is a lecturer at the Ghana Institute of Journalism, Accra. His research interests include the language of news, news readability and comprehension, media and journalism education, media and society in Ghana, and similar socio-political societies.

Itohan Mercy Idumwonyi is a university lecturer at the University of Benin, Nigeria and a doctoral student at Rice University, Houston, US. Her research interests encompass women and gender studies, African religions, and African Christianity and Pentecostalism with an emphasis on women and gender dynamics in Nigerian Pentecostalism and Benin religion. She has had articles published on culture, gender and African religions. Her work has appeared in *Orita: Ibadan Journal of Religious Studies* and *African Journal of Legal Studies*. She is a fellow of the prestigious American Association of University Women (AAUW) and the Forum for Theological Exploration.

Ijeweimen Solomon Ikhidero is a researcher who holds an MA in African religion. His research interest revolves around the re-awakening of African value systems in the modern world. His work has been published in the *Ilorin Journal of Religious Studies*. He is the author of *The Matrimonial Oath of Fidelity among the Benin of Southern Nigeria: Its Ethical Implications for Postcolonial Nigeria* (2014).

John Lwanda has lived in Zimbabwe, Malawi and Scotland. A physician and social historian, his research interests include collecting, archiving and recording popular and traditional music. His PhD examined culture, politics and medicine with reference to HIV/AIDS in Malawi. His books include: *Kamuzu Banda of Malawi* (2010), *Politics, Culture and Medicine in Malawi* (2005), *Music, Culture and Orature: The Malawi Public Sphere, 1949–2006* (2008), and *Promises, Power Politics and Poverty: Democratic Transition in Malawi, 1961–1999* (forthcoming, 2015). He has contributed book chapters, including 'Politics, Culture and Medicine: An Unholy Trinity?' in Kalipeni et al. (eds) *HIV/AIDS in Africa: Beyond Epidemiology* (2004), as well as a variety of academic and scholarly papers.

Brilliant Mhlanga holds a PhD from the University of Westminster, London, UK. He is a member of the Mass Communications Group and Lecturer in Media Cultures at the University of Hertfordshire, UK. He remains affiliated to the National University of Science and Technology (NUST), Zimbabwe. He is working on a number of projects including a book titled *Bondage of Boundaries and the 'Toxic Other' in Postcolonial Africa: The Northern Problem and Identity Politics Today* and another project, provisionally titled 'On the Banality of Evil: Cultural Particularities and Genocide in Africa'. His research interests include media and development communication, community radio, ethnic minority media, ethnicity, nationalism and postcolonial studies, and the media policies and political economy of the media.

Uzoma Chukwuemeka Okugo is an associate professor in the Department of Mass Communication at Abia State University, Nigeria. He holds a doctorate in Mass Communication. His areas of interest include media theories, effects and radio/TV production. He is a renowned and prolific scholar, with well over 50 international and local publications, and is a member of the African Council for Communication Education (ACCE).

Philip Oburu is Assistant Professor in the School of Social Communication at Saint Paul University, Ottawa, Canada. His research revolves around interactive digital media and social activism in transitional democracies, including the roles of media in conflict transformation and humanitarian intervention.

Chimaobi Dick Onwukwe is a lecturer in the Department of Linguistics and Communication Studies/Igbo at Abia State University, Nigeria. He is a doctoral candidate in the same department. His work is widely published in the fields of both linguistics and communication. He is a member of the African Council for Communication Education (ACCE) and the Linguistics Association of Nigeria (LAN).

Abiodun Salawu is Professor of Journalism, Communication and Media Studies at North-West University, South Africa. His writing on the subject of African language media has been widely published. He edited the seminal book *Indigenous Language Media in Africa* (2006).

Oloruntola Sunday is Senior Lecturer in the Department of Mass Communication, University of Lagos, Nigeria. He holds a PhD in agricultural communication from the Federal University of Agriculture, Abeokuta, Nigeria, and a BSc and MSc in communication from the University of Lagos, Nigeria. He worked as a reporter and production sub-editor in different media houses in Nigeria before becoming an academic. He has a number of published local and international articles to his credit. His areas of interest include the ethics of mass communication, editorial writing and theories of mass communication. He is also interested in print and Development Journalism, conflict transformation and humanitarian intervention.

Introduction: Language, Structure and Agency: Optimising Media Diversity in Africa Using the Indigenous Languages

Monica B. Chibita and Abiodun Salawu

Language plays a crucial role in the media as a key public domain, to the extent that the languages people use in the media determine their chances of getting heard. However, there are numerous forces determining which languages are used in the public domain and the hierarchy of their deployment. This point has been debated extensively in the literature of language ideology. In her seminal work in this area, Woolard (1992, pp. 235–236), for instance, suggests that to the extent that language is the vehicle of large proportions of media content, it is linked to expression and to power. According to Woolard, "language stands in dialectical relation with, and thus significantly influences, social, discursive and linguistic practices". There also exists a dialectical relationship between language attitudes and the roles different languages are assigned in the public domain. Because of the important role of language, this relationship constitutes an important issue for discussion in the context of the media's role in inclusion and exclusion and in the overall democratisation project in Africa. Political economy scholars have for over two decades made the same point about the relationship/s between language, diversity, expression and democracy (see, for instance Golding and Murdock 1991; Goldsmith Media Group 2000; Gurevitch 2000; McChesney 2000; Bagdikian 2014). Curran's seminal argument (1991, p. 23) has been fundamental to this argument. He says:

> A basic requirement of a democratic media system should be that it represents all significant interests in society. It should facilitate their participation in the public domain, enable them to contribute to public debate and have an input in the framing of public policy. The media should also represent the functioning of representative

organisations and expose their internal processes to public scrutiny and the play of public opinion. In short a central role of the media should be defined as assisting the equitable negotiation or arbitration of competing interests through democratic processes.

There is no denying that language plays a key role in facilitating this kind of participation as it enables people to express themselves in ways that most represent their views and experiences. This book seeks to place indigenous language media in Africa in a particular socio-historical context with a view to highlighting their role in enhancing Africans' political participation and cultural expression in their local environs.

Typically, the roles African languages play in the public domain in Africa have been linked to colonial policies of marginalisation, and to a large extent, accepted as the norm. Thus, by force of historical circumstance, it is believed that certain sections of the population in Africa have had privileged access to public information and expression because of their linguistic competencies. While it is important to look at language competence and access as structurally conditioned, one must also pay attention to agency: the language choices that individuals or communities make at the micro level in spite of policy, colonial history and other structural factors. Such choices can work hand in hand with structural factors to enhance the kind of participation that increases chances of political participation and cultural expression. Thus, beyond seeing African peoples as victims of language hegemony, both at micro and macro levels, this book is interested in considering human agency in the choice and use of language in the media. The point here is that people can actually be protagonists of cultural assertiveness through the promotion of their local languages in ways that are innovative. In this book we examine the manner and the extent to which the indigenous languages continue to be deployed in liberalised media environments by government, civil society and individuals in Africa, and the impact of this. Thus, while the book grapples with the language of politics, it also considers the *politics of language*, that is, the motives behind the choice of languages used in the political and cultural domains.

It is true that the politics of language in Africa today is, to a great extent, part of the legacy of colonialism (see for instance, Bamgboṣe 1991; Mamdani 2001; Salhi 2002; du Plessis 2011; Meeuwis 2011). Meeuwis (2011) in particular presents an insightful analysis of different colonial approaches to language. While England, Germany and Belgium adopted a policy of adaptationism (also called acculturationism or indirect rule), which involved the colonised peoples taking on the language and aspects of the culture of the colonial power *alongside* their own, France and Poland adopted assimilationism, which required the colonised peoples to adopt the language and culture of the colonisers in exchange for the privilege of citizenship to the latters' countries. These positions influenced the deployment of the colonial languages vis-à-vis the indigenous languages in key sectors, notably the media.

In Anglophone Africa, the English language media today remain the mainstream media, particularly in the print sector. In the Francophone world of Africa, French is the predominant language of the media as well (Diallo 2011). Portuguese dominates mediated communication in Lusophone Africa. Wali, however, argues that "the whole uncritical acceptance of English and French as the inevitable medium for educated African writing is misdirected and has no chance of advancing African literature and culture" (Wali 1963: 13–15). Building on this argument in the context of the history of Kenya's language policy, Ngugi wa Thiong'o writes, "English became more than a language: it was *the* language and all the others had to bow before it in deference" (wa Thiong'o 1986: 11). Wa Thiong'o offers an explanation of the positions of West European languages and African languages:

Today, the West European languages and African languages are where they are in relation to one another, not because they are inherently progressive or backward but because of the history of oppression on the one hand, and the resistance to that oppression on the other. (1993: 36)

Recognising that the West European languages are the languages of power yet they are spoken by a minority in most African communities, wa Thiong'o further contends:

English, French and Portuguese are the languages in which the African people have been educated; for this reason the results of our research into science, technology and of our achievements in the creative arts are stored in those languages. Thus a large portion of this vast knowledge is locked up in the linguistic prison of English, French and Portuguese. Even the libraries are really English (or indeed French or Portuguese) language fortresses inaccessible to the majority. So, the cultivation of these languages makes for more effective communication only between the elite and the international English-speaking bourgeoisie. (1993, p. 37; see also wa Thiong'o 2014)

Wa Thiong'o's decision to do his subsequent creative writings in his native Gikuyu language was predicated on the argument stated above. He also strongly recommends to fellow African writers to produce their literature in African languages.

Ngugi's stance, however, has been faulted by some African writers and literary critics, notably Chinua Achebe. Achebe contends that he has no choice but to write in English (Achebe 1976; Jalali and Ansaripour 2014). Achebe argues that the colonial language is the language that can reach the whole country, like English in Nigeria or Portuguese in Angola. He further argues that European languages can be Africanised to serve African ideas and interests. Achebe adds, however, that the price a world language must be prepared to pay is submission to many different kinds of use (Achebe 1976; see also Achebe 1997; Jalali and Ansaripour 2014). Others who have argued against Ngugi's stance include Moore (2004) and Vakunta (2010).

This book deals with the often neglected link between indigenous languages, the media and democracy in Africa. It explores the politics associated with the use or lack of use of indigenous languages in Africa. Language enables both political and cultural expression as well as identity formation. The book recognises that the media indeed play a key amplifying or "publicising" role without which modern-day expression, public participation and ultimately democracy would be inconceivable. It recognises that the majority of African nations today have, at the formal level, opened up to a multiplicity of media channels and to a variety of political views. However, whether this plurality equals diversity in different African contexts remains a matter for more specific scrutiny. Mirroring the argument of the Goldsmith Media Group, the authors of several of the chapters in this book recognise that one must make a distinction between access that enables consumption as opposed to access that enables plurality and diversity. The Goldsmith Media Group (2000, p. 54) put it this way:

The media, as forms of communication at a distance, raise issues of participation which are not reducible to questions of consumer choice. It is not normally an issue, let alone an issue of public importance, whether you had the opportunity to participate in the production of the clothes you wear. It is an issue, and one of fundamental public importance, what opportunities you had to participate in the representation to others of your living conditions, your opinions, your forms of cultural expression. The latter are fundamentally issues not merely of choice, but of control; they are issues of freedom, which must be addressed at the social level.

The volume places indigenous language media in Africa in a particular socio-historical context with a view to highlighting their role in enhancing Africans' cultural and political participation in their local environs. The chapters in the book fall into three broad areas: (i) Indigenous languages, media and democracy in Africa; (ii) the media, language, inclusion and exclusion in Africa; and (iii) the indigenous language media in political and cultural expression in Africa.

In Part I, Salawu and Chibita's chapters discuss the contribution of the indigenous language media to political participation and to democratisation. In "Indigenous Language Media and Democracy in Africa" Salawu argues that language plays a crucial role in the media as a key public domain. He contends that there is a link between roles assigned to different languages and the attitudes towards these languages, and the extent to which the speakers of these languages can make themselves heard through the media. Contrary to the view, however, that colonialism has doomed the African languages to taking an inferior position, he argues that Africans can, and have, become agents of empowering their languages to increase their political participation and efficacy. Chibita's chapter, "Indigenous Language Media and Freedom of Expression in Uganda", based on an empirical study of Ugandan listeners' and viewers' perceptions of the media's performance on a range of counts, including the enhancement of freedom of expression, demonstrates that while there is some truth in the argument that the more media outlets a polity has, the greater the chances that a more diverse set of views and cultures will be accommodated, this depends on a number of other structural and symbolic factors. Chibita therefore discusses public perceptions of constraints including the architecture of media ownership, the linguistic accessibility of the media, the manner in which the media are regulated, the capacity of citizens to own and to use the media and the extent to which Ugandan citizens perceive themselves as actually free to enjoy freedoms such as media freedom and freedom of expression.

In Part II, Buthelezi's chapter, "IsuZulu Language and the *Ilanga* Newspaper as Catalysts for Participatory Democracy in South Africa", discusses how isiZulu language and media "became reflective tools through which the colonised critically and collectively reflected on their "neophyte colonised identities and their African identities". Using a language and power framework, and taking the *Ilanga* newspaper as a case, Buthelezi argues that being able to reflect on and critique the colonial experience in their own language was key to the Zulu people's preservation of their identity and culture.

In "The Return of the local: Community Radio as Dialogic and Participatory", based on an empirical study, Mhlanga tackles the important subject of community media as a participatory, dialogic forum. He questions the gap between the ideal and reality, asking to what extent community media in South Africa are icons of equality, community participation and representation. Based on the case of XK FM, which serves the !Xû and Khwe communities of South Africa, Mhlanga argues that because community radio operates as an "alternative" medium, it offers local communities an opportunity to critique cultural "distortions inherent in the majority-controlled media", and to participate in and own the process of social transformation. He places the indigenous languages at the centre of this empowerment process.

Onwukwe and Chukwuemeka's chapter, "The Englishisation of the World Wide Web: Implications for Indigenous Languages in Nigeria" draws to our attention the fact that the English language is the predominant language of the world wide web. Hardware and software are configured to process data in English. The majority of websites are in the English language. They argue that considering the over 400 languages in Nigeria, this situation poses serious challenges in the development of the indigenous languages in Nigeria. The chapter examines the prospects of using the indigenous languages in Nigeria for information and communication on the web. The authors agree that this is a positive move towards expanding the frontiers of usage of Nigerian languages and encouraging their appreciation in the light of the rising nonchalant attitude towards indigenous languages, particularly among the youth. However, they identify technological and human requirements as possible set-backs to any move towards the standardisation and expanded use of Nigerian languages on the world wide web.

Akpojivi and Fosu's chapter, titled "Indigenous Language Broadcasting in Ghana: Retrospect and Prospect", also based on an empirical study, argues that although the media in Ghana were liberalized, starting in 1992, plurality has not equalled diversity. In particular, they point out the marginalisation of the indigenous languages leading to the exclusion of large sections of the population. Akpovi and Fosu, however, see some hope in the form of the Guidelines for Local Language

Broadcasting by the National Media Commission, whose introduction, they argue, has enabled the broadcast media to increase the use of the indigenous languages, thus allowing more of the underprivileged members of society to participate in the media.

The chapters in Part III focus on the importance of the indigenous language media's significance for political and cultural expression, and sometimes for a combination of both. They bring out the intricacies and implications of deploying these languages in multi-media settings. Onguny's chapter, "Indigenous Language Radio in Kenya and the Negotiation of Inter-Group Relations During Conflict Processes", explores the extent to which indigenous radio frames influence inter-group relations during conflict processes in Kenya with a focus on the 2007/08 conflicts. The chapter reveals how indigenous-language radio frames may inform attitudes leading to the kinds of alliances that people form during elections, with far-reaching consequences.

The next chapter, by Oloruntola, titled "Mobilising Nigerians Towards National Population Census: The Role of Indigenous Language Media", examines the history of censuses in Nigeria and the problems associated with census exercises, especially the misconceptions surrounding them. It further highlights the importance of the mass media in sensitising and mobilising the people for purposes of ensuring successful census exercises. Oloruntola observes that although indigenous language media may be contributory to effective communication and advocacy ahead of a census, it is not the only means by which that goal may be achieved, and urges that indigenous language media usage for this purpose be engaged strategically, taking advantage of the latest technological developments in the media.

Idumwonyi and Ijeweimen's chapter discusses how African Independent Churches in the context of Nigeria used indigenous languages to adopt to a more globally accessible and sustainable form of Christianity. They argue that "translating" Christianity breaks cultural boundaries, resulting in a "richer and more global Christianity".

The book ends with Lwanda's chapter, "Poverty, Prophets and Politics: 'Marxist' Discourses in Malawi music, 1994–2012", which discusses how Malawi's oral culture competes with other forms of mediated expression in the various public spheres. It traces popular musicians' engagements with issues of class, labour, poverty, oppression and politics between 1994, when Malawi became a multi-party state, and 2012. The chapter highlights the role of popular music in articulating the living conditions of the *azimwale* (peasantry) since 1994. Lwanda's chapter seeks to "bust" the myth of a warm and friendly Malawi, as portrayed in official discourses, by juxtaposing this against the "lyrical discourses" of Malawi musicians reflecting *azimwale* realities.

In total, the book contributes to a more situated understanding of the roles of the indigenous language media in Africa, the obstacles they meet in fulfilling these roles, and the innovative ways Africans have devised of subverting these obstacles. It highlights Africans' efforts at optimising the opportunities the indigenous language media afford them to enhance the democratization process and preserve or promote cultural identities.

References

Achebe, C. 1976. *Morning Yet on Creation Day*. Garden City, NY: Anchor Press.

Achebe, C. 1997. English and the African Writer. *Transition*, pp. 342–349.

Bagdikian, B. H. 2014. *The New Media Monopoly*. Boston, MA: Beacon Press.

Bamgboṣe, A. 1991. *Language and the Nation: The Language Question in Sub-Saharan Africa*. Edinburgh: Edinburgh University Press.

Curran J. 1991. Rethinking Media as a Public Sphere, in *The political Economy of the Media*, vol. ii, edited by P Golding and G. Murdock. Cheltenham: Edward Elgar. 120–150.

Diallo, I. 2011. "To understand lessons, think through your own languages". An analysis of narratives in support of the introduction of indigenous languages in the education system in Senegal. *Language Matters: Studies in the Languages of Africa*, 42(2), pp. 207–230.

Du Plessis, T. 2011. Editorial. *Language Matters: Studies in the Languages of Africa*, 42(2), pp. 171–172.

Golding P. and Murdock G. 1991. Culture, communications and political economy, in *Mass Media and Society*, J. Curran and M. Gurevitch (Eds). London: Edward Arnold, pp. 15–32.

Goldsmiths Media Group. 2000. Media organisations in society: Central issues, in *Media Organisations in Society*, J. Curran (Ed.). London: Arnold, pp. 19–65.

Gurevitch, M. 2000. The globalization of electronic journalism, in P Marris and S Thornham (Eds). *Media Studies: A Reader*, 2nd edition. New York, NC: New York University Press, pp. 676–686.

Jalali, M. and Ansaripour, E. 2014. Post-Colonialism and Critical Language Awareness (Chinua Achebe, L2, and Identity). *Procedia-Social and Behavioral Sciences*, 98, pp. 713–718.

Mamdani, M. 2001. Beyond settler and native as political identities: Overcoming the political legacy of colonialism. *Comparative Studies in Society and History*, 43(4), pp. 651–664.

McChesney, R. W. 2000. *Rich Media, Poor Democracy: Communication Politics in Dubious Times*. New York, NC: The New Press.

Meeuwis, M. 2011. The origins of Belgian colonial language policies in the Congo. *Language Matters: Studies in the Languages of Africa*, 42(2), pp. 190–206.

Moore, D. C. 2004. Response to Ngugi wa Thiong'o. *Macalester International* 14, pp. 48–55.

Salhi, K. 2002. Critical imperatives of the French language in the Francophone world: Colonial legacy–postcolonial policy. *Current Issues in Language Planning*, 3(3), pp. 317–345.

Vakunta, P. W. 2010. Aporia: Ngugi's fatalistic logic of the unassailable position of indigenous languages in African literature. *Entrepreneur*, 10 May, pp. 74–81.

Wali, O. 1963. The dead end of African literature. *Transition* 10: 13–15.

wa Thiong'o N. 1986. *Decolonising the Mind: The Politics of Language in African Literature*. London: James Currey.

Woolard KA. 1998. Language Ideology as a Field of Inquiry, in *Language Ideologies: Practice and Theory*, edited by BB Schieffelin, KA Woolard and PV Kroskrity. New York: Oxford University Press: 3–47.

Part I
Indigenous Languages, Media and Democracy in Africa

1
Indigenous Language Media and Democracy in Africa

Abiodun Salawu

Introduction

The origin of the African language press is usually associated with Christian missionaries. They chose to establish a press in the local language for their evangelical activities (Akinfeleye, 1985; Tsumba, 2002; Salawu, 2003, 2007). The missionaries knew that the only way they could, effectively, diffuse the beliefs and tenets of their religions among the natives was to communicate with them in the indigenous languages. For instance, the Church Missionary Society (CMS) did this in the Yoruba language; the Dutch Reformed Church Mission (DRCM), later known as the Church of Christ among the Tiv or the Nongo U Kristu Ken Sudan Hen Tiv (NKST), in the Tiv and Chiyanja languages; the United Mission for Central Africa (UMCA) in Chiyanja; the Catholic Church in isiZulu, Chichewa and Ewondo; the Overtoun Institute of the Free Church of Scotland in Chiyanja; the Wesleyans and Presbyterians in isiXhosa; the Church of Scotland Mission in Efik; the former Qua Iboe Mission, now the United Evangelical Mission, in Igala, etc.

It is the same idea of effective communication in indigenous languages (McNamara, 1965; Mlama, 1978 in Okombo and Rubgumya, 1996; Fafunwa et al., 1989; Djite, 1993; Prah, 1996; Salawu, 2004) that made local language press a veritable tool for democratic mobilisation. Political theorists (Herbst, 1993; Olukotun, 2000; Entman, 2003; Jamieson and Waldman, 2004; Kovach and Rosentstiel, 2007; Voltmer and Koch-Baumgarten, 2010) have established a connection between democracy and the media. The media are increasingly replacing political parties in stimulating and organising the participation of broad masses in the political system. Issues of participation, which are central to the democratic project, have evolved around the creation of alternative media as well as the use of creoles and local languages. In this vein, an effective public sphere is created when there is a press established as a genuinely critical organ of a public engaged in political debate (Habermas, 1989).

The public sphere is the source of public opinion needed to "legitimate authority in any functioning democracy" (Rutherford, 2000:18). This chapter attempts to place indigenous language media in Africa in a particular historical context with a view to highlight their role in enhancing the participation of Africans in the political process in their local environs. It looks at the involvement of the African language media in Africa mainly in the two epochs of nationalist struggle and post-independence politics. It also considers the pitfalls of the participation of local language media in ethnic politics.

Local language media in the nationalist struggle

African politicians in the colonial period regarded the local language media as an important tool for mobilisation against colonialism. Folarin and Mohammed (1996), for instance, remarked that a major purpose of the early local language newspapers in (colonial) Nigeria was the expression of nationalism. Yoruba newspapers like *Eko Akete* (1923), *Eleti Ofe* (1923) and *Akede Eko* (1931) proclaimed in their mottos that they were for liberation and the defence of people's rights (Olunlade, 2006). A foremost nationalist, Chief Obafemi Awolowo, also established *Iroyin Yoruba* in 1945 to further the nationalist struggle and later his own political agenda among the Yoruba people. Political parties in colonial Malawi similarly recognised the need to have their own media in the battle for the minds of the African masses (Kishindo, 2006). The Nyasaland African Congress (NAC) began *Kwacha* (Dawn) in 1955 for the purpose of counteracting damaging propaganda emanating from newspapers established by the colonialists. *Kwacha* had enormous influence. It was, for example, credited for being responsible for mobilising massive support for the Congress candidates in the first elections that took place in the country in 1956 when five Nyasas were elected into the Legislative Council. When *Kwacha* was banned in 1959 during the State of Emergency, it was replaced by another indigenous language newspaper, *Mtendere Pa Ntchito* (Freedom at Work) to continue the political agitation. The NAC was replaced by the Malawi Congress Party, which within a month of its formation launched *Tsopano* (Now) as its unofficial organ. *Tsopano* was a militant mouthpiece which was widely accepted by the people. The United Federal Party also saw the virtue of publishing in the indigenous language. It published a Chinyanja monthly journal called *Timvane* (Let's Listen to Each Other).

In Kenya, during the struggle for independence starting in the early 1920s to the late 1950s, nationalist leaders like Mzee Jomo Kenyatta, Harry Thuku and Tom Mboya started news publications in various local languages, which they used as forums to galvanise the support of the African constituency against the existing oppressive political conditions (Ugangu, 2006). Since the colonial administration did not permit African leaders to organise formal political meetings, the indigenous language press platform became a useful forum through which they could explain African grievances against the colonial administration in a manner and language that local people understood. The indigenous language press thus became the vehicle through which the emerging class of political leaders were able to communicate the central issues of African grievances like land, poor wages for African workers, harassment by local authorities, lack of self-determination and the need for liberation. The early African-owned indigenous language press succeeded not only in reaching out to the masses; they also succeeded in making the struggle a collective responsibility for the majority of Kenyans.

Overtime, this created a critical mass of Africans with a growing sense of awareness of their rights such that in later years they would organise and arm themselves to fight the colonialists during the Mau-Mau rebellion in the 1950s. The fervent political atmosphere, in turn, provided ample ground for the mushrooming of the indigenous language press. Even though *Isigidimisama Xosa* (The Xhosa Express) and *Imvo Zabantsundu* (Native Opinion) were categorised under the missionary press in the first phase of the local language press in South Africa (Johnson, 1988; CCSU, 1996), they were part of the anti-colonial struggle. One of the editors of *Isigidimi* was John Jabavu, an important figure in the early phase of African nationalism. It was the same Jabavu who later started *Imvo*. The second phase (1880–1930) of the indigenous language press in South Africa was tagged the 'Independent Press'. This phase witnessed the realisation by the black elites that "mission overlordship" was not necessarily in their best interests. They saw the need for a press that would be independent of the influence of the missionaries and the colonialists. The newspapers in this phase included *IkwezeLe Afrika* (1928–1932),established by Pixley Seme, African National Congress (ANC) President-General (1930–1937); *Lwase Afrika*, set up in 1928 and published by A. W. G. Champion on behalf of a splinter group of the Natal Industrial and Commercial Workers' Union of South Africa; and *Ankanyiso Yase Natal* (The Natal Light).

A major newspaper in the third phase, dubbed the 'Commercial Press', was *Ilanga* (established in 1903). *Ilanga*, like other newspapers during this phase, sought to exploit the black market for consumer goods. It played this role in Natal until 1978, when it was bought out by the Inkatha Freedom Party. The newspapers in the fourth phase, tagged the 'Progressive Press', were platforms for the expression of community struggles. They were located in the wider struggle for democracy. This phase started in the 1980s. The newspapers in this phase were connected to popular political movements. They were not-for-profit and largely relied on subsidies and grants from churches, foundations and trade unions. *Ukusa*, published in Natal between 1982 and 1985, was a newspaper during this phase. Communication, Culture and Society Unit (CCSU) (1996: 30) noted that *UmAfrika* had been moving in a progressive direction since 1986.

Local language media in the post-independence period

In Kenya, there was a lull in the indigenous language press in the period immediately after independence. This lasted from 1963 to 1987. These years (1963–1987) saw the gradual development of a very conformist mainstream press in Kenya and very little indigenous language press development. However, the agitation for multi-party democracy from the late 1980s to the early 1990s saw the re-emergence of the indigenous language press as a tool in the agitation for greater democracy and political change in the country. As a result of the conformist stance of the mainstream press, even under the Moi regime, many Kenyans in need of more objective and courageous reporting started moving towards a re-emerging alternative press for news on what was happening in the country. At the height of agitation for democracy in the mid-1980s up to the early 1990s, many publications – some in English, but many others in the various native languages (particularly Kiswahili) spoken in Kenya – started appearing on the newsstands as the alternative press. *Pambana* was one such newspaper.

The publisher of *Alaroye* newspaper in Nigeria said that he started the newspaper (in 1996) to fill a gap that existed because there was no independent and in-depth coverage of the political development of the time in Yoruba newspapers (Adedayo, 2006). This was a time when there was fervent agitation for the de-annulment of the June 12, 1993 presidential election and for the establishment of democracy. The election happened to have been won by M. K. O. Abiola, a Yoruba man. Therefore, it was understandable that the struggle was more alive in

Yorubaland. The publisher noted that the people yearned for information and a thorough analysis of events as they unfolded. Olukotun (2002a, 2000) catalogued the protest in popular culture in the Yoruba area of Nigeria during the years of agitation against military rule following the 1993 presidential election annulment. Similarly, Williams (1999: 76) wrote about the traditional Yoruba protest media during the struggle for democracy:

> they fuelled the climate of popular outrage which led to the precipitate and unceremonious departure of General Babangida following the infamous annulment of the presidential election. Two of these artistes, LanrewajuAdepoju and GbengaAdewuyi, much lionised as Yoruba Ewi poets, were so daring in their personal attacks, so liberal with savage excoriations that between them they probably cost the Babangida government its remaining authority and legitimacy in Yorubaland.

Olukotun (2002b) remarked that this experience showed how in times of repression, when the regular channels of expression are closed or suppressed, civil society falls back on indigenous modes of communication to express dissent and to censure the authorities. Meanwhile, Williams (1995) had noted that Adepoju and others were inheritors of a rich tradition of using popular literature, arts and performance to offer critical comments on the prevailing political climate. Williams recalled that before the military coup of 1966 (staged because of the excesses of the Nigerian politicians of the first republic [1960–1966]) there was "the upsurge of local theatre with explicitly political motives. The local Yoruba dramatists simply took over the rich indigenous tradition and converted it to a vehicle against autocracy and political perfidy" (Williams, 1995: 71). Both Williams (1995) and Olukotun (2002a) recalled the late Hubert Ogunde's 'Yoruba Ronu', which was a biting satire of the misrule of the then premier of the Western Region of Nigeria, Chief Samuel Ladoke Akintola. The drama was subsequently banned by the regional government.

Oso (2003) pointed out that protest arts and performances are rooted in Yoruba traditional culture. According to him, Yoruba traditional artistes exercise a lot of poetic licence to censure an erring ruler and/ or any other member of the community. Traditional festivals across Yorubaland provide platforms for such performances. These festivals include the Oro and Eluku among the Ijebu and Remo and the Oke-Ibadan in Ibadan. Olukotun (2002a) referred to an insight provided by

Chief Adebayo Faleti, who said that whenever an Oba went off course in the Oyo empire and Yorubaland, in general, the Egungun will enact some sketches to abuse or reprimand the Oba. Using a drama video as a springboard, Salawu (2008) attempted an analysis of the impact of these traditional or folk media in bringing about order and justice in society.

The poets also employed the wide reach of radio to get their message across to a wider audience. Olukotun (2002a: 178) remarked that radio professionals majoring in Ewi occupied a strategic position in the legitimation contests. Olukotun (2002a) observed that even normally establishment musicians like Ebenezer Obey and the late Sikiru Ayinde Barrister produced albums critical of the military rule and the socio-economic hardships being suffered by the people as a result of misrule.

Olukotun similarly recognised the contribution of the local language press to the political discourse of the anti-military struggle. He noted:

> Alongside this querulous popular media was the resurgence of a vernacular press, published in Yoruba, of which *Alaroye* is the most distinct. These emergent vernacular media tried to fill a gap in discourse by translating popular political debates into vernacular and by giving the grassroots a voice in those debates – a development accentuated by the emergence of private radio stations in the mid-1990s. (Olukotun, 2002a: 167)

He specifically remarked on the contribution of *Alaroye* thus:

> *Alaroye* founded in 1992 and which rapidly became a success in circulation terms has shown the possibility of a more politically flavoured, critical journalism in vernacular as the paper contributed its quota to the anti-military ferment in the 1990s. (Olukotun, 2002a: 167)

Pitfalls

Interestingly, the indigenous language press could also be used to counter democratic movement and agitation. For instance, *Bwalo la Nyasaland* (Nyasaland Forum) was a European settler newspaper published (1953–1962) to disseminate propaganda, extolling the virtues of colonialism and counteracting the liberation movement in Malawi. Similarly, *Gaskiya Tafi Kwabo* (a Hausa language newspaper in Northern Nigeria) was used to counter anti-colonial propaganda from the Southern press. Ahmad (2006: 96) notes that *Gaskiya* "was founded by a colonial administration with the sole aim of promoting colonial objectives of propaganda". To achieve this, MrL. C. Giles, a colonial officer, was appointed deputy to Abubakar Imam, the editor (Ahmad, 2006: 102).

Fingers were pointed at indigenous language radio stations as major culprits in the violence that greeted the 2007 election in Kenya. Wachanga (2011) reports that these radio stations were chastised for constructing and disseminating narratives of hate, using embellished metaphors. Wachanga acknowledges the presence of the metaphors and the ethnicised stereotypical humour they provided before the election. The author recalls:

> Metaphors, therefore, became substitutes for past ethnic grievances. They served as a rallying cry and a call to arms, not because of the totality of what can be inferred from them, both positive and negative, but their signification of aspects of difference.

It is this difference that was exploited during the election violence, not because of the metaphors but in spite of them. With the background of political tension that suffocated the country, metaphors became materials to propagate ethnic identities and a basis for ethnic nomenclature (Wachanga, 2011: 109).

Wachanga (2011: 116–117) gave a detailed analysis of offensive metaphors used against rival ethnic groups in the broadcast media before and during the 2007 general election in Kenya. The metaphors were drawn from the Kikuyu, Luo and Kalenjin languages.

Similarly, indigenous language radio was used in the 1990s in Rwanda for the incitement of the Hutus against the Tutsis in a war that horrified the whole world as genocide was committed on a grand scale. The radio broadcasts were made in the Kinyarwanda language (Callahan, 2013). Before the use of radio for incitement, it was the *Kangura* newspaper that started publishing anti-Tutsi articles and cartoons from 1990 (Melvern, 2000). Somerville (2014) also reports how a local language radio is being used to spread hate against the Banyamulenge in the ongoing civil war in the Democratic Republic of Congo. A similar scenario is being played out in the ongoing civil war in South Sudan, where radio is being used to incite ethnic violence (Somerville, 2014). Salawu (2004) notes that indigenous language newspapers are ethnic-based newspapers, which, of course, have primordial interests in the ethnic groups whose (indigenous) languages the newspapers use. According to him, "these newspapers can lead and modify the opinions of their peoples forming stereotypes for them about other ethnic groups; thereby fuelling further the social conflicts" (Salawu, 2004: 259).

In his analysis of identity politics concerning the 2003 presidential election in Nigeria, Salawu (2004) reports that *Alaroye Magasini* (a magazine published in Yoruba, a Southern Nigerian language, with sister publications such as the *Alaroye* newspaper and *AkedeAgabaye*) of October 2002 screams on its cover page: *"L'odun 2003: Nigeria yoofosiwewe"*, meaning "2003: Nigeria Will Break Up". The story, which runs from page 7 to page 10 of the issue, gives the following three major reasons why Nigeria will split up in 2003:

1. Political analysts reason that if the then President Obasanjo is not re-elected and either a Hausa or an Ibo wins the election, the outcome will not be pleasant for Nigeria with the possibility that Nigeria will break up. (p. 7)
2. As matters stand –Obasanjo is in power and the Peoples Democratic Party (PDP) (the ruling party) leaders are behind him; Anyim (the then Senate President) holds sway in the Senate and GhaliNa'Abba (the then Speaker of the House of Representatives) is in the House of Representatives; Babangida (a former military president and major opinion leader in the North where the Hausa ethnic group is based) and the Hausa elders are plotting against the return of Obasanjo for a second term – what is obvious is that the year 2003 does not appear as a year of peace in Nigeria. It is a year that will be as volatile as 1983 and 1993 (there were horrific political crises in Nigeria in those years). (p. 8)
3. However, some Igbo are already examining the scheming of the Hausa and are saying that if the Hausa were to allow one of theirs (the Igbo) to be Nigeria's president, and such a president was assassinated while still serving as happened in the case of Ironsi (a military head of state who was assassinated in a military coup led by soldiers of northern origin) in 1966, that is the end of Nigeria and everything will become fragmented. (p. 10)

Alaroye newspaper's front page story of November 24, 2002 provides another example of the journalism of identity politics. Here, it is the use of words to refer to ethnicity that is of interest. The cover title reads: *"Ibo Aare 2003: EseObasanjo n mi – Awon Hausa ta ku: Won l'Ekuemelawonfe"*, meaning "Presidential Election 2003: No assurance for Obasanjo – The Hausa insist: They say they prefer Ekwueme". The politics of identity are manifest in this headline with reference to the Hausa tribal group. In the body of the story, Dr Alex Ekwueme is referred to as the "igbo man" (p. 5).

The "impeachment saga" was an adjoining issue to the 2003 presidential election. In August 2002, the House of Representatives, led by AlhajiGhaliNa'Aba, served the President, Chief Olusegun Obasanjo, a notice of impeachment. This resulted in a political crisis, and political watchers in the southern part of the country, particularly in the southwest, saw the impeachment bid as a ploy by the Hausa/Fulani, and by extension, the north, to wrest power from Obasanjo, and by extension, the south-west. All this, the political watchers reasoned, was a ploy to spoil Obasanjo's chance in 2003.

On this issue, the *Alaroye* newspaper of November 19, 2002 published a letter to the editor. The letter has the headline: "President Obasanjo, it is you we blame". Reacting to the issue, part of the letter reads:

> This dividend of democracy, you (Obasanjo) must share it into three (for the three major ethnic groups) so that everybody will go his own way. It is enough. Come back home and rest.
>
> The madman has his belly filled and breaks the dish of pounded yam: the goat eats up the cassava and upturns the cassava tray; the Gambari has his belly filled and want to turn Abuja to motor-park. Our father, Obasanjo, what are you holding on to that you won't leave these animals and come back to Lagos to lead the children of Oduduwa. (p. 4)

Here, we note the liking of the Hausa to the madman and the goat. We also note the use of the derogatory word, "Gambari", for the Hausa and, of course, the reference to them as "animals". Again, the newspaper made it clear that it knew the motive behind the House of Representatives Speaker's insistence, despite various interventions, to see the President's impeachment through:

> GhaliNa'Aba who turns himself to Obasanjo's enemy and is carrying out the Arewa agenda.(p. 5)

The above story occurs in the cover story of November 19, 2002 with the headline, "*Anyim, oloriawonasofinkowo je!*", meaning "Anyim, the Senate President in fraud scandal!" The 2002 Miss World Beauty Pageant-induced crisis in Nigeria was another nerve-racking issue (see also Salawu, 2009, 2013). It was linked to the 2003 presidential election as it was alleged to be yet another ploy by the north to discredit the Obasanjo regime as not being able to ensure peace in the country and, therefore, spoil the incumbent's chance in the 2003 election. *Alaroye* magazine played up the politics of identity in its November 2002 issue. The story headlined *"RogbodiyaniluKaduna"* ("Mayhem in Kaduna) included the following statements:

> What the crisis brought to the fore is the difference between the Hausa and other tribes in Nigeria. The Hausa are greatly different from us; their conduct is not the same as ours. (p. 5)

Referring to what led to the mayhem – a story published on November 16, 2002 by *This Day*, which was alleged to be blasphemous of the Prophet Mohammed – the magazine writes:

> If such a statement angers the Yoruba, what they would do is to write a strong rejoinder, and explain issues to the writer ... But the Hausa do not do this, in particular their leaders... The religion of this Hausa is different from that of the Yoruba. (p. 5)

Similarly, in its editorial published on page 4 of the December 10 issue, *Alaroye* newspaper writes:

> We are opposed to the Hausa's crazy fight, we are opposed to their stupid conduct. We are equally opposed to the idea of perpetrating evil under the guise of Islam... If a Hausa person were to be in power, we know the Hausa would not start the Sharia system ... there are many people in Hausa land who can slaughter their mothers because of politics... there are many Satanic children among them.

The same issue of the newspaper carried a very blunt cover title: *"Ija Kaduna: Yoruba niHausa fee bajagun"*, meaning "Kaduna mayhem: The Hausa want to engage the Yoruba in war". We shall refer to a portion of the cover story that appears on page 5:

> In actual fact, churches and the non-Hausa are the target of (the evil of) the rioters, but the fight was different from those of the past because they say among themselves that the Yoruba were the actual target.

There are outright calls for dismemberment of the nation. This is evident in a letter published in *Alaroye* of November 19, 2002. Yet, a similar letter appeared in the same month in *AlaroyeMagasini*. The letter, published on page 3 of the issue has the headline: *"Imoran mi fun gbogboomo Nigeria"*("My advice to all Nigerians"). It includes the following:

My first advice to Nigeria is that we should break so that each ethnic group will go its own way, because if we say a Hausa, or Ibo or Yoruba will do it well, we are only deceiving ourselves. As Yoruba is doing it now and peace is not allowed to reign, when it is the turn of Hausa or Igbo, they will do the same. Instead, let everybody answer to his father's name, that is the only way peace can reign.

Meanwhile, Salawu (2004) notes that *Alaroye* news publications are not the only ones capable of the journalism of identity politics. Other publications owned by people of other ethnic groups and based in other regions are equally known for this (see Abati, 2000: 87–121).

Conclusion

Notwithstanding these challenges, indigenous language media still remain a potent vehicle for mobilising people for positive (developmental) goals that include democracy. Colonialism may have been dislodged in Africa but there is still the need to ensure effective participatory democracy so that people can be involved in their own governance, make informed decisions and make governments accountable.

A major factor that can militate against local language media playing this positive role is the growing phenomenon of the corporatisation of the local media. In order to ensure the profitability of the media business, corporate media organisations that venture into this kind of publishing end up pampering the readers/audience to 'funky' contents that more often appeal to base instincts (Salawu, 2015).

However, in this age of New Communication Technologies, the crusading role of local language media can be extended to the new and social media (for example, blogging, mobile telephony and social networking sites). Unfortunately, many African languages are not present in the cyberspace as many Africans are reluctant to use their languages for socialising online. It is therefore not unsurprising that researches into the use of African languages in the social and digital media are a rarity. This, for instance, is in contrast to what obtains for minority languages in Europe, which already enjoy a number of researches into their use in social media (Cunliffe and apDyfrig, 2013; Cunliffe et al., 2013; Dolowy-Rybinska, 2013; Johnson, 2013; Johnson and Callahan, 2013; Jones et al., 2013; Wagner, 2013; Cru, 2014). Although there have been a number of studies done on the use of social media and mobile technologies for democratic and civil activist purposes (Moyo, 2009; Tanja, 2010; Axford, 2011; Kperogi, 2011; Olorunnisola and Martin,

2013; Breuer et al., 2014), none of them is about the use of African indigenous languages in the (social and digital) media. The inference that can be made here is that there is little or no use for the indigenous languages in the media and for democratic purposes. This is without prejudice to the existence of Swahili (though not an indigenous African language) blogs in Tanzania. Most blogs in Tanzania are in Swahili and they cover diverse issues such as politics, entertainment, culture, sports, health etc. The blogs include Issa Michuzi, WanamuzikiWa Tanzania, Wanajenje, Fununu, Tutoke etc.

The United Nations Educational, Scientific and Cultural Organization (UNESCO) realised the importance of indigenous language media to the advancement of democracy when it included the module Indigenous Language Media and Democracy in Africa in its four-course Reporting Africa syllabus. The specific objective of the particular module is to experiment with culturally and linguistically innovative media forms that lend themselves to a more democratically engaged journalistic practice. The indigenous language media have played, and continue to play, a key role in Africa's democratisation. The Indigenous Language Media and Democracy in Africa course is described thus:

> This course seeks to place the indigenous language media in Africa in a particular historical context with a view to highlighting their role in enhancing the participation of Africans in the political process in their local environs. It interrogates the extent to which such media can be innovatively extended to journalistic production. (UNESCO, 2010: 35)

A meeting was held in October 2010 with four South African universities adjudged by UNESCO in 2009 as potential centres of excellence in journalism training regarding the ways and means of implementing the module. Regrettably, there has been no follow-up action since that meeting. We express our hope in this chapter that UNESCO will still be able to galvanise action on this important matter.

References

Abati, R. 2000. The Press, Politics and Society in Nigeria. In T. Oseni and L. Idowu (eds) *Hosting the 140th Anniversary of the Nigerian Press*. Lagos: Tosen Consult, pp. 87–121.

Adedayo, A. 2006.The Story of Alaroye. In A. Salawu (ed.) *Indigenous Language Media in Africa*. Lagos: CBAAC, pp. 196–205.

Ahmad, G. 2006. *Gaskiya Ta Fi Kwabo*: From Colonial Service to Community Beacon. In A. Salawu (ed.) *Indigenous Language Media in Africa*. Lagos: CBAAC, pp. 95–113.

Akinfeleye, R. 1985. Religious Publications: Pioneers of Nigerian Journalism. In O. Nwuneli (ed.) *Mass Communication in Nigeria: A Book of Readings*. Enugu: Fourth Dimension Publishing Co. Ltd, pp. 34–47.

Axford, B. 2011. Talk about a Revolution: Social Media and the MENA Uprisings. *Globalizations*, 8(5): 681–686.

Breuer, A., T. Landman and D. Farquhar 2014. Social Media and Protest Mobilisation: Evidence from the Tunisian Revolution. *Democratization*. Available at http://dx.doi.org/10.1080/13510347.2014.885505.

Callahan, C. 2013. Radio in the Rwandan Genocide. *The Devil's Tale: Dispatches from the David M. Rubenstein Rare Book and Manuscript Library*. Available at http://blogs.library.duke.edu/rubenstein/2013/05/10/radio-in-the-rwandan-genocide (Accessed 2014/06/03).

CCSU 1996.*Community and the Progressive Press: A Case Study in Finding Our Way*. Durban: Contemporary Cultural Studies Unit, University of Natal.

Cru, J. 2015. Language Revitalisation from the Ground Up: Promoting Yucatee Maya on Facebook. *Journal of Multilingual and Multicultural Development*, 36(3): 284–296. Available at http://dx.doi.org/10.1080/01434632.2014.921184.

Cunliffe, D., D. Morris and C. Prys 2013. Investigating the Differential Use of Welsh in Young Speaker' Social Networks: A Comparison of Communication in Face-to-face Settings, in Electronic Texts and on Social Networking Sites. In E.H.G. Jones and E. Uribe-Jongbloed (eds) *Social Media and Minority Languages: Convergence and the Creative Industries*. Bristol: Multilingual Matters, pp. 75–86.

Cunliffe, D. and R. apDyfrig 2013. The Welsh Language on YouTube: Initial Observations. In E.H.G. Jones and E. Uribe-Jongbloed (eds) *Social Media and Minority Languages: Convergence and the Creative Industries*. Bristol: Multilingual Matters, pp. 130–145.

Djite, P. 1993. Language and Development in Africa. *International Journal of the Sociology of Language*, 100/101: 148–166.

Dolowy-Rybinska, N. 2013.Kashubian and Modern Media: The Influence of New Technologies on Endangered Languages. In E.H.G. Jones and E. Uribe-Jongbloed (eds) *Social Media and Minority Languages: Convergence and the Creative Industries*. Bristol: Multilingual Matters, pp. 119–129.

Entman, R.M. 2003. *Projections of Power: Framing News, Public Opinion, and U.S. Foreign Policy*. Chicago: University of Chicago Press.

Fafunwa, A.B., I. Macauley and F. Sokoya 1989. *Education in Mother-tongue: The Ife Primary Education Research Project 1970–1978*. Ibadan: UPL.

Folarin, B. and J.B. Mohammed 1996.The Indigenous Language Press in Nigeria. In O. Dare and A. Uyo (eds) *Journalism in Nigeria*. Lagos: NUJ, Lagos State Council, pp. 99–112.

Habermas, J. 1989. *The Structural Transformation of the Public Sphere: An Inquiry into a Category of Bourgeois Society* (trans. Thomas Burger with Frederick Lawrence). Cambridge, MA: MIT Press.

Herbst, S. 1993. History, Philosophy and Public Opinion Research. *Journal of Communications*, 43(Autumn): 140–145.

Jamieson, K.H. and P. Waldman 2004. *The Press Effect: Politicians, Journalists, and the Stories that Shape the Political World*. Oxford: Oxford University Press.

Johnson, I. 2013. Audience Design and Communication Accommodation Theory: Use of Twitter by welsh-English Biliterates. In E.H.G. Jones and E. Uribe-Jongbloed (eds) *Social Media and Minority Languages: Convergence and the Creative Industries*. Bristol: Multilingual Matters, pp. 99–118.

Johnson, J.L. and C. Callahan 2013. Minority Cultures and Social Media: Magnifying Garifuna. *Journal of Intercultural Communication Research*, 42(4): 319–339.

Johnson, S. 1988. Historical Overview of the Black Press. In *The Limits of Dissent: Resistance, Community and the Press in South Africa*. ed. K. Tomaselli, R. Tomaselli and J. Muller, 19–35. Johannesburg: R. Lyon.

Jones, R.J., D. Cunliffe and Z.R. Honeycutt 2013.Twitter and the Welsh Language. *Journal of Multilingual and Multicultural Development*, 34(7): 653–671.

Kishindo, P. 2006. The Development of Indigenous Language Press in Malawi. In A. Salawu (ed.) *Indigenous Language Media in Africa*. Lagos: CBAAC, pp. 21–41.

Kovach, B. and T. Rosenstiel 2007.*Elements of Journalism: What Newspeople Should Know and the Public Should Expect* (2nd Edition). New York: Crown Publishing.

Kperogi, F. 2011. Webs of Resistance: The Citizen Online Journalism of the Nigerian Digital Diaspora. PhD thesis, College of Arts and Sciences, Georgia State University.

McNamara 1965. The Problem of Solving Difficulties of Bilingual Children. *Bulletin of the British Psychological Society*, XVIII: 58–59.

Melvern, L. 2000. *A People Betrayed: The Role of the West in Rwanda's genocide*. London: Zed Books.

Moyo, D. 2009. Citizen Journalism and the Parallel Market of Information in Zimbabwe's 2008 Election. *Journalism Studies*, 10(4): 551–567.

Okombo, O. and C. Rubgumya 1996.Synopsis of Research Findings on Languages of Instruction and their Implication for Educational Policies in Africa. *ADEA Newsletter*, 8(4): 11–14.

Olorunnisola, A.A. and B.L. Martin 2013. Influences of Media on Social Movements: Problematising Hyperbolic Inferences about Impacts. *Telematics and Informatics*, 30: 275–288.

Olukotun, A. 2002a. Traditional Protest Media and Anti-Military Struggle in Nigeria 1988–1999. *African Affairs*, 101: 193–211.

Olukotun, A. 2002b.*State Repression, Crisis of Democratisation and Media Resistance in Nigeria (1988–1999)*. Ibadan: College Press Limited.

Olukotun, A. 2000.Governance and the Media. In H. Goran et al. (eds) *African Perspectives on Governance*. Trenton, NJ: World Press Incorporated, pp. 91–121.

Olunlade, T. 2006. Yoruba Newspapers' Mottos: A Literary Analysis. In A. Salawu (ed.) *Indigenous Language Media in Africa*. Lagos: CBAAC, pp. 71–85.

Oso, L. 2003. Voices on Stage: Popular Performances as Communication. In L. Oso (ed.) *Community Media: Voices of the Oppressed*. Abeokuta: Jedidiah Publishers, pp. 197–213.

Prah, K.K. 1996. The Language Factor in the Scientific and Technological Development of Africa. In H. Griesel (ed.) *The Feasibility of Technical Language Development in the African Languages*. Pretoria: Department of Arts, Culture, Science and Technology/National Terminology Services, pp. 21–38.

Rutherford, P. 2000. *Endless Propaganda: The Advertising of Public Goods*. Toronto: University of Toronto Press.

Salawu, A. 2015. A Political Economy of Sub-Saharan African Language Press: The Case of Nigeria and South Africa. *Review of African Political Economy*. Available at http://dx.doi.org/10.1080/03056244.2014.988695, pp. 299–313.

Salawu, A. 2013.Recall of Politics of Identity in the Narratives of the Nigerian Press. *Journal of Communication*, 4(1): 41–48.

Salawu, A. 2009.Media Narrative Construction of Ethno-Religious Conflicts in Nigeria. *Communication Studies (EstudosemCommunicao)* (5): 75–93.

Salawu, A. 2008.*AyanAgalu*: Art, Media and Social Crusade in Nigeria. *Pula: Botswana Journal of African Studies*, 22(1): 89–101.

Salawu, A. 2007.The Religious Essence of Indigenous Language Press in Nigeria. In R. Taiwo et al. (ed.) *Perspectives on Media Discourse*. Germany: Linus Communication Studies, pp. 140–155.

Salawu, A.S. 2004.Identity Politics and the Indigenous Language Press: A Case Study of the *Alaroye* Publications. In Duro Oni et al. (ed.) *Nigeria and Globalisation: Discourses on Identity Politics and Social Conflict*. Lagos: CBAAC, pp. 257–274.

Salawu, A.S. 2003. Essentials of Mother-tongue Newspapers to the UBE Scheme. *Journal of Nigerian Languages and Culture*, 5(1): 106–111.

Somerville, K. 2014. South Sudan: How Hate Radio Was Used to Incite Bentin Massacres. Available at http://africanarguments.org/2014/04/24/south-sudan (Accessed 2014/06/03).

Tanja, B. 2010. Digital Journalism and Online Public Spheres in South Africa. *: South African Journal for Communication Theory and Research*, 36(2): 265–275.

Tsumba, Y. I. 2002. Literacy in Indigenous Languages in Nigeria: The Tiv Experience. *Literacy and Reading in Nigeria*, 9(2): 211–224.

Ugangu, W. 2006.The Development and Political Mobilisation Role of Kenyan Indigenous Language Press. In A. Salawu (ed.) *Indigenous Language Media in Africa*. Lagos: CBAAC, pp. 86–94.

UNESCO 2010. *Reporting Africa: A Selective Syllabus*. Windhoek: UNESCO.

Voltmer, K. and S. Koch-Baumgarten 2010. Introduction: Mass Media and Public Policy–Is there a Link? In S. Koch-Baumgarten and K. Voltmer (eds) *Public Policy–and Mass Media. The Interplay of Mass Communication and Political Decision-Making*. Abingdon: Routledge, pp. 1–13.

Wachanga, D.N. 2011. Kenya's Indigenous Radio Stations and their Use of Metaphors in the 2007 Election Violence. *Journal of African Media Studies*,3(1): 109–125.

Wagner, M. 2013. Luxembourgish on Facebook: Language Ideologies and Writing Strategies. In E.H.G. Jones and E. Uribe-Jongbloed (eds) *Social Media and Minority Languages: Convergence and the Creative Industries*. Bristol: Multilingual Matters, pp. 87–98.

Williams, A. 1995. The Fictionalisation of Democratic Struggle in Africa: The Nigerian Example. In D. Olowu et al. (eds) *Governance and Democratisation in Nigeria*. Ibadan: Spectrum Books Ltd, pp. 67–82.

Williams, B. 1999.Literature in the Time of Tyranny. In D. Olowu et al. (eds) *Governance and Democratisation in West Africa*. Dakar: Codesria Press, pp. 65–80.

2
Indigenous Language Media and Freedom of Expression in Uganda

Monica B. Chibita

Since the liberation of Uganda's broadcast media sector two decades ago, the sector has seen considerable growth. The number of channels has multiplied and the programming menu has taken on a more global and commercial(ized) character as local media houses have had to compete for audiences with regional and global media. At the same time, there has been significant growth in the volume of programming in the indigenous languages across the broadcast spectrum as most media owners acknowledge the need to be relevant to local audiences. Information and Communication Technologies (ICTs), and particularly the mobile phone, have flourished, notwithstanding persistent urban–rural disparities in access. In this context, it is pertinent to evaluate the performance of the electronic media in enhancing freedom of expression.

Media freedom, typically characterized by freedom of the media to operate without undue interference from government, big business or other powerful forces, is central to the media's democratizing role as it makes it possible for a variety of voices to be heard in and through the media. Media freedom is closely linked to media diversity. In summarizing the concept of media diversity, van Cuilenberg (1999, p. 183) relates it to media content, and in particular to (i) reflection of population preferences and (ii) openness and equal, uniform media access for divergent population preferences. Media diversity pre-supposes a degree of media freedom. Therefore, in this chapter media freedom and diversity refer to evidence of tolerance of difference in the media. Freedom of expression on the other hand simply refers to the freedom to communicate or exchange information through a variety of channels. These all relate to the proper functioning of a democratic polity.

Scholars have long debated the extent to which the liberalization of media spaces equals expanded opportunities for diversity and freedom

28

of expression(Curran 1991, pp. 29–30; van Cuilenberg1999; Goldsmiths Media Group 2000, p. 22, pp. 53–54; Article XIX 2003, p. 3; see also White 2008; Meadows 2013). In particular, critical political economy scholars underscore the media's democratic potential while also arguing that people's capacity to participate freely in public debate through the media is typically constrained by a number of obstacles, some structural and some symbolic.[1] Critical political economy literature relates socio-economic conditions, and particularly poverty, to the capacity to access the democratic benefits that the modern media bring and emphasizes the need to look not just at the global factors affecting access to the media, but also local ones (Murdock and Golding 1989, pp. 192–193; Verstraeten1996; Goldsmith Media Group 2000, pp. 24–25; Wasko 2012; see also Golding 1990, p. 85).

Therefore, while the liberalization of the media in Africa has been hailed for ushering in a new wave of democracy (Hyden, Leslie and Ogundimu 2003), empirical inquiry into specific contexts is useful in pointing out public perceptions of the extent to which this outcome is actually being realized.

Common denominators in defining democracy

Diamond and Morlino (2005, pp. ix–xliii) have identified six useful markers of democracy, namely: greater equality of opportunity; strengthening the rule of law; greater citizen participation in all aspects of government decisions; freedom of competitive political proposals; vertical and horizontal accountability to reduce corruption and greater public control over elected officials.

Norris (2009) argues that the media play three key roles in attaining the above and therefore contributing to democratization and good governance: being a watchdog over those in power (see also Curran 2000; Leibman 2005; Cooper 2006); providing a civic forum for political debate (Garnham 1995; Mwesige 2004; Nabunya 2009; Meadows 2013); and setting the agenda for policy-makers (McCombs and Shaw 1972; Scheufele and Tewksbury 2007). For the media to play these roles optimally, it is important that they permit the expression of diverse political and cultural perspectives. However, in this regard, White (2008, p. 270) contends that although this relationship between the media and democracy is considered a given in elite discussions about the democratizing role of the media in the African context, there has been little research relating the media to the enhancement of these key markers of democracy in the African context where access to the media cannot be taken for granted. What research there is on the relationship between the media and democracy has taken a broader, continental or regional perspective as opposed to a more local one. Examples include Ocitti (1999); Tettey (2001); Hyden, Leslie and Ogundimu (2003); Nyamnjoh (2005); Nisbet (2008); Wasserman (2010); Wasserman (2011); and Blankson and Murphy (2012).

The empirical findings presented from Uganda help illuminate in a specific way the close connection between a free media, a diverse media and freedom of expression. They also help point out hindrances to media freedom and freedom of expression that ordinary people in contexts like Uganda's encounter in the context of a liberalized media environment.

An overview of the media landscape in Uganda

Uganda's broadcast sector has been influenced by changes in the sector at the global level. The liberalization of the broadcast sector in Uganda starting with the early 1990s reduced the influence of government and introduced a range of private players who have established radio stations, TV stations and internet service provision facilities in the different regions of the country (Broadcasting Council 2004; Kibazo and Kanaabi2007; Mwesige and Tabaire2010). Between 1992, when the broadcast sector was liberalized, and 2004, the channels of broadcasting grew from one television and one radio station to nine television stations and over 80 radio stations broadcasting in English, French and Kiswahili, as well as various indigenous Ugandan languages, to different parts of the country.

Today, according to the Uganda Communications Commission (www.ucc.org), there are over 270 licensed FM stations, with 192 of them on air. There are 55 registered television stations, including 35 that are operational. While most television programming is in English, the majority of radio airtime is shared between Luganda, the language spoken by the largest number of Ugandans (17%), and English. There are approximately 34 other languages. Of these, four are designated regional languages along with Luganda. They include Runyakitara for Western Uganda, Luo for Northern Uganda and Ateso and Ngakarimojong for North-Eastern Uganda. The Uganda Broadcasting Corporation (UBC) broadcasts in 24 of the languages of Uganda. The privately owned stations, however, choose what language to broadcast in, apart from the predominant regional language, based on commercial viability.

There has been great growth in the mobile telephony sector as well, with a significant increase in mobile phone service providers and mobile telephone lines reported. According to the Commissions website (www.ucu.ac.ug) by June 2013, there were approximately 17 million mobile telephone subscribers in a country of 34 million inhabitants. While this growth has been phenomenal, it has not been systematic, and, as the discussion following will show, neither has it been perceived by the majority of Ugandans as significantly increasing their chances of freedom of expression in English or the indigenous languages.

The regulatory context for the broadcast media in Uganda

Article 29 (a) of the Constitution of the Republic of Uganda (Uganda 1995) states: "Every person shall have the right to—(a) Freedom of speech and expression which shall include freedom of the press and other media." Article 41of the constitution further guarantees the right of access to information in the possession of government departments.

These constitutional provisions are guided by international instruments including the Universal Declaration of Human Rights (UDHR), whose Article 19 states:

> [E]veryone has the right to freedom of opinion and expression; this right includes freedom to hold opinions without interference and to seek, receive and impart information and ideas through any media and regardless of frontiers.

Related provisions are found in the International Convention on Civil and Political Rights as well as in the African Charter on Human and People's Rights.

The enjoyment of the right of access to information and communication is, for critical political economy, fundamental to the appreciation and enjoyment of civil and political rights in particular (Murdock and Golding 1989, pp. 183–184; Skoufias, Narita and Narayan 2014; Wasko 2014). Civil rights include freedom of speech and opinion, the exercise of which is closely linked to the media, while political rights include the right to participate in the exercise of political power, hence holding public office, voting, and participating in the making of the laws by which one consents to be governed. Access to adequate information and to a diversity of debate is a basic pre-condition for the effective functioning of a democratic polity and for the full exercise of citizens' rights. Thus, communication systems (and therefore the media) should provide people with access to the information, advice and analysis they need to know and pursue their rights and provide the broadest possible range of information, interpretation and debate in areas related to political choice. This would enable them to choose, or to dissent and propose alternatives (Murdock and Golding 1989, p. 183; Golding and Murdock 1991, pp. 21–22; see also Chibita 2006, p. 36, White 2008).

The freedoms promised by the broadly liberal provisions in Article 29 (a) and Article 41 of the Constitution of the Republic of Uganda (Uganda 1995) are to be read in the context of Article 43 of the same document, which sets the parameters within which freedom of expression and the right of access to information should be enjoyed. It states: "In the enjoyment of the rights and freedoms enshrined in the constitution, no person shall prejudice the fundamental or other human rights and freedoms of others or the public interest." Constitutionally, therefore, the boundaries for freedom and regulation of the media in Uganda appear well laid out. However, it is also at the intersection of Articles 29 (a) and 41 and Article 43 that most debates about freedom of expression in Uganda have occurred, as the media's attempt to expand the boundaries of their freedom have collided with government's efforts to reign them in "in the public interest".

The major and most current piece of legislation with regards to the regulation of the electronic media in Uganda is the Uganda Communications Act (2013). The Act affirms the convergence of the sector, lays out the modalities for the appointment and constitution of the regulator, and provides for the regulation of radio, television, data/internet, video and cinematography and postal services. It lays out licensing conditions, provides for fair competition and provides for dispute resolution. It should be noted, however, that according to Section 7 of this Act, the line Minister may give "policy guidelines" to the Commission regarding the execution of its responsibilities and the Commission "shall be obliged to comply", even though Section 8 purports to grant the Commission autonomy.

Other legislation that affects the operation of broadcasting in Uganda includes the Access to Information Act (2006), which provides for access to information in the hands of government officials, the Penal Code Act (Amendment) 2007, which criminalises media offences including libel and defamation, and the Public Order Management Act (2013), which proscribes the right of journalists to cover "undesirable" political gatherings. Others are the Official Secrets Act (1964), the Anti-Terrorism Act (2002), the Uganda Broadcasting Corporation Act (2005), the

Referendum and Other Provisions Act (2005), the Presidential Elections Act (2005), the Parliamentary Elections Act (2005) and the Interception of Communications Act (2012).

There are other forms of subtle regulation imposed via government departments and operatives such as the Uganda Media Centre, the police, and local political and security officials. Each of these pieces of legislation is intended to cure some perceived ill and safeguard the public interest, but aspects of the same laws also have a bearing on the free operation of the media. In some cases, such as, for instance, the Anti-Terrorism Act, where the maximum penalty for being associated with perceived "dissidents" could be death, or the Public Order Management Act, which has the potential to proscribe otherwise legitimate gatherings, the sanctions for any breach are so severe as to place a degree of restraint on the exercise of freedom of expression. This in turn has a bearing on the ability of Ugandans to fully enjoy their freedom of expression. Hence, Tabaire's observation that the contradiction between perceptions of freedom of expression and the experience of media organisations is related to the state's desire to appear liberal before the international community in an era where it is no longer "honourable" to openly repress the media. Tabaire adds that the Ugandan executive has taken advantage of International Instruments "in order to maintain a positive reputation with Uganda's international friends". However, he notes that "in terms of domestic politics this is a strategy that carries risks for [President] Museveni, and so he has been quick to clamp down on the press when the need arises" (Tabaire 2007, p. 204).

Attempts at self-regulation have not been very successful. There exists the Independent Media Council (IMC), a non-statutory body that represents an attempt by the journalism fraternity to regulate itself. However, the IMC, established in 2010, has not secured the necessary buy-in from its principal stakeholders to have any significant effect on the regulation of the sector, and is considered moribund or even dead by many media practitioners.

There was a National Broadcasting Policy passed by cabinet in 2007. However, this policy has never been fully implemented. Ernst and Young (2012) in their evaluation of the National Broadcast Policy (2004) argue that whatever its legal status, as it stands now, this policy has been overtaken by events. As such, it is limited in its potential to guide the regulation of the media in its execution of its many mandates, including that of providing a platform for the expression of diverse political opinions.

Chibita 2006 has observed that the contribution of language is often ignored in discussions of policy to enhance freedom of expression. In this regard, Chibita (2006, p. 42) says:

> Communication policy is often not specific on the roles that different languages may play in the media. This has a bearing on which people are able to participate in the political (and cultural) process and with what degree of ease through the media. It is important for people to recognise themselves and their aspirations in the range of representations offered within the major communication sectors as well as to contribute to the development of these representations.

Thus, from the above context it is clear that although the framework for the operation of a liberalized media is in place, there is also great potential for constraint to the free operation of the media as well as to the full enjoyment of freedom of expression. The degree of control the state wields over the media also remains a potential obstacle.

The following section discusses findings obtained as part of a larger study, the National Electronic Media Performance Study (NEMPS) (2014), on the broadcast media's capacity to provide a platform for the enjoyment of freedom of expression in Uganda, and the Ugandan public's perception of key obstacles to the fulfilment of this role.

Methodology of the National Electronic Media Performance Study (2014)

The NEMPS (2014) was commissioned by Uganda's converged regulator, the Uganda Communications Commission. The current author was the Principal Investigator and was assisted by a co-researcher/statistician. This level of involvement in the study provided the Investigator an opportunity to closely observe perceptions of media diversity in Uganda among a cross-section of Ugandan citizens. At the same time, she acknowledges that because of her direct involvement in the said study, there was a risk that this could blunt her critical edge. In order to mitigate this risk, the findings of the NEMPS are, as far as possible, related to findings from related recent studies and literature on the Ugandan and other media.

The objectives of the NEMPS(2014) were to solicit the public's views on the general performance of the broadcast media in Uganda and to establish to what extent the media are perceived to be meeting the needs of the Ugandan public. The study also sought to identify gaps in broadcast policy, regulation and performance and to draw conclusions to inform ongoing policy review and regulation processes.

The study investigated station and programme preferences, perceptions of the role of the media in promoting freedom of expression; met and unmet needs and satisfaction with the volume and quality of local content. The study focused mostly on radio and television although it also explored awareness, access to, and use of the internet and mobile phones along with the traditional media. This chapter specifically focuses on findings on public perceptions of media freedom and the media's role in enhancing freedom of expression.

In order to ensure national representativeness, the country was divided into four regions: North, Central, East and West. Three districts[2] were purposively selected from each of the four traditional regions of Uganda (i.e. Northern, Eastern, Western and Central). The main criteria for selecting the three districts from each of the regions for the study were the district population sizes and representation of ethnic diversity within that region. Based on these criteria, the districts of Lira, Zombo and Moroto were selected from Northern Uganda; Iganga, Mbale and Katakwifrom Eastern Uganda; Kibaale, Mbarara and Kasese from Western Uganda; and Kampala, Masaka and Nakasongola from the Central region. The sample for the household survey was 1,440. Two-thirds of the sample respondents were drawn from the rural areas and one third from the urban areas, in keeping with the population patterns.[3] A multi-stage stratified cluster sampling design was used to select the study areas as well as the households that were included in the study. To the extent possible, the researchers ensured that 50% of the respondents to the survey were female, although this was not always possible to attain with the Focus Group Discussions (FGDs). Half of the respondents consisted of younger people (15–29 years) and the other half older people (30 years and above). At household level, only one respondent falling in the above specified categories was selected for inclusion in the survey sample.

Key informant interviews

In each study district, in-depth interviews were conducted with district officials, media owners, managers and practitioners, local content producers, religious leaders and representatives of the disabled on the obligations, roles, performance and regulation of the electronic media. In order to further clarify, triangulate and supplement data from the districts and obtain a national position, additional in-depth interviews were conducted at national level with key policy-makers, technocrats and various categories of electronic media service providers. The key informant interviews at the national level targeted top officials in the ministries of Information and National Guidance and of ICT, members of parliament, media trainers, artists, journalists and managers of major media outlets that have a national reach, media regulators, sports officials and representatives of the disabled. In all, there were more than 175 key informant interviews conducted for the study.

Focus Group Discussions

From each study district, four to six FGDs were conducted among people 15–29 years old and four to six with people 30 years and above in each of the study districts. All FGDs were held in one urban and two rural sub-counties per district. As much as possible, there was an attempt to have equitable representation by age, gender and location across the board. In total, 68 FGDs were conducted.

Findings

Media ownership and its implications for freedom of expression

The literature of critical political economy extensively addresses the link between media ownership and media freedom. Relevant to this discussion, the central argument is that the current media environment dictates that those who are politically connected also tend to control the media (McChesney 2000 Wasko, Murdock and Sousa 2011, pp. 1–10). The literature further posits that due to an overriding desire to remain profitable, media owners tend to influence their stations' programming priorities in a direction that filters out all controversial or commercially non-viable programming thus stifling diversity and potentially interfering with freedom of expression (Jenkins 2004; Baker 2006). A key constituent of so-called "commercially non-viable programming" is programming in numerically smaller indigenous languages. Considering that Uganda, like many African countries, has more of these than the larger language blocs constituting their population, this tends to produce a degree of uniformity in programming and to stifle diversity, and, most importantly, to marginalize indigenously produced content that would otherwise enable people to participate more actively in important mediated discourse and generally exercise their freedom of expression.

The findings of the NEMPS (2014) suggest that the predominant public perception among Ugandans is that the prevailing ownership patterns are not conducive to the maximum exercise of freedom of expression. A similar study, conducted approximately ten years after Uganda's broadcast sector had been liberalized, indicated that the media in Uganda were owned by "the rich and/or politically connected, private business individuals or entities, and, to a certain degree, NGOs [non-governmental organizations] /religious organisations" (Broadcasting Council 2004, p. 24). The findings of the NEMPS(2014) confirm this as they suggest that media are still largely owned by business people, politicians sympathetic to the ruling party, and religious leaders or organizations, most of whom also openly support the ruling party.

The UBC is officially *the* public broadcaster, but several studies (Kibazo and Kanaabi 2007; Lugalambi, Mwesige and Bussiek 2010) conducted to assess its performance as a public broadcaster have found it wanting. There are a few community radio stations, which struggle to stay afloat amidst competition from the commercial broadcast sector. Government also owns majority shares in the Vision Group, whose stable includes five newspapers, three magazines, five radio stations, three television stations and a printing press. Two of its papers, one in English and the other in Luganda, each have the highest circulation in their respective markets. Together, the Vision Group's media outlets cover all the regions of Uganda in the country's five major languages (Ateso, English, Luganda, Luo and Runyakitara).

The Nation Media Group controls *The Monitor*'s weekly and weekend newspapers; also, NTV, and KFM radio which broadcast predominantly in English; and Dembe FM, a youth radio station broadcasting in Luganda. Other privately owned print media include the *Red Pepper* (daily), the *Observer* (tri-weekly) and the *Independent* (weekly).

The products of the Vision Group and the Nation Media Group together command the largest portion of the Ugandan audience in the newspaper, radio and television sector. NTV, according to Uganda All Media Products (UAMPs) (2013), commands the largest share of viewership across the country (71%) followed by the UBC (the state broadcaster) and the Vision Group's Bukedde TV, a lower-market Luganda-language station. These are followed closely by Urban TV (an English-language youth-oriented station, which also belongs to the Vision Group). These results are confirmed by those of the NEMPS (2014). The Nation Media Group and the Vision Group thus command a lion's share of television. Most other media are private commercial ventures, and their listenership/viewership is highly fragmented.

Because of the scale of investment required in the telecommunications sector, there is more foreign ownership here than in the traditional media sector. There is significant foreign investment in internet service provision, and none of the five major mobile telephone service providers (Mobile Telephone Network (MTN), Orange, Airtel and Uganda Telecommunications (UTL) are controlled by Ugandans.

There has been no regulation of mergers and acquisitions in the electronic media sector, and both the Vision Group and the Nation Media Group have expanded across the country unhampered by any laws over the last decade. When interviewed, a spokesperson for a government communication agency, whose docket covers the media, expressed concern about this as well as the rise of what he referred to as media "cartels", warning that they negatively affect diversity. He cited the Vision Group and the Nation Media Group, but also mentioned that media owners have learnt to beat broadcast radius regulations by linking up with friendly media to cover as much of the country as possible, even though on the surface the stations look discrete, each with a limited reach.

This informant added that because of the nature of media ownership, there is limited concern about the quality of content, provided it promotes or conforms to the owners' ideology. Several key informants shared these views, arguing that the ideology question relates to politics, religion or ethnicity, and sometimes to a combination of these.

While several other key informants acknowledged a link between unregulated ownership and diversity, there were varied responses to the question of whether or not it is necessary or prudent to regulate particular aspects of media ownership such as foreign ownership and cross-media ownership at this point in the growth of the industry. It emerged that media owners in particular see a delicate balance between promoting media diversity and preserving Uganda's national cultural sovereignty on the one hand, and attracting much-needed investor capital on the other. One Corporate Affairs Officer for a large media house noted that capital is a particularly important consideration as there are increasing demands on media houses for sophisticated technology to catch up with the rest of the world. Several media managers who were interviewed argued that what is important is to have clear but broad regulation objectives before adopting specific regulation measures in this area. One senior manager at the Vision Group put it this way:

> I think the thing people should worry about is not ownership regulation; it is content regulation, irrespective of who the owner is. Once you have put those rules in place and you can enforce them equally,

then the ownership won't matter. The problem is failure to impose order in the house. If there was order, the question of dominance would not arise.

The majority of respondents in the NEMPS (2014) both at the household and the national level said they did not think the private media were diverse enough either in terms of ownership or content. A number of key informants, for instance, thought there were deliberate efforts by government to block the opposition from owning private media, which they argued impacted negatively on the diversity of the sector. This view was echoed in FGDs in all four regions of the country. Asked whether he thought an opposition person with the means would be allowed to set up a station, one manager had this to say:

> It will be complicated and there are incidences that can be quoted to that effect. It is said (and I am sure that it is very true) that for example Garuga James Musinguzi who was once a very active politician in FDC [Forum for Democratic Change—the strongest opposition party] wanted to put a radio station in Kinkiizi West and he was not allowed so it may be hard for an opposition [person] to put up a radio station.

Other opposition leaders have publicly made this allegation, though the Executive Director of the Uganda Communications Commission denies that there is a policy barring people from owning stations based on their political affiliation. Nonetheless, government and its supporters are perceived by many key informants to have an advantage over media owners to the degree that government wields control over the UBC and has majority shares in the Vision Group (both of which have a national reach), and through its direct or indirect influence, dominates the ownership of the private media licences in the electronic media sector as well. This is perceived to have a significant effect on the diversity of the sector.

One veteran journalist who belongs to the ruling National Resistance Movement (NRM) party concedes that there may be an imbalance, but attributes it to the "far-sightedness" rather than "high-handedness" of the ruling party. This is his explanation:

> For some strange reason, the owners of the radio stations in particular and the TV stations are supporters of the ruling establishment. My suspicion is that somebody told them that this is the platform of the future and they invested in it. And I am not very much aware of a deliberate attempt to erect obstacles for opposition-leaning

politicians to establish radio stations. I just think, as it is happening with the ordinary political platforms, they just shied away. They didn't think it was worth investing in [...] Now the market is almost saturated with the NRM-leaning radio stations around the country.

The above media ownership landscape seems to confirm the argument of critical political economy regarding the link between media ownership, media diversity and freedom of expression (McChesney1999; Baker 2006). It also demonstrates that Ugandan audiences are not oblivious to this link, and indeed see it as an important determinant in the performance of the media with regards to diversity of content and freedom of expression, as the following section illustrates.

Media ownership, media content and freedom of expression

It emerged from the NEMPS findings that although radio in Uganda is the most attended to medium, with nearly 100% of respondents reporting that they listen to it, only 40% claim to have ever watched television. This is consistent with recent findings such as UAMPs (2013), which found that twice as many people listen to radio regularly as watch television, and Bratton, Mattes and Gyimah-Boadi, (2005, pp. 210–211 cited in White 2008, pp. 276–277), who found that while the majority said radio was an important source of political information, only one in four thought the same about television and even fewer (one in nine) about newspapers.

While most people interviewed acknowledged the significant increase in the number of channels available to them, many did not think this equalled more diversity. Only half of those interviewed, for instance, said the media were promoting a variety of political views in their programming. It is also important to note that 29% (more than one in four) declined to comment or said they had no opinion on this matter. The number of respondents who said they had "no opinion" not only signals possible disenchantment with the media's performance in providing a platform for the expression of diverse political views, it could also suggest that a considerable number of Ugandans are afraid to take a position on this matter in case of possible victimization by the state.

The following up-country media manager's response highlights the tight-rope situation that some Ugandans find themselves in with regard to freely expressing their views in the media:

We have a political situation where anything we do might backfire. When it comes to the government we carefully choose what to do and what not to do. This is where our independence comes in because we look at the consequences of what we do.[4]

It should be noted that these kinds of fears appear more prominently the further out of the capital city one moves. Wasswa (2011) and Mwesige and Tabaire (2011) make similar observations. On the whole, what emerges is that in a context like Uganda's, the political realities dictate that enjoying freedom of expression includes the wisdom to know what to say or not to say, and whom to host or not to host in the course of your duty as a journalist. Furthermore, it emerges that the upcountry stations, which broadcast mostly in the indigenous languages, seem more vulnerable to this type of interference—perhaps because of their perceived political influence with the majority of voters.

While it may seem as if there are many channels and therefore more opportunities for the expression of diverse political views, a considerable number of Ugandans interviewed appear uncertain or negative about the extent of this diversity. These findings are made more significant by their consistency with the findings of similar recent studies by Kibazo and Kanaabi (2007), Nassanga (2008), Kalyango (2009), Bussiek, Lugalambi and Mwesige (2010), Wasswa (2011), all of which indicate that particularly due to the twin pressures to be commercially viable and remain politically safe, the media in Uganda are not as free to allow a variety of political views to be aired as they could be. The fact that the pressure is highest on upcountry stations to be politically safe also means political programming in the indigenous languages bears the brunt as most of these stations broadcast partly or wholly in these languages. This has implications for a large section of the population who either do not have access to the more urban stations, or even if they did, can only participate in their own languages. This may partly explain why nearly one-third of respondents to NEMPS were cautious in their views on the broadcast media's political diversity, which reflects directly on freedom of expression.

Local content and freedom of expression

Defining local content locally

Several jurisdictions, including Australia, South Africa and Rwanda, have synthesized the definition of local content down to "content produced under the creative control of a national". The NEMPS (2014) also investigated understandings of local content as well as perceptions of its importance and adequacy in Uganda. In a context as ethnically diverse as Uganda's, any discussion of diversity and freedom of expression would need to take into account local content. According to McNair and Goldsmith (2015, p. 18), the democratic importance of local content, particularly in a country with great diversity, is undisputed. Besides its commercial significance, they point to local content's contribution to community cohesion and identity, "simply keeping people informed about their immediate environment". They further argue:

> where national news organisations rarely report on the routine affairs of state, regional and city governments, local media must ensure that citizens are aware of and understand the issues on which their locally elected representatives make policy and take decisions. Such scrutiny, a manifestation of the Fourth Estate and watchdog roles deemed to be core functions of the media in a democracy, is just as important at the local level as the national.

McNair and Goldsmith are cognizant of the fact that freedom of expression refers both to political and cultural expression.

The majority of Ugandans interviewed for the NEMPS (2014) seemed familiar with the notion of local content. In trying to define it, the focus was repeatedly on aspects such as the thematic content, language, talent, the location of production and the source of funding. The most common perceptions of what constitutes local content emerging out of the interviews included content that "exhibits any aspect of Ugandan culture, language or music". Many FGD participants dismissed as "not local content" anything that was in a non-Ugandan language. Other characteristics of local content that emerged out of the household survey included "a programme produced by a local group", "something done in the local language", "local songs (and drama) of local artists", "a programme reflecting people's needs", "the traditional way of doing things", "when a programme is not aired on the national station", "something done in the local language," "one produced within or by a particular region, area or group" and "a programme designed to tackle community issues". A few said "a programme that talks about concerns of all Ugandans". The local definitions were in many respects consistent with generic definitions of local content while underscoring the centrality of the local or the indigenous.

Perceptions of adequacy of local content provisions

The majority (80%) of respondents across the regions said they were getting enough local content on radio, while 15% said they were not (5% did not have an opinion). The Central region registered the lowest percentage of the population who said they were receiving adequate local content on radio despite the region having the highest density of radio stations. The reasons given for saying they were not receiving adequate local content included the perception that presenters preferred foreign programmes to local ones, and that local drama and oral literature were absent on radio.

In the current context, the most plausible reason for dissatisfaction with levels of local content on radio appears to be the ethnic mix, particularly in cosmopolitan Kampala. This makes it imperative for stations to try to reach as many different ethnic groups as possible. This in turn results in presenters switching languages in the course of programmes (from English to Luganda, or between different local languages), which frustrates some listeners. Another level to the problem is that while there are several stations broadcasting largely in Luganda in the Central and Eastern regions, there are not that many stations broadcasting exclusively in any of the other languages representing the diverse peoples of these two regions. Instead, the other stations have snippets of several local languages during the day, which also may frustrate listeners.

Only a third of the respondents indicated that they receive enough local content on television. Furthermore, there were wide regional differences in the responses. Three out of four respondents in the Central region said they were receiving enough local content, but less than one in ten in the Northern region held this opinion. In Western Uganda, close to a half of television viewers said they were getting enough local content on television, while only about a quarter (27%) of TV viewers in Eastern Uganda said they were happy with the amount of local content they were receiving on television. This may be attributed to the fact that in the less affluent parts of the country (the Eastern and Northern regions), not many individuals own television sets. Most viewing is in public facilities like bars or video-halls that have a digital/satellite signal. These tend to focus on foreign movies, news and sports, most of which are imported.

There was consensus about the fact that a fundamental ingredient of local content is that it should tackle local issues in a language that is accessible to local audiences. Managers who were interviewed argued that with or without regulation, stations that want to survive must tackle local issues, because this is what sells. While all interviewees acknowledged new regional dynamics, such as the emergence of the East African Community, that might affect perceptions of local content and local content regulation, there was consensus that a distinction needed to be made between local (Ugandan) and local (regional). The key element in distinguishing these two seemed to hinge around the language in which the content was produced.

It is also worth noting that where people said they were not satisfied with the adequacy of local content in the media, the most common explanation given for their dissatisfaction, particularly in reference to television, was that most programming was in English. The importance people attach to programmes in their own languages is further illustrated by statements such as this one by a respondent in Nakasongola, one of the study districts:

> People prefer to watch in a language they can understand; they want to understand certain statements about the events they are watching on the TV. When they watch the local programmes in the local language, it gives them a sense of ownership; they see that TV belongs to them[...]

All informants at the national level agreed that there is a high degree of ethnic diversity in content particularly on radio, though they observed that there are still a few languages that dominate the airwaves. In particular they singled out Luganda and English, and in a second tier, Runyakitara and Luo. The latter group are more commonly used on upcountry-based radio stations in their respective regions (Runyakitara for the West and Luo for the North). The private commercial stations, which would be a great platform for freedom of expression for the rural communities, are under the greatest pressure to use the more widely spoken languages in order to maximize profits.

Perceptions of the limits of media freedom

White (2008, pp. 269–270) contends that the public needs information to enable them to participate meaningfully in their governance through the media (see also Bucy 2001; Effing, van Hillegersberg and Huibers 2011). However, for the media to be partners in the fulfilment of this need, they must be free from undue interference from the state, business and other powerful interests.

One-in-two people interviewed in the household survey said they perceived the broadcast media as free to air facts without undue interference. However, direct responses to this question were less forthcoming, particularly in FGDs conducted in the rural areas.

The views from media owners and managers on the issue of media freedom were varied. While some media managers said they enjoyed a degree of freedom from political interference, others stated the contrary. The following response from an FM station manager whose station broadcasts in English and Luganda typifies one of the more positive responses:

> I think we are doing very well [...] because there is freedom of speech which is not the same like our neighbor[s]. Like when you go to Rwanda, there is a lot of regulations [sic]. Here there is a lot more freedom to talk about things, which also helps people understand certain things better because people are free to talk about anything. [There are] some medias [sic] of course, a few, where there is inflation [meaning exaggeration] and all, and some things are not well dispersed off [sic] or balanced so there is need for balance in terms of discussion of issues which is either political, or it can be social.

The following response from another Kampala-based programmes manager, however, is less straightforward and captures the complexity of gauging media in a context where the rules are both written and unwritten:

> I think whereas they [the media] have the platform, there is a level at which they cannot realize this freedom of expression and this level varies between different media houses. If you are talking about government-owned media houses like the UBC, there is a limit beyond which they cannot go. There are issues they cannot touch. You have seen that some people have been sacked for hosting people in opposition. But even privately owned media houses, they are not also safe because many times they are also intimidated, especially when you go in the villages and it is election time. The RDC[5] can easily call in and tell the manager of Luweero FM that "My friend, if you are going to host Besigye [the opposition leader] whom we have learnt is in the area, I think you are making a big mistake that you will regret for [the rest of] your life". So there are such threats that are going on and certainly they remain a big issue in the freedom of expression.

The findings also indicated that political pressure on stations varies from season to season, reaching its peak at election time. The interviews revealed that upcountry journalists are victimised both by law-enforcement officers and by fellow citizens. Some key informants at the grassroots level reported, for instance, that it is not unusual for *boda-boda*[6] cyclists to gang up and beat up a reporter whose work appears not to support their political affiliation. This was also confirmed by other key informants at the national level.

The views on this issue among national-level key informants did not differ significantly from those at the grassroots. It emerged, therefore, that if there is a degree of freedom of expression, the media certainly have learnt not to take it for granted.

Perceptions of the performance of the public media in enhancing freedom of expression

One of the ways in which diversity is achieved is the demarcation of broadcasting into different tiers (typically public, commercial and community). The general perception among managers of private media houses in Uganda is that the private stations offer better quality, and that they have more "dynamic" programming ideas because they are not as constrained to tow the government line or become bogged down by bureaucracy, and are more able to take risks. The public broadcaster UBC, which is expected to cater to the majority of Uganda's population in their various languages, has suffered the same technical, human resources and funding constraints that several other public broadcasters in Africa suffer (see Lugalambi, Mwesige and Bussiek 2010 and Friedrich Ebert Stiftung 2012c, Uganda 2012, p. 47 for a recent comprehensive discussion on the state of the UBC; see also Friedrich Ebert Stiftung 2012b, Democratic Republic of Congo, p. 103; Friedrich Ebert Stiftung 2013a, Kenya p. 44; Friedrich Ebert Stiftung 2013b, South Africa, p. 54). A key informant from the UBC admitted that as a result of these challenges, they are only able to meet a few of the needs of their audiences.

The issue of signal interference for the UBC stations in particular was mentioned repeatedly in the poorer areas of the country, notably Northern and Eastern Uganda. This problem, considered to be a major hindrance by many of the interviewees, is attributed to the fact that the UBC's transmitters in these areas are in a state of disrepair, while the private stations have the resources to buy more powerful transmitters. This is compounded by the fact that the regulator does not consistently enforce the use of filters.

The UBC's other challenges, according to the UBC media manager, include the fact that their policy is to be cautious and not to "over-sensationalize" issues. This is perceived to result in a loss of audiences, since the competitors—the private FM stations—seem to have more room for daring programming. Even though government funding to the UBC has decreased steadily since they were re-structured into a "public" broadcaster, the UBC still suffers from a degree of complacency that comes from being state funded. For instance, the key informant reported that they have not conducted much audience research in the last decade. As a result, they do not always have a clear picture of the needs of their audiences. In addition, the UBC suffers from being viewed as a state broadcaster rather than a public broadcaster by government and by some of its audience. This compounds the expectations and pressures of the station. The key informant from the UBC put it this way:

> Not that it is written but it is again this culture that you find. So if you are a news reporter and you bring in your well-balanced news story, so how does the editor treat it? Because the editor is more graded [more high-ranking] [...] than you, a news reporter, in terms of what the government will think when that particular story airs [...] with time a reporter obviously learns what your editor may not want in your story.

This informant admits that although they do invite opposition politicians, they must be selective.

> So you can see that then there [is] some kind of concern that when you are inviting somebody from the opposition, who are you exactly inviting from that opposition? So when you are drawing the list of invitees, yourself [sic] consider "who am I going to bring?" And in fact for here in UBC every guest who is invited for a talk-show, any type of talk-show, has to be vetted by the Managing Director himself. So it is like you fill a form in which you state that "Sir, I have a guest in this show and the guest is called this, and this is his telephone number, this is where he works", and then you submit it to the manager for approval so that you do not get these radical persons who might unfairly, in the view of the corporation, come and bash for example on government interests and something like that, and there is the connectivity of government interests in UBC. Not state interests, but government interests.

That the UBC still operates like a state broadcaster and is not entirely free of direct government interference is consistent with a number of recent studies and evaluations (see, for instance, Kibazo and Kanaabi 2007; Lugalambi, Mwesige and Bussiek2010). However, while the "public broadcaster" may be constrained by official or non-official government regulation and internal inefficiencies, it still has a role to play since public broadcasters by their nature, no matter how imperfect, tend to be more inclined towards public affairs broadcasting than their FM, often privately owned counterparts. Besides, public broadcasters are designed to accommodate more linguistically diverse programming than other stations and have the potential to provide a forum for debate for the majority of citizens, who may not be able to express themselves freely in English. Indeed, the key informant at the UBC was positive about the potential of the public broadcaster to enhance political diversity. He said he saw the UBC as meeting a unique need for information and analysis for the 25–50-year-old age-group who do not feel satisfied with the offerings of the typical FM (private) station. This is how he put it.

> These listeners expect analysis or breakdown of national public-interest issues. You know if you made a comparison with a typical FM radio, largely you find that talk is really little. A typical radio station say in Kampala [...] will have just one talk-show in a day. They may have these simple topics about celebrities but not these ones about, say, policy, law and implementation [level]. But for us [sic] we really try, and of course we have more than one language. We have [programmes] along those serious topical issues.

Perceptions of the performance of community media in enhancing freedom of expression

Community media have the potential to make a significant contribution to freedom of expression to the extent that they serve local, often lower-income sections of the population, are not bound by the need for professionals in their running, are low budget and typically broadcast in the indigenous languages and address the needs of the less affluent (Opubor 2000; Wanyeki 2000). Recent research on community media in Uganda suggests that the sector is poorly understood; it is weak because it is poorly resourced; and it is not independent enough. As a result, the sector is perceived as not having fulfilled its mandate of serving the unique needs of geographical or interest communities in the lower income strata of the country in a liberalized media environment (Dralega 2009; Nassanga2009). A key informant from Maama FM, one of the oldest community media stations in Uganda, said lack of staff and dependence on volunteers has characterized this sector since its inception. For instance, despite being one of Uganda's longest surviving community stations, Maama FM has only four permanent staff compared to 38 volunteers. The biggest impediment to the community media in Uganda contributing to freedom of expression, however, appears to be their lack of financial sustainability. Many of them are entirely dependent on donor funding or are funded by local politicians. This has undermined the core purpose of community media, and given rise to a degree of disillusionment.

The key informant from Maama FM, for instance, said it would be "important for government to support the establishment and running of community radio stations". She also recommended that the regulator relax regulation that bars community media from soliciting advertising, and instead compel these stations to ensure the proceeds are ploughed back rather than shared by owners or shareholders. Otherwise, she said, community broadcasting in Uganda would be untenable. However, such compromises, practical as they may appear, would come at a cost—a possible loss of independence. Besides, the proposals of the key informant seem to contradict most of the literature on the independence of community media from the control of government, What they do, though is (i) echo some of the findings at the grassroots level; (ii) echo the findings of the Broadcasting Council (2004), where one policy-maker, asked about the viability of community media depending on community contributions replied, "Community broadcasting would be desirable, but everybody is still preoccupied with survival. The community spirit therefore is lacking. There is no stability in the social structure"; and (iii) underscore the complexity of identifying viable mechanisms for financial sustainability for the survival of the sector, a problem that dogs community media in several African countries.

Thus one may conclude that even with the knowledge of how community media should ideally run, the pressures of survival can push the most ardent advocates of community broadcasting in its pure form to concede some ground to secure the sustainability of this tier of broadcasting and perhaps their own jobs. As a result of this, the sector may suffer as the former advocates of its independence from government and other powerful interests, pushed into a corner, are forced to compromise on those ideals that are supposed to secure the sector's contribution to freedom of expression.

Perceptions of the performance of the new media in enhancing freedom of expression

The performance of the new media (particularly mobile telephones and the internet) with regard to diversity and freedom of expression have received mixed reviews from researchers. While several studies have hailed the new media as the new frontier that will unleash Africa's democratic and developmental potential, superseding the traditional media in their accessibility and versatility (see, for instance, Ekine 2008), others (for instance, Alzouma 2010; Etzo and Collender 2010) caution that exuberance about the contribution of these new media is perhaps misplaced. They point out structural obstacles such as technical infrastructure, inability to afford access, language and others that still hinder the majority of ordinary citizens in developing countries from enjoying the potential benefits of these new technologies.

The findings of the NEMPS confirm that while a relatively large number of (especially) urban residents in Uganda have heard of the internet, considerably fewer reported ever having used it. Similarly, although 85% said they had used mobile phones, only 69% said they owned a mobile phone. The findings also revealed that while the mobile phones are more accessible and affordable and have great potential to draw ordinary citizens into public discourse on issues of political interest, particularly in synergy with indigenous language radio, internet access and the skills to use it remain the privilege of a few, reducing its potential to play a similar role.

All key station managers who were interviewed acknowledged that the technology of the media is changing rapidly and that their stations felt obliged to keep up with the times. Unlike managers of upcountry stations, all the media managers based in Kampala (the capital city) who were interviewed said their stations were harnessing synergies between the new and old media to extend their services, and that audience evaluation was positive. They also said that this had helped audiences to participate more in programmes through the internet and the use of mobile phones to call in. There were many upcountry (rural) stations where this was not yet the case, but still the majority of informants said they were aware of the democratic potential of the new media.

However, the findings of the study also reveal that there are still significant disparities in how many people have heard about the new media technologies, how many have used them and in the case of the phone, how many actually own them. For instance, there are many who would not even agree to be interviewed about, particularly, the internet, because they said they had never heard of it, let alone used it. Of those interviewed in the household survey, only 13% said they had ever used the internet. There were significant disparities based on gender and location (urban vs. rural) as well.

While 85% said they had used mobile phones, only 69% reported owning a phone. This notwithstanding, there was consensus that the mobile phone had made it easier for people to access the broadcast media and to express their views. It did emerge, though, that even with this facility i) stations select what calls to accept or reject, particularly during political talk-shows and ii) the capacity to afford air-time remains an obstacle, leading some callers to accept air-time from well-resourced politicians who then expect them to call in to promote or defend a particular ideological position.

Digital migration and implications for diversity and freedom of expression

There is a digital migration policy in place and Uganda is on course for the mandatory migration from analogue to digital broadcasting. Ideally this should make more media outlets accessible, increase content diversity and improve the quality of reception. This in turn should increase the capacity of the media to serve as forums for debate and self-expression. However, the experience in neighbouring countries has been that most new digital stations following digital migration tend to be devoted to light entertainment.

With the country moving towards digitalization, it may be necessary to refine regulation to further secure freedom of expression. Such refinement would seek to address the reduction in the traditional gate-keeping role of editors, for instance, without unduly infringing on fundamental rights to information and expression within the context of the laws of Uganda. It will also seek to address the regulation of the new mobile and versatile converged platforms that were previously not regulated at all or regulated in a discrete rather than converged manner.

A policy-maker who was interviewed pointed out that it would be necessary to make set-top boxes affordable in order not to lock out the majority of Ugandans after digital migration. Considering that many cannot afford television sets in the first place, it is unlikely that set-top boxes will be a priority for the majority, particularly the rural poor. It would also be necessary to boost local content production to populate the many new channels that would arise from digital migration. This could in turn strengthen the media's contribution towards enhancing freedom of expression, with cultural, economic and political dividends.

Conclusions

The concepts of media freedom, media diversity and freedom of expression are interlinked. While there is some truth in the argument that the more media outlets a polity has, the greater the chances that a more diverse set of views will be accommodated, this depends on a number of other factors, both structural and symbolic. These, in the case of Uganda, include the new commercial logic of the media industry and the architecture of media ownership. Uganda's media landscape is dominated by the Vision Group and the Nation Media Group but has a large number of radio stations broadcasting in one or more of the indigenous languages. Coupled with television and the emerging new media of the internet and mobile telephone, these stations could be a great opportunity for enhancing freedom of expression. However, the manner in which the media are regulated and the double message that the regulatory regime sends to media owners and citizens poses a considerable obstacle to the full enjoyment of freedom of expression. There are concerns about government interference in the editorial operations of the media. It also emerges that both the public and community broadcasting sector are weak and therefore are not able to "stand in the gap" where the commercial media fail to satisfy the needs of audiences. Practical concerns like the capacity of citizens to own and to use the media also have an impact on the extent to which citizens are free to enjoy freedoms such as media freedom and freedom of expression.

At the symbolic level, one notes that in a context like Uganda's the indigenous languages are potentially some of the greatest enablers of media-related freedoms. It is also clear that Ugandans enjoy a degree of local content on radio. However, the local content provisions on television are still perceived as inadequate except in a few, dominant, commercially viable languages. This has implications for the citizens' ability to access information available in the media, as well as to express their views or their lifestyles in the media. The structural and symbolic factors combined have a bearing on the potential of the media i) to operate freely (without undue interference) and ii) to serve as a platform for the free expression of a variety of voices and cultures for all citizens.

Acknowledgements

The National Electronic Media Performance Study (2014) was made possible by funding from the Uganda Communications Commission. Monica B. Chibita was the Principal Investigator; Richard Kibombo was the co-researcher.

Notes

1. Symbolic barriers in an African context typically include language barriers created by the position of English vis-à-vis the indigenous languages.
2. Uganda currently has 112 districts.
3. According to the Uganda Bureau of Standards (www.ubos.org), nearly 80% of Uganda's population live in the rural areas.

4. Government has on several occasions in the past closed down stations for broadcasting material that it found displeasing.
5. Resident District Commissioner, a high-ranking politically appointed district official.
6. A bicycle or motorcycle taxi commonly used in East Africa.

References

Alzouma, G. 2010. Media, technology, and democracy in Niger: What did the advent of ICTs change? In C.U. Nwokeafor and K. Langhmia (Eds). *Media and Technology in Emerging African Democracies*, pp. 23–42.

Alzouma, G. 2013. Dimensions of the mobile divide in Niger. In C. J. Witte and S. E. Mannon (Eds). Massimo Ragnedda and Muschert, Glen W. The *Digital Divide*, pp. 297–308.

Article XIX. 2003. *Broadcasting Policy and Practice in Africa*. London: Article XIX.

Baker, C. E. 2006. *Media Concentration and Democracy: Why Ownership Matters*. Cambridge: Cambridge University Press.

Blankson, I. A. and Murphy, P. D. (Eds). 2012. *Negotiating Democracy: Media Transformations in Emerging Democracies*. New York: State University of New York Press.

Bratton, M., Mattes, R. and Gyimah-Boadi, E. 2005. *Public Opinion, Democracy and Market Reform in Africa*. Cambridge: Cambridge University Press.

Broadcasting Council. 2004. *National Electronic Media Performance Study*. Kampala: Makerere University Printery.

Cammaerts, B. and Carpentier, N. (Eds). 2007. *Participation and Media. Reclaiming the Media: Communication Rights and Democratic Media Roles*. Bristol: Intellect.

Chibita, M. B. 2006. Indigenous language programming and citizen participation in Ugandan broadcasting: An exploratory study (Doctoral dissertation). Retrieved from uir.unisa.ac.za/bitstream/handle/10500/2473/thesis.pdf?sequence=1.

Cooper, S. D. 2006. *Watching the Watchdog: Bloggers as the Fifth Estate*. Marquette: Marquette Books.

Curran J. 1991. Rethinking media as a public sphere, in *The Political Economy of the Media*, vol. ii, edited by P Golding & G Murdock. Cheltenham: Edward Elgar. 120–150.

Curran, J. 2000. Rethinking media and democracy. *Mass Media and Society*, 3(1), 120–154.

Diamond, L. J. and Morlino, L. (Eds). 2005. *Assessing the Quality of Democracy*. Baltimore: Johns Hopkins University Press.

Dralega, C. A. 2009. Participatory ethos, multimedia experiments, and disjunctures in community media in Uganda. *Ecquid Novi*, 30(1), 24–41.

Effing, R.C., van Hillegersberg, J. and Huibers, T.W.C. 2011. Social media and political participation: Are Facebook, Twitter and YouTube democratizing our political systems? In *Third IFIP WG 8.5 International Conference on Electronic Participation*, ePart2011, 29 August–1 September 2011, Delft, the Netherlands, pp. 25–35.

Ekine, S. 2008.Women's responses to state violence in the Niger Delta. *Feminist Africa*, 10, 67–83.

Ernst & Young. 2012. *Review of the Draft National Broadcasting Policy (DRAFT)*. (Unpublished).

Etzo, Z. and Collender, G. 2010. The mobile revolution in Africa: Rhetoric or reality? *African Affairs*, 109(439), 659–668.

Friedrich Ebert Stiftung. 2012a. African Media Barometer. Democratic Republic of Congo. Retrieved from https://www.google.com/#q=african+media+barom eter+2012.

Friedrich Ebert Stiftung. 2012c. African Media Barometer. Uganda. Retrieved from https://www.google.com/#q=african+media+barometer+2012.

Friedrich Ebert Stiftung. 2013a. African Media Barometer. Kenya. Retrieved from https://www.google.com/#q=african+media+barometer+2013.

Friedrich Ebert Stiftung. 2013b. African Media Barometer. South Africa. Retrieved fromhttps://www.google.com/#q=african+media+barometer+2012.

Garnham, N. 1995. The media and the public sphere. In C. Calhoun (Ed.). *Habermas and the Public Sphere.* Cambridge, MA: MIT Press, pp. 359–376.

Golding, P. 1990. Political communication and citizenship: The media and democracy in an inegalitarian social order. In M. Ferguson (Ed.). *Public Communication: The New Imperatives: Future Directions for Media Research.* London: Sage, pp. 84–100.

Golding, P. and Murdock, G. 1991. Culture, communications and political economy. In J. Curran and M. Gurevitch (Eds). *Mass Media and Society.* London: Edward Arnold, pp. 15–32.

Goldsmiths Media Group. 2000. Media organisations in society: central issues, in *Media Organisations in Society*, edited by J Curran. London: Arnold:19–65.

Hyden, G., Leslie, M. and Ogundimu, F. F. (Eds). 2003. *Media and Democracy in Africa.* New Brunswick, NJ: Transaction Publishers.

Ipsos/Synovate. 2013. *Uganda All Media Products Survey.* Kampala.

Jenkins, H. 2004. The cultural logic of media convergence. *International Journal of Cultural Studies*, 7(1), 33–43.

Kalyango, Jr, Y. 2009. Political news use and democratic support: A study of Uganda's radio impact. *Journal of Radio & Audio Media*, 16(2), 200–215.

Kibazo, P. and Kanaabi H. 2007. *FM Stations in Uganda: "Quantity without Quality." East African Media Institute Examines the State of FM Stations in Uganda on Professional Standards and Information Dissemination.* Kampala: East African Media Institute.

Liebman, B. L. 2005. Watchdog or demagogue? The media in the Chinese legal system. *Columbia Law Review*, 105(1), 1–157.

Lugalambi, G.W., Mwesige, P. G. and Bussiek, H. 2010. *On Air: Uganda Public Broadcasting Corporation Survey Report.* Nairobi: AfriMAP, OSIEA, OSMP. Retrieved from www.issuelab.org/resource/on_air-uganda-public-broadcasting-corporation-survey-report.

McCombs, M. E. and Shaw, D. L. 1972. The agenda-setting function of mass media. *Public Opinion Quarterly*, 36(2), 176–187.

McNair, B. and Goldsmith, B. 2015. Local content and the ABC. *The Conversation.* Retrieved from http://creativecommons.org/licenses/by-nd/4.0/.

Meadows, M. 2013.Putting the citizen back into journalism. *Journalism*, 14(43), 43–60.

Murdock, G. and Golding, P. 1989. Information poverty and political inequality: Citizenship in the age of privatized communications. *Journal of Communication*, 39(3), 180–195.

Mwesige, P. G. 2004. *"Can You Hear Me Now?":* Radio Talk Shows and Political Participation in Uganda. Bloomington: Indiana University.

Mwesige, P. and Tabaire, B. 2011. *Overview of the State of Media Freedom in Uganda*. Kampala: African Centre for Media Excellence.

Nabunya, C. 2009. The Role of Radio Talk Shows in the Transition to Multi-Party Politics and Democracy in Uganda. A Case Study. Retrieved from http://uta32-kk.lib.helsinki.fi/bitstream/handle/10024/81328/gradu04101.pdf?sequence=1.

Nassanga, L. G. 2008. Journalism ethics and the emerging new media culture of radio talk shows and public debates (Ekimeeza) in Uganda. *Journalism*, 9(5), 646–663.

Nassanga, L. G. 2009. As Assessment of the changing community media parameters in East Africa. Equid Novi: African Journalism Studies, 30, pp. 42–57.

Nisbet, E. C. 2008. Media use, democratic citizenship, and communication gaps in a developing democracy. *International Journal of Public Opinion Research*, 20(4), 454–482.

Norris, P. 2000. *A Virtuous Circle*. Cambridge: Cambridge University Press.

Norris, P. 2009. *Public Sentinel: News Media and Governance Reform*. Washington, DC: World Bank.

Nyamnjoh, F. 2005. *Africa's Media: Democracy and the Politics of Belonging.* London: Zed Books.

Ocitti, J. 1999. Media and democracy in Africa: Mutual political bedfellows or implacable arch-foes (Doctoral dissertation, Weatherhead Center for International Affairs, Harvard University).

Opubor, A. E. 2000. If community media is the answer, what is the question? Promoting community media in Africa. Retrieved from http://www.unesco.org/webworld/publications/community_media/pdf/chap1.pdf.

Scheufele, D. A. and Tewksbury, D. 2007. Framing, agenda setting, and priming: The evolution of three media effects models. *Journal of Communication*, 57(1), 9–20.

Skoufias, E., Narita, R. and Narayan, A. 2014. Does access to information empower the poor? Evidence from the Dominican Republic. (1 May 2014). World Bank Policy Research Working Paper, (6895).

Tabaire, B. 2007. The press and political repression in Uganda: Back to the future? *Journal of Eastern African Studies*, 1(2), 193–211.

Tettey, W. J. 2001. The media and democratization in Africa: Contributions, constraints and concerns of the private press. *Media, Culture & Society*, 23(1), 5–31.

Uganda. 1964. Official Secrets Act. Kampala. Government Printers.

Uganda. 1995. Constitution of the Republic of Uganda. Kampala. Government Printers.

Uganda. 1995. The Press and Journalists' Act. Kampala. Government Printers.

Uganda. 1996. The Electronic Media Act. Kampala. Government Printers.

Uganda. 2002. Anti-Terrorism Act. Kampala. Government Printers.

Uganda. 2004. The Draft National Broadcast Policy. Kampala. Government Printers.

Uganda. 2005. Parliamentary Elections Act. Kampala. Government Printers.

Uganda. 2005. Presidential Elections Act. Kampala. Government Printers.

Uganda. 2005. Referendum and Other Provisions Act. Kampala. Government Printers.

Uganda. 2005. Uganda Broadcasting Corporation Act. Kampala. Government Printers.

Uganda. 2006. Access to Information Act. Kampala. Government Printers.

Uganda. 2007. Penal Code Act (Amendment). Kampala. Government Printers.

Uganda. 2012. Interception of Communications Act. Kampala. Government Printers.

Uganda. 2013. Public Order Management Act. Kampala. Government Printers.

Uganda. 2013. The Communications Act. Kampala. Government Printers.

Uganda. 2014. National Electronic Media Performance Study. Unpublished.

Uganda. Uganda Communications Commission.www.ucc.co.ug.

Universal Declaration of Human Rights. www.un.org/en/documents/udhr. Accessed on 28 July, 2014.

Van Cuilenberg, J. 1999. On competition, access and diversity in media, old and new. *New Media and Society.* 1(2), 183–207.

Vartraeten, Hans. 1996. The media and the transformation of the public sphere. *European Journal of Communication,* 11(3), 347–370.

Wanyeki, L. M. 2000. The development of community media in East and Southern Africa. Promoting community media in Africa. Retrieved from https://scholar.google.no/scholar?q=The+development+of+community+media +in+East+and+Southern+Africa.+Promoting+community+media+in+Africa&bt nG=&hl=en&as_sdt=0%2C5&as_vis=1.

Wasko, J. 2014. The study of the political economy of the media in the twenty-first century. *International Journal of Media & Cultural Politics,* 10(3), 259–271.

Wasko, J., Murdock, G. and Sousa, H. 2011. Introduction: The political economy of communications: Core concerns and issues. In J. Wasko, G. Murdock and H. Soussa (Eds). *A Handbook of the Political Economy of Communication.* Hoboken, NJ: Wiley-Blackwell.

Wasserman, H. (Ed.). 2010. *Popular Media, Democracy and Development in Africa.* London: Routledge.

Wasserman, H. 2011. Mobile phones, popular media, and everyday African democracy: Transmissions and transgressions. *Popular Communication,* 9(2), 146–158.

Wasswa, J.B. 2011. Media in an era of advertiser recession: rethinking the business models. *Uganda Media Review,* 11, 27–32. White, R. A. 2008. The role of media in democratic governance in Africa, 1(3), pp. 269–328.

Part II
The Media, Language, Inclusion and Exclusion in Africa

3
IsiZulu Language and the *Ilanga* Newspaper as Catalysts for Participatory Democracy in South Africa

Thabisile Buthelezi

Introduction

When writing about language matters, Gilmartin (2004) states that language was crucial in the establishment and maintenance of both colonial rule, and the new postcolonial identities. In such colonial systems, the colonisers used language, among other things, as a colonising and civilising tool, where the colonised (deemed civilised) assimilated the language of the coloniser, most often at the expense of their indigenous languages. Even today, that is, centuries after colonialism ended in Africa, we still see colonial languages such as English and French remaining dominant in many African countries. Examples are the Malawian government that adopted English as an official language immediately after independence in 1964 (Moyo 2001); the Cameroon, where the two official languages are the foreign English and French (Ngefac 2010); Tanzania, where English and Kiswahili are languages of education (Swilla 2009), and many others.

However, language is connected to one's identity. When one loses one's language, one may subsequently lose one's sense of self. Alexander (2005) also confirms that the "source of power of language is its function as a transmission mechanism of 'culture' or more popularly, its role in the formation of individual and social identities". On the contrary, experience has taught us that even though South Africa was colonised, not all Africans learnt the English language, and not all people who learnt English attained adequate competence in that language. This means that the continued use of English in administration, education, and economy renders the majority of Africans excluded and powerless, as Alexander (2005) argues:

> If one does not command the language, one is automatically excluded and disempowered [...] The self-esteem, self-confidence, potential creativity, and spontaneity that come with being able to use the language(s) that have shaped one from early childhood (one's mother-tongue) is the foundation of all democratic polities and institutions. To be denied the use of this is the very meaning of oppression.

In this sense, it means that an opportunity to use one's home language is empowering and liberating. Tabata (2006) identifies the three pillars of identity as history, anti-imperialism, and language. Accordingly, one may argue that a nation's struggle to preserve its history, heritage and language, is actually a struggle for identity preservation. My thesis in this chapter is that in South Africa while English was used as a civilising, colonising and educational tool, isiZulu language maintained its position as a language of communication through isiZulu print media (for example; *Bona Magazine*, *Ilanga* newspaper), and radio (such as Ukhozi FM). Particularly, *Ilanga* newspaper became a reflective tool through which the colonised people critically and collectively engaged with their own neophyte colonised identities and their African identities. As they used isiZulu language through isiZulu media, the colonised people critically deliberated on the laws that were imposed upon them by the colonial masters. The critical engagement of amaZulu people about their origins, their heritage, and through their language kept their identity and nationality, to a certain degree, checked.

Using evidence from *Ilanga* newspaper editions of the period 2010–2013, I further argue that in the new democratic South Africa, *Ilanga* newspaper provides a dialogic, consultative and educational space among citizens themselves through which readers engage with debates and discourses about their origins and identity and the social issues affecting their lives. This means that ordinary citizens have a medium through which to express their views and the newspaper provides a connection between the needs of people from the low socio-economic groups of society and the available resources in communities, within and outside government, for addressing such needs. Therefore, the chapter will discuss the following main issues:

- Language, power and the policy context in South Africa.
- The history and development of isiZulu language.

- The role of isiZulu language and media in the colonial era.
- The role of isiZulu language and media in contemporary South Africa.

Language, power and the policy context in South Africa

In South Africa, the long period of apartheid rule, which started in 1948 and contributed to the underdevelopment of African languages, ended with the first democratic elections that occurred in 1994. During this time, African languages were neglected. However, the neglect of African languages started much earlier with the entry of European languages into South Africa, which occurred in 1652 when Jan van Riebeeck arrived at the Cape, with a subsequent establishment of a Dutch trading station of the Dutch East India Company (De Groef 2010). During this Dutch influence period, which Kamwangamalu (2000) terms the Dutchification period (1652–1795), a variety of languages were spoken at the Cape; however, as De Groef (2010) further states, only the knowledge of the Dutch language enabled one to access resources and employment in civil service. In 1795 when the British Government took over South Africa from the Dutch for the first time, and then later during re-annexation in the years 1806–1948, it successfully anglicised the colony, replacing the Dutch language with English, and this marked the beginning of the hegemony of English (De Groef 2010).

When discussing the relationship between language and power, Scott and Ng (1999) argue that in colonial systems, language routinises power. During colonisation the colonists' impositions of power over weaker nations are often coupled with the imposition of the master's language over the native people since the native people are required to learn and use the master's language for their own survival and social mobility. In this sense, the colonial language gains power because of its imposed use on the natives. Along these lines, De Kadt (1996) argues that language in itself does not possess power, but that "it is individual languages, in their individual societal locus, which exercise power, and this power is a function of the roles of these languages in 'their' society". Therefore, in South Africa English gained its power because African nations were forced to learn it so that they could access employment in civil service.

Alongside colonisation in South Africa was the Christian missionary work that was introduced in the country; for instance, the Christian mission stations were established "in the nascent colonial order of Natal in the 1850s and 1860s" (Gilmour 2007). Through their mission schools, the missionaries provided education for Africans. This facilitated the teaching of English to African children, as it was one of the school subjects. Through the missionary education, a new educated group of Africans emerged. Since missionaries provided education, education itself became associated with religion and thus the emerging group of educated Africans became known as *amakholwa* (the believers) (Mokoena 2009). This group became regular readers of *Ilanga Lase Natali*.

However, keen to spread their religion, the missionaries also learned local languages such as isiXhosa and isiZulu and translated some of their religious documents into local languages. This promoted the development of African languages into written languages (Houser 2010). Therefore, Africans who participated in missionary education learnt the written form of their home languages. However, during the missionary epoch the use of indigenous languages was limited to communication, mainly for religious purposes, and African languages were not used to access economy or as official languages, or as languages of learning and teaching.

In colonised societies, if the natives learn the master's language in addition to their own native language, this leads to additive bilingualism. This happened in South Africa where educated Africans learnt English as well as their indigenous languages, and became bilingual. However, Scott and Ng (1999) argue that in this situation of bilingualism, the two languages are unequal as the master's language "commands more social prestige and utility". Furthermore, the widespread use of the master's language affects "political dominance to the native culture, making it a natural part of everyday life". Ng and Bradac (1993) refer to this state of social change as the linguistic routinisation of dominance.

The Afrikaners (Nationalist) Government took power in 1948, and throughout its rule (1948–1994) sought to challenge the hegemony of English by promoting the Afrikaans language, elevating its status to that of an official language and a language of learning and teaching (Kamwangamalu 2000). Thus, alongside English, Afrikaans became the official language of the country.

When the democratic government of the African National Congress (ANC) took over in 1994, it sought to correct the status of languages, and embarked on multilingualism, which Kamwangamalu (2000) dubs the democratisation period. The country adopted 11 official languages as one of the Founding Provisions in its New Constitution (Green 2008). Although the progress regarding the implementation of this policy is beyond the scope of this chapter, it is important to note that the policy provides for the promotion, development and use of African languages.

Further development of African languages in the current context is possible because most already developed into written languages during the missionary era in South Africa.

A brief history and development of isiZulu language

Like other African indigenous languages, isiZulu language is a medium of expression and communication of ideas, a repository of customs, traditions and literature. As one of the 11 official languages in South Africa, and as the Census 2011 shows (Statistics 2011), isiZulu is the language with the largest number of speakers, constituting about 23% of the total population, and its speakers are concentrated in KwaZulu-Natal.

Its relation to other languages in the Nguni cluster (isiXhosa, isiSwati, isiNdebele), where similarities in grammar and syntax exist (Gowlett 2004), means that a person who knows any one of the four languages in the Nguni cluster understands all other Nguni languages. According to Statistics South Africa (2011), the Census 2011 reports show that a combined total number of speakers of the four Nguni languages (isiZulu, isiXhosa, isiNdebele and isiSwati) is approximately 44% of the total South African population.

IsiZulu language has a well-developed orthography. The 19th-century missionaries in the then Natal colony, for example the Church of England's Bishop, J. W. Colenso (1814–1883), Springvale Mission Bishop, H. Callaway, L. Grout and others started to put together a written isiZulu language using the old orthography (Houser 2010). As they developed the written form of the African languages, the missionaries determined what would constitute a specific language orthography and standardisation although this was along the lines of political practice and evangelical rivalry (Gilmour 2007).

Since isiZulu has been a written language, many whites and Zulu writers have been enthusiastic in formulating and publishing isiZulu grammar books, and among these are the pioneers of isiZulu grammar books, L. Grout (Rogerson 2013), Dr C. M. Doke and Professor C. L. S. Nyembezi (Green 2008). In addition, many authors have written reference materials (such as dictionaries); a well-developed body of fiction material has been published in isiZulu language over the years, and many more authors are published every day. New isiZulu newspapers have appeared, and some titles have continued to flourish as they increase their sales. I will discuss this point in detail in the following section.

An overview of isiZulu newspapers and the research strategy

Switzer and Switzer (1979) argue that in South Africa it was difficult to have an effective black ownership and editorial control of newspapers as African-financed newspapers had not survived the test of time. However, Berger (1998) states that the Natal newspaper, *Inkundla Ya Bantu* (the People's Forum), which was founded in 1938 by African entrepreneurs Paul Knox Bonga and Phillip Goduka Katamzi, owners of the Verulam Press, survived for an effective 13 years. It served as a space that the youth wing of the ANC utilised for intellectual engagement (Berger 1998).

According to Mokoena (2008), in the 19th century the missionary Bishop Colenso established a printing press at his mission station, where isiZulu books, dictionaries and translations were published. In 1876, the missionary printing press "ventured into the newspaper business" by establishing a mostly religious isiZulu newspaper, *Ubaqa* (the Torch) (Mokoena 2009), which later folded. According to Switzer and Switzer (1979), another isiZulu newspaper, *Inkanyiso Yase Natali*, was

> [t]he first newspaper that gained a reputation as a protest journal because although it was originally established in 1889 as an Anglican mission product it was not restricted to religious matters, and after being handed over to its African editors in 1895, it operated beyond the confines of mission censorship.

Another isiZulu newspaper, which was founded in 1898 under the editorship of Mark Radebe, was *Ipepa Lo Hlanga* (Mokoena 2009). Furthermore, a controversial figure, A. W. G. Champion, founded his own newspaper, *Udibi Lwase Afrika*, in the 1920s to counter the influence of *Ilanga Lase Natali* newspaper, which was owned and edited by his political rival, J. L. Dube ((Mokoena 2009); *Udibi Lwase Afrika* closed down in 1929. IsiZulu newspapers that have survived for centuries are *UMAfrika* and *Ilanga*.

Abbort Gerard, who was appointed Provost in the Marrianhill Monastery, situated in Pinetown, established UMAfrika, which started as *Izindaba Zabantu*, in 1911; and an excellent isiZulu linguist, Father John Baptist Sauter, ordained in 1909 at Marrianhill as a Trappist, became the chief editor of the paper in 1923. The paper changed its name to *UMAfrika* in 1929 and has been published without a break to the present day (Marrianhill Monastery, Pinetown).

A recent but flourishing daily newspaper, *Isolezwe* (the Eye of the Nation), was launched in 2002; and a very recently established religious weekly newspaper, *Inkazimulo* (the Glory) profiles itself as bringing back humaneness (*Ibuyisa Ubuntu*).

While most South African print media slightly declined their circulations after the 2009 recession, isiZulu newspapers continue to flourish, with sales rising since readers in isiZulu language are growing in the newspaper market (Tabelo 2011). Part of the reasons for the rise in isiZulu media is that the language can be understood by speakers of other Nguni languages (used by about 44% of the total South African population). *Isolezwe* is even read by foreigners (for example, Zimbabwean Shona) when they want to learn isiZulu. The current tabloid styles of isiZulu newspapers, *UMAfrika* (the African), *Isolezwe* (the Eye of the Nation), *Ilanga* (the Sun) and *Inkazimulo* (the Glory) are the cheapest papers on the market, selling for R3.00 each (that is, about 40 US cents or 30 Euro cents), and this makes the newspapers affordable to ordinary South African citizens. *Isolezwe* and *Inkazimulo* are the youngest of the four newspapers. Launched in 2002, and according to the Audit Bureau of Circulation and Tabelo (2011), *Isolezwe* is now one of the growing daily newspapers: sales of its daily edition have risen to more than 104, 320, and those of its Sunday edition, *Isolezwe NgeSonto* (the Eye of the Nation on Sunday), exceeded 74,916. A recently established weekly newspaper at KwaZulu-Natal, *Inkazimulo*, targets Christians and sells 35,000 copies every week.

Started by the first president of the ANC (the current ruling party in South Africa), John Langalibalele Dube, in 1903, *Ilanga* is published twice a week and has a circulation of 500,000 per edition (Tabelo 2011). It also has a Sunday edition, *Ilanga LangeSonto* (the Sunday Sun), and a community supplement, *Ilanga LeTheku* (the Durban Sun).

To determine the role of *Ilanga* newspaper during the colonial period, I reviewed historical literature sources relating to *Ilanga Lase Natali*, the original title of the newspaper in question. Regarding its role during the democratic rule in South Africa, I analysed selected editions of *Ilanga* newspaper; its community and Sunday editions, *Ilanga LeTheku* and *Ilanga LangeSonto*, respectively, for the period 2010–2013. Based on the thematic analysis, I show how isiZulu media have provided a reflective and dialogic space where readers engage with discourses about their origins, their identity, and other social issues that affect them.

However, since a discussion of the past isiZulu media would not be complete without including *amakholwa*—the converted Zulu people—who were readers and authors of such media, I briefly discuss this group of people below.

Amakholwa: The mission-educated and converted Zulu elite

Houser (2010) tells us that the American missionaries of the 19th century initially struggled to convert the Zulu people in Natal and Zululand to Christianity. Even 22 years after the first missionary arrived in Natal, they reported no converts (Houser 2010). This was partly because to the Zulu people the gospel of the missionaries was irreconcilable with their own beliefs, and the missionaries' behaviour (for example, their racial discrimination) was contradictory to the proclamation of love in their preaching (see criticism of the missionaries in Bakke 2012). Similarly, the Zulus punished pregnant girls as they believed this was a sin; yet the missionaries accepted these girls when they ran away from home in fear of punishment. Struggling to convert the Zulu people through preaching, the missionaries resorted to education and employment as strategies to "coerce" people to convert to Christianity: children in mission schools were indoctrinated with religion, and servants, obliged by employer–employee power relationships, were forced to attend the preaching of the missionaries (Houser 2010). Engrossed with their strict religious worldview, where people were either Christians or heathens (Houser 2010), the missionaries alienated their converts (*amakholwa*) from the non-converts (known as *abahedeni* or *iziqhaza*, the heathens). The *amakholwa* elite of the 19th and 20th centuries then became a class of their own; as defined by Mokoena (2008, 2010), they were the educated, converted Africans "who were neither 'tribal subjects' nor 'colonial citizens'" but who soon became African intellectuals.

Having mastered reading and writing skills, the mission-educated *amakholwa* elite engaged with a broader literature, and through their writings they managed to build a network of readers and writers who shared thoughts, had a sense of togetherness and were referred to as *ibandla* (an assembly of readers and writers) (Mokoena 2009). They conquered space by using alternative spaces of interaction, such as newspapers, books and pamphlets; and having a common isiZulu language through which interactions, conversations and debates took place, they were able to comment, reflect upon and articulate their views on social, political, intellectual and economic situations. The isiZulu press, particularly *Ilanga Lase Natali* played a major role in the struggles against colonisation and apartheid. I will discuss the role of isiZulu newspapers below.

The role of isiZulu language and media during the colonial era: The voice of the African voices

When John Langalibalele (J. L.) Dube established *Ilanga Lase Natali* newspaper for the first time on the 10 April 1903 (Gasa 1999), he was strategically creating a space where Africans could freely engage among themselves on issues that affected them. With such a vision, J. L. Dube kept the newspaper insulated from influences that might have swayed the newspaper focus, as he seized the editorship of the newspaper and sourced its funding from friends in addition to subscriptions from readers. The media have the power to influence the public, and as a result, there is the potential for powerful business or political sectors with vested interests to manipulate the newspapers and channels to take sides while presenting facts (Dutta 2011) to serve their own agendas. In the case of *Ilanga Lase Natali*, J. L. Dube prevented such manipulation as he effectively controlled the funding sources of the newspaper until 1935, when the Bantu Press bought 50% of the subsidiary *Ilanga Lase Natali*, which was formed specifically for that purpose (Gasa 1999). The International Printing Press initially printed the newspaper until October 1903, when Ohlange Industrial School, also founded by J. L. Dube, took over the printing of the newspaper (Gasa 1999). He also took control of the editorship of the newspaper for an effective 17 years (1903–1920) (Gasa 1999).

J. L. Dube was the first President of the ANC, which was initially known as the South African Native National Congress and established in 1912, and he thus founded the paper with a political motive (Gasa 1999). Therefore, his control of the newspaper could be perceived as the ANC's (in)direct control of the newspaper. However, there is a lack of research-based evidence reporting that the paper was, at that time, the mouthpiece of the ANC in the same way as the newspaper *Inkundla Ya Bantu* was (as a space for ANC Youth engagement). This does not mean that *Ilanga Lase Natali* newspaper did not publish articles debating and discussing political issues and those relating to the ANC. For example, an article written by Pixley Ka Isaka Seme specifically discussed the South African Native National Congress (the then name of the ANC) (*Ilanga Lase Natali* 1912).

Similarly, when *Ilanga* newspaper was bought from the Argus Company by Mandla-Matla, a company owned by the Inkatha Freedom

Party (IFP) (a rival political party to the ANC) in 1987 (Gillwald and Madlala 1988), there is still a lack of research-based evidence that the paper was solely serving the interests of the IFP. Although Ndlovu (2011) implies that *Ilanga* newspaper has been a mouthpiece of the IFP in his statement "despite *Ilanga*'s history as a political mouthpiece of Inkatha", he does not provide evidence for this one-line claim. In addition, R. W. Johnson provides contrary views. For example, he states:

> *Isolezwe* had a strong ANC bias but *Ilanga* could be relied on to inform its readers of all the latest details of Zuma's unfolding marital dramas as well as news about Inkatha that sometimes upset Buthelezi. (*Sunday Times*, 11 November 2012)

In other words, it is yet to be ascertained whether being controlled by a president of a political party or by a company controlled by a political party made *Ilanga* newspaper a mouthpiece of either organisation in relevant periods. Research has also still not clarified what it means for a newspaper to be a mouthpiece of a political party or organisation, particularly because it is doubtful if any media can claim to be completely independent of any outside influence, whether business, political or any sector of the community. However, such discussions about the political context of *Isolezwe* and *Ilanga* are beyond the scope of this chapter, and Johnson (2012) engages with these in the newspaper article.

Based on the increased sales of *Ilanga* newspaper (Gillwald and Madlala 1988), which have survived centuries, it is argued here that the newspaper has continually served public interests and has drawn regular readers and writers from prominent and influential leaders—not only local isiZulu readers but also in the African continent. This was particularly so in earlier issues of the newspaper as these used both English and isiZulu languages (Gasa 1999).

Ilanga Lase Natali having a broader focus

The 19th and 20th centuries were times of social transformation in South Africa. Many people were adopting the Western religion, which required them to abandon their cultures and way of life, but it did not satisfactorily answer all their queries. Therefore, through *Ilanga Lase Natali* newspaper, isiZulu-speaking literate people of Southern Africa "communicated current affairs while also debating the very 'essence' of Zuluness and the meaning of their Zulu cultural heritage" (Mokoena 2010). However, while some of the articles published in *Ilanga* newspaper were/are dedicated to issues relating to amaZulu cultural heritage;

there is no evidence that the newspaper has been at any stage limited to such a focus. Articles published in both earlier and contemporary issues of *Ilanga* are varying and cover a number of topics affecting not only amaZulu but also Africans and world issues. For example, between 23 April 1938 and 20 March 1943, Jordan K. Ngubane published a number of articles on various social, political and educational topics in the weekly column of *Ilanga Lase Natali*, titled "Gleanings from Life" under his pseudonym "Jo The Cow". The following example is an excerpt from an earlier issue of *Ilanga Lase Natali*, where he wrote about parliamentary elections:

> They have come at last and prospective legislators are moving up and down the country making most solemn promises to alleviate the sufferings of white South Africa, should they be returned to Parliament. And I am not surprised that these men should appear so public spirited just now. It is always the case when elections approach [...] But now, I feel a little unrestful when I, Jo The Cow, and those of my colour are made the object of scorn, ridicule and condemnation by prospective members of Parliament only to catch the vote of the Plattelanders [...] I hear that One Big man says that I, Jo The Cow, and those who are unfortunate to be black should be segregated and when completely segregated [which experience and common-sense show to be impossible] the Government should not "waste the people's money" [the fabulous sum of £100,000, for six million Bantu] on me and the black man, but should use it to alleviate distress among the Whites [and only a fraction of the two-million whites— the farmers have received £20,000,000 from the Government] (*Ilanga* 16 April 1938).

In addition, between 16 December 1939 and 27 February 1943, Ngubane published articles on world issues, in a *Ilanga Lase Natali* column titled *"Ezomhlaba Jikelele"* (World Affairs). The following example is an excerpt from one of the articles published under this column, titled *"OHulumeni Bama Allies"* (Allied Governments):

> *Le mpi kuzokhumbuleka ukuthi yaqalwa oHulumeni Bama Allies bephethwe ngamanye amadoda. I-Ngilandi yona yayiphwethwe nguMnu. Neville Chamberlain, i-France yona iphethwe nguMnu. Daladier. Bobabili ke laba kabasekho ezinhlaka zoHulumeni. E-Ngilandi kukhona manje uMnu. Winston Churchill, e-France kukhona uMnu. Paul Reynaud. Yilowo nalowo ke uthe ukuba angene esikhundleni kwaba khona okuningi*

akuhlelayo [...] sibona kuthiwa uHulumeni wamaNgisi uguquliwe....
Ukwenza kwawo amaDemocracy. Wona inxa umuntu engafiki lapho
kufuneka khona uyagudluzwa nje abekwe eceleni kungene omunye esik-
hundleni sakhe, kuqhutshekwe nomsebenzi. (Ilanga 1 June 1940)

It could be remembered that Allied Governments ruled by certain
men started this war; Mr Neville Chamberlain led England, and
Mr Daladier led France. These two are not in government structures
anymore. Now in England it is Mr Winston Churchill, in France it is
Mr. Paul Reynaud. Each of them has made certain changes soon after
assuming their positions [...] we see changes in English Government [...]
This is how the Democrats work. If a person does not meet the expectations, s/he is removed from position and put aside and another one
assumes the position, and the work continues. (Translation)

Amakholwa were at the forefront of community discourses and they
reflected upon their nationalism, their conflicted identity brought
about by conversion to Christianity and acculturation to mission life
(Mokoena 2010). Therefore, my argument is that this reflective experience contributed to most of the *amakholwa* community adopting
Western religion and education while choosing to retain some of their
African cultures and customs, much against the preaching of missionaries who condemned all African cultures as heathen. Hence, Mokoena
(2008) argues that this class of *amakholwa* "represented both the success of mission acculturation and failure of imperial liberalism and
humanitan-anism".

From 1915 onwards, Magema Magwaza Fuze, a columnist and an
assistant to Bishop John William Colenso of Natal, led the discourses
and debates on the African origins. He published serialised articles
for the newspaper *Ilanga Lase Natali*, including the popular *"Abantu
Nemikuba Yabo Bengaka Biko Abelungu"* (The Black People and their
Customs before the Coming of the Whites) (Mokoena 2008). Having
been established with a political motive, the newspaper thus functioned
as "an organ of the intellectual and cultural aspirations of the *amakholwa* elite" (Mokoena 2008).

Protest, dialogue and consultation

In South Africa in the 19th and the 20th centuries, amidst the mission
work there were political changes that occurred when the government passed new legislation that would negatively affect the Africans.
Although J. L. Dube published educational articles, he mainly designated *Ilanga Lase Natali* for political issues and political education that

empowered the masses to fight against white oppression (Gasa 1999). For example, Jordan K. Ngubane published a number of articles under the column *"ISouth Afrika Lakusasa NabaNsundu"* (the Future South Africa and the Blacks). The following are examples:

"Amalungelo epolitiki" (Political rights). (*Ilanga Lase Natali* 18 October 1941)
   "Amaholo" (Wages). (*Ilanga Lase Natali* 11 October 1941)
   "Umhlabathi nokulima" (Land and ploughing). (*Ilanga Lase Natali* 25 October 1941)
   "Isizwe esifayo nempilo" (A dying nation and health). (*Ilanga Lase Natali* 1 November 1941)
   "Imfundo nesizwe esikhulayo" (Education and the growing nation). (*Ilanga Lase Natali* 8 November 1941)

J. L. Dube kept Africans informed of the new developments by publishing "government or official notices, new acts, and legislation measures and reports of commissions, which were sometimes accompanied by his comments" (Gasa 1999). Writing either in isiZulu or in English, the readers used the columns of *Ilanga Lase Natali* newspaper to criticise government policies. They articulated their plight both to the government that dictated oppressive laws and to the missionaries who complied with the laws of the government. Gasa (1999) asserts that through *Ilanga Lase Natali* J. L. Dube vigorously opposed the practical implementation of the 1913 Native Lands Act. Jordan K. Ngubane was also vocal about the land issue. For example, an excerpt in his article titled *"Umhlabathi Nokulima"* (Land and ploughing), which was published in *Ilanga Lase Natali* in 1941 under the column *"ISouth Africa Lakusasa NabaNsundu"* (the Future South Africa and the Blacks) stated:

Udaba olubahlupha ngamandla abansundu yilolu lwezwe [...] Umthetho kaHulumeni kawumvumeli onsundu ukuba athenge izwe noma kuyiphi indawo. Unezindawo lapho elithenga khona izwe, ebese kuthi emadolobheni angaze avunyelwa ukuba alithenge khona [...] Emakhaya, konokhesheni kanye nakoRizevu izwe selicinene ngokwesabekayo [...] leli zwe abansundu abanikwa lona kuyo yonke iNyunyana, okuthiwa licela ku 54, 000 square miles, kakukho lutho olukhombayo ukuthi uma banda abantu lona liyokukwazi kanjani ukubaphilisa. (Ilanga Lase Natali 25 October 1941).

The main issue troubling Blacks is that of the land [...] The government law prevents Blacks from buying land anywhere. There are specific areas where [a Black person] can buy land, and then in cities [a Black person] is not allowed to buy land. In the rural areas, farms and reserves the land is too densely populated [...] this land given to Blacks in the entire Union totals to 54,000 square miles, there is no indication that when they [Blacks] increase in number, how this land will make them survive. (Translation)

A. W. G. Champion, a controversial columnist and a nationalist, effectively wielded the power of the newspaper using his column *"Okubonwa NguMahlathi"* (Mahlathi's Views), which was dedicated to topical political issues and contributed to the re-kindled Zulu ethnic nationalism (Tabata 2006). Some of the topics he raised were the early marriage of Prince Goodwill Zwelithini (the current King of the Zulus) in 1969 and he wrote extensively, arguing for the acceptance of Uzibuse, which was the establishment of homeland governments in South Africa (Tabata 2006). Mokoena (2009) has written extensively about Magema Fuze's writings, which were published in *Ilanga Lase Natali* in the 19th century.

According to Hadebe (2003), the Zulus regarded *Ilanga Lase Natali* as an authentic representation of their history. J. L. Dube's *Ilanga Lase Natali*, through his reportage of the treason trial of King Dinuzulu (Hadebe 2003), became the voice that spoke to maintain King Dinuzulu's innocence regarding the *Impi Yamakhanda* (Head War) of 1906 in the midst of the noise by colonialists who sought to vilify the King of the Zulus. *Ilanga* also reported many articles relating to the *imali yamakhanda* (head tax) and the aforementioned *Impi Yamakhanda*. For example, an excerpt from *Ilanga Lase Natali* stated:

Igazi elibangelwe ilentela yekhanda lendoda licitekile enhla ne Lovu, kwe-sakwa Mveli, indodana ka Hemuhemu, kwa Mafuze. Isixukwana sawo nongqayi sasitunywe ukuyobamba abantu ababili, abahlomele iMantyi mhla iyotelisa kuleyo ndawo. Bati nxa sebefikile onongqayi bekwele ama-hashi, bababamba labo bantu, zanikela kona izinsizwa sezitele inswani yazo ne mibhumbhuluzo. Zati bayeke, kwa pikiswana njalo uMr Hunt oyena beyinduna yabo ebona umkonto usude umenyeze ubengezela eduze naye, lowo mfo wamshaya wamlahla phansi nge volo-volo, yadumelana njalo bayipisela ngomkonto induna yawo nongqayi no munye, omunye waba inkubele, kwafa abantu abayisikombisa, bayisusa babaleka o non-gqayi, beshiya ababili babo. (Ilanga 16 February 1906)

The man's head tax has caused the spillage of blood in the upper Mid Illovo, in the area of Mveli, the son of Hemuhemu, at Mafuze.

A small contingent of policemen was sent to arrest two people who were armed against the magistrate when he went there to collect tax. When the mounted police arrived, captured those people, young men went there carrying their *inswani* (collection of *assegais*) and *imibhumbhuluzo* (large war shields). They said, leave them alone, the argument started and Mr Hunt, their leader, seeing the glinting on the spear next to him, he shot the man dead with a revolver, fighting then started and *induna* (leader) of the mounted police was stabbed with an assegai as well as another policeman, the other one was crippled, seven people died, the policemen started the fighting but fled, leaving the two of them behind. (Translation by Moses Hadebe in his unpublished paper, titled *"Isidumo sokulwa e Richmond"*)

Through *Ilanga Lase Natali*, J. L. Dube aimed at making Africans aware of their rights and privileges as well as the whites' thoughts. A column was therefore set aside for comments on articles and editorials appearing on English white-owned newspapers (*Natal Mercury, Witness,* and *Natal Advertiser*) (Gasa 1999).

In the context of policies and religion that sought to divide Africans and thus weaken them, J. L. Dube used *Ilanga Lase Natali* to give "effective and powerful backing to the idea of an African United Front" (Gasa 1999). He insisted that Africans should confront their weaknesses, make progress in education and lead their own political and socio-economic advancements instead of relying on missionaries. J. L. Dube criticised Africans for their backwardness, and in his article titled *"Isita Esikhulu Somuntu Nguye Uqobo Lwake"* (the Biggest Enemy of the Black Person is Himself or Herself), which appeared in *Ilanga Lase Natali* newspaper, he made the following points to the blacks:

It was their lack of thrift, their altitude towards labour, their want of perseverance, and even more, their lack of cooperation and unity due to petty jealousy, which were the main factors militating against their progress. However, while JL Dube was critical of his fellow Africans, he also encouraged them to aspire to greater heights, to develop improved working habits, to buy land, to form companies, to establish schools and colleges (Gasa 1999).

Ilanga Lase Natali also had articles and editorials written in English, which were intended for the consumption of the white settler community, the Department of Native Affairs, and the Natal Government to help them "keep in touch with native thought" (Gasa 1999).

The role of *Ilanga* newspaper in the contemporary democratic South Africa

Since 1994, South Africa has had a legitimate government elected by the majority, and therefore all people have a social responsibility to develop leaders who will alleviate poverty, guard against the abuse of power, and protect and promote human rights culture. Media have the power to tell a society's stories and thereby influence thinking, beliefs and even behaviour. The use of isiZulu media has been to share information, preserve history, generate identities and share resources that enable collective political and social causes to be realised, and *Ilanga* newspaper acts as a voice for the people.

Ilanga as space for people's views in a democratic system

Ilanga newspaper has acted as a dialogic space in the South African democratic system whereby it unearths the system's various shortcomings. Its investigative reporting has helped in exposing the large-scale corruption that has robbed the nation, and, thus, *Ilanga* regularly calls government and its departments to account on many issues affecting the citizens. For example, under the title *"Sisele Gengelezi Esomphakathi"* (The community building structure has been abandoned), *Ilanga* exposes the unused building structure, known as the "Farmers' Market" that was built in Ixopo area under Sisonke Council, using more than twenty-five million rands; it also describes how the company that obtained the tender illegally obtained a loan from the government department and did not complete the work. Thami Shangase writes:

> *Sesiphenduke isibaya sezinkomo isikhungo sezigidi zamarandi esakhiwe edolobheni eXobho wumkhandlu iSisonke okuphendulwe umkhandlu umashonisa ukuze sakhiwe. ILanga lingakusho ngaphandle kokwesaba ukuthi isikhungo esaziwa ngeFarmers Market kasisebenzi emva kokumoshwa kwemali yabakhokhi bentela. Lesi sikhungo besakhelwa ukusiza abalimi bakule ndawo ukuze babe nayo indawo yokuhambisa imikhiqizo yabo.* (*Ilanga* 14–16 June 2012, p. 12)

The structure that was built with millions of Rands by Sisonke Council and where the department was turned into a loan shark has turned into a cattle kraal. *Ilanga* can state without fear that this structure known as The Farmers Market is not being used after wasting the taxpayers' money. This structure was built to help the local farmers to sell their produce. (*Ilanga* 14–16 June 2012, p. 12)

Opinion columns that regularly publish articles critical of government practices, policies, strategies and other societal issues include *"Ngibukela Ngikude"* (I Observe from a Distance), *"Ezaseziko"* (Those for the Fireplace) and *"Sivubela Ngosiba"* (We Mix with the Pen). A large space dedicated for *Izindaba* (News) is also used for criticising or applauding the government when necessary. Other examples of topics that drew critical views on the government include the following:

> *Ubhimbile UMnyango WezeMfundo* (The Department of Education made a mistake). (*Ilanga* 13–15 August 2012, p. 14)
> *Ungabazane ngokudedelwa kweziboshwa ngoshwele* (Scepticism about the release of inmates through amnesty). (*Ilanga LangeSonto* 29 July 2012, p. 18)
> *Ngeke lusize ngalutho udaba luka-US\$ 2bln* (The matter of US\$ 2 bn will not help with anything). (*Ilanga LangeSonto* 24 June 2012, p. 18)
> *Kunukwa inkosikazi yemeya ngamanyala* (The mayor's wife is suspected of corruption). (*Ilanga* 5–7 July 2012, p. 9)

Dutta (2011) states that a democratic system of government runs best if there is wide participation and this participation is possible if people are informed about various issues. *Ilanga* uses isiZulu, a language that is understood by the majority of the population, to inform the public about developments that are taking place. The following are examples of information sharing topics published in *Ilanga* newspaper:

> *Kusazothatha iminyaka ukuqeda isibhedlela* (It will still take years to complete the hospital); *Kusekude phambili kuhulumeni nezinyunyana* (It will still take time for the government and unions to reach an agreement). (*Ilanga* 5–7 July 2012, p. 8)
> *Imeya ezinhlelweni zokusiza abafundi basemakhaya* (The mayor in planned projects to help learners in rural areas). (*Ilanga* 29 July 2012, p. 13)
> *Umkhankaso wokugqugquzela ukufunda* (A campaign to promote reading). (*Ilanga* 16–18 August 2012, p. 13)
> *Ingase ihlomule intsha yasoNdini* (Ulundi youth might benefit). (*Ilanga* 24 June 2012, p. 8)

Furthermore, Dutta (2011) states that media can conceal facts, and this happens in situations where the media are manipulated by groups that have their own agendas to sway the public against the government. In such cases, the media only criticise the government and conceal facts from the public about the developments made by the government. However, *Ilanga* newspaper's critical voice about the government is balanced by its objective information sharing about government projects and the applause that it gives to the government when reasonable or good service delivery has occurred. The following are examples of non-critical topics that have been published:

> *Siyathokozisa isimemezelo sikangqomgqoshe* (The minister's announcement is pleasing). (*Ilanga* 13–15 August 2012, p. 14)
> *Umasipala ugwema ukuhlukunyezwa kogogo* (The municipality prevents the rape of grandmothers). (*Ilanga* 29–31 July 2012, p. 13)
> *Malisetshenziswe ithuba elivulwa ngumongameli* (The opportunity that the president has opened must be used). (*Ilanga LangeSonto* 16 September 2012, p. 18)

The government also uses isiZulu media to inform people about their objectives and make them aware of various initiatives aimed at development. This happens through the SIMAMA (Be sustained) supplement, which is inserted into some issues of *Ilanga* newspaper, particularly because even after vigorous attempts to get control of *Ilanga*, the ANC has been unsuccessful (see Johnson 2012). There is not yet evidence that the distribution of the SIMAMA supplement is the result of the government's influence on the newspaper. The possibility is that *Ilanga* treats this supplement in the same way as many other advertising pamphlets from business and academic institutions. However, given that the current government is that of the ANC, this distribution of the pro-government supplement through *Ilanga* newspaper, in a way challenges the perceived influence that the IFP has on the newspaper.

Ilanga as a point of connection between needs and resources

The apartheid system of government in South Africa took effectively 45 years (1948–1994) to run its course. With regard to the Africans in the country, this means 45 years of purposeful trampling on their rights and development. As a result, the problems of poverty, unemployment and inequality in income distribution are constant irritants facing the current democratic government. Thus, many lives could be improved if not only the government, but also societal members, institutions and organisations participate in social uplifting. *Ilanga* newspaper brings societies, social institutions and cultures closer to each other for the benefit of societal members. It routinely publishes stories of individuals or families needing urgent intervention to improve their lives and who cannot wait their turn for government-planned projects. This is one of the initiatives to promote participatory communication from the grass-roots rather than from the top down. For example, in *Ilanga LangeSonto* (23 September 2012, p. 20), under the column *"Phonsa Esivivaneni"* (Add Your Contribution), three poor families (Ms Ncamisile Buthelezi with her eight children; Ms Buyi Gcabashe with her partner who is sick with TB; and Ms Ivy Shezi with her late daughter's two children) voiced their plight due to lack of housing. Many other individuals or families are able to tell their stories of desperation via the newspaper under *"Phonsa Esivivaneni"*.

When readers of *Ilanga* newspapers become aware of such situations, they intervene as individuals or organisations to assist in improving the lives of the people on the lowest socio-economic band. *Ilanga* newspaper regularly publishes feedback on the interventions by community members in the same column (*"Phonsa Esivivaneni"*). For example, in *Ilanga LangeSonto* of 19 August 2012 (p. 20), the Gigaba family in need, at Adams Mission, a rural area south of Durban, received groceries from TV1 Express organisation. Nhlanhla Mathonsi of *Ilanga* news also wrote an article titled *"Amandla Elanga LangeSonto"* (Power of the Sunday Sun) to show *Ilanga*'s ability to connect people who are in need with the people and organisations that have resources to help such members of the society. Nhlanhla writes the following:

> *Usethole ikhaya Elisha owesilisa waseFolweni eningizimu yeTheku, obekhala ngokuhlukunyezwa ngudadewabo nendodakazi yakhe. Umnu Khuphukani Luthuli Ilanga Lange Sonto libike ngaye engosini, Phonsa Esivivaneni, ukuthi ufisa ukuthola ikhaya labadala, ukuze aphumule ukuphila impilo ebuhlungu esandleni sikadadewabo abemsola ngo-kuthi unqwahe nekhadi lakhe lomholo [...]. Emva kokufunda udaba iziphathimandla zesibhedlela i-Hillcrest entshonalanga YeTheku zingenel-ele walandwa njengoba esehlala esibhedlela impilo yakhe yonke, aphinde alashwe khona.* (Ilanga LangeSonto 19 June 2011, p. 16)

> The *Ilanga LangeSonto* reported in the column *"Phonsa Esivivaneni"* that Mr Khuphukani Luthuli, a man from the Folweni area who complained that he was abused by his sister and her daughter, needed a better home. He has now found a home. After reading the story, the management of Hillcrest Hospital intervened and fetched him. (Translation)

Since *Ilanga* readers span a wide range of classes and socio-economic standing, on reading the story of a desperate person or family, readers who have the means, even without government intervention, could address the plight of such a person or family. This was also evident in Nokuthula Nxumalo's article, titled, *"Behluleke wukukhuluma bethola usizo"* (They were speechless when they received help). The following is an extract from the article:

> *Wehluleke nokukhuluma umndeni wakwaXulu eMakhabeleni maphakathi nekwaZulu-Natali onamalunga ayi-13 ILanga LangeSonto lilethe usizo[...].* *ILanga LangeSonto belihamba naMadoda Aqotho, okungabaculi bokholo, usomabhizinisi waseMgungundlovu uMnu Themba Njilo, usomahlaya u-Celeste Ntuli, uMasipala wesiFunda uMzinyathi, nomasipala uMvoti bebeyise usizo kulo mndeni ngemuva kokuba leli phephandaba libike ngosizi lwawo.* (*Ilanga LangeSonto* 21 August 2011. p. 20.)
>
> The Xulu family with 13 members at EMakhabeleni was tonguetied when *Ilanga LangeSonto* brought resources to help the family. *Ilanga LangeSonto* was with Real Men, who are Gospel Singers, businessman Mr Njilo from Pietermaritzburg, the comedian Celeste Ntuli, Mzinyathi and UMvoti Municipalities who sent help to this family after this newspaper reported on the family's predicament). (Translation)

Ilanga as a dialogic space among citizens

Ilanga provides space for its readers to present their opinions and comments in the *"Imibono"* (Opinion) section. In addition, *Ilanga* encourages and invites readers to comment via the SMS cell phone system in the column *"Umqhafazo"*. An article is published here and readers are invited to comment on it by sending a text message to SMS *Ilanga* 34351. Selected SMS comments (between 10 and 15) are then published in the next issue of *Ilanga*. The SMS section encourages interactive communication between readers and the newspaper. The following are some of the SMS comments that were responding on the article about a herbalist whose car killed a person, yet he was denying it:

> *Uyazi yini Mnu. Ndebele uNkulunkulu akahlulwa yilutho? Le nyanga noma ingaqamba hlobo luni lwamanga kepha iqiniso lihlala liyiqiniso.* Babalwa Chitelo, Tshuze, EBIZANA.
>
> You know what Mr Ndebele, nothing is impossible with God. Even this herbalist can tell any kind of lies, truth is always the truth. Babalwa Chitelo, Tshuze, EBIZANA. (Translation)
>
> *Noma ngabe usewukhokhovu lwenyanga uMatatazela, akanalungelo lokuthatha impilo yomuntu bese edala amaqhinga abhedayo. Amaphoyisa*

aseZilozini mawenze umsebenzi wawo. Thandiwe Mzolo, Kwanyavu, Emkhambathini.

Even if Matatazela is a big herbalist he does not have a right to take one's life and then tell bad dispeakable lies. The police of Zilozini must do their job. Thandiwe Mzolo, Kwanyavu, Emkhambathini. (Translation) (*Ilanga* 17–19 June 2013)

Dutta (2011) also states that in democratic societies where there is widespread poverty and underdevelopment, the media take on the education of the masses in order to help their advancement in society. *Ilanga* newspaper has educated the masses by informing them about law, health and other topics that are relevant to ordinary citizens. In the column *"Ezomthetho"* (Legal Matters), legal experts regularly educate the public about laws and legal issues. For example, in *Ilanga* 4–6 October 2012, p. 2, the published article titled *"Okumele kwenziwe ngofuna uku-faka isehlukaniso"* (Steps that need to be taken by a person who wants to file for divorce), written by the Khanyile Incorporated Legal Firm was about divorce and the Divorce Act No. 70 of 1979. Other titles on law that have appeared in the newspaper are the following:

Yincwadi yefa ekhipha isixazululo efeni (The will (letter) provides a solution). (*Ilanga* 12–14 July 2012, p. 2)
Ukwabiwa kwefa nezingane ezingekho kulowo mshado (The inheritance distribution with children outside marriage). (*Ilanga* 5–7 July 2012, p. 2)

Ilanga LeTheku of 15 November 2012, p. 1–3 featured an educational article (with illustrative pictures) on diabetes: the statistics of people affected by the condition: its causes, signs and symptoms: and ways of living and controlling diabetes. Many other articles on health, first aid and healthy living are regularly published, for example,

Ibhokile i-sinusitis kula makhaza (Sinusitis is common with this cold); *Zilaphe ngengxube yoju nogaliga* (Treat yourself with a mixture of honey and garlic). (*Ilanga* 18–20 June 2012, p. 10)
Izimpawu kowezidakamizwa (Signs of drug abuse); *Ukuphalaza kakuhlangene nokuqhumisa* (Vomiting is not linked to teething). (*Ilanga* 2–4 July 2012, p. 12)

Much space has been devoted to the culture and history of the people in the *Ilanga* newspapers. Different cultural practices are explained in the column, Amasiko Nemikhuba / Lithini isiko often authored by Nhlanhla Mathonsi and Zethu MaPhoswa Khumalo, separately. Examples, of topics that have appeared in this column are the following:

> *Umemulo womuntu oseshonile* (*Umemulo* for the deceased). *(Umemulo is a feast for a daughter who has reached marriageable stage).* (*Ilanga LangeSonto* 8 August 2010, p. 18).
> *Ukugezwa koshonelwe* (Cleansing the survivor). (*Ilanga LangeSonto* 21 August 2011, p. 20)

In 2011 and 2012, serialised articles about Zulu surnames appeared under the column *"Awungisho Wethu!"* (Give me my praises, my peer!). These were authored separately by Menzi Jele, Zethu MaPhoswa Khumalo and Daisy Mncwango. Each article fully discussed one surname, giving its history and origin, and information on how the surname became related to other surnames; at the end there were *izithakazelo* (clan names) for that particular surname. Examples are as follows:

> *AbakwaMkhize* (the Mkhizes). (*Ilanga* 15–17 August 2011, p. 8)
> *AbakwaMpungose* (the Mpungoses). (*Ilanga* 28–30 May 2012, p. 8)
> *AbakwaHlophe* (the Hlophes). (*Ilanga* 5–7 November 2012, p. 8)

In addition, under the news column, *Ilanga* published lengthy articles (mostly authored by Eric Ndiyane) discussing the history of several nations. Each article would discuss one nation in detail. For example, where the particular nation came from, its movements over the years, wars it was involved in, and different amaKhosi (leaders) from various periods. The following are some of the titles of articles that were published:

> *AbakwaMngomezulu bafike kwezwakala kubeNguni* (The Mngomezulus came and made an impact to the Ngunis). (*Ilanga* 10–12 September 2012, p. 9)
> *Bebengazwani nempi abakwaDube* (The Dubes did not like war). (*Ilanga* 3–5 September 2012, p. 9)
> *Sibuthwalile ubunzima isizwe sakwaCele* (The Cele nation experienced great difficulties). (*Ilanga* 25–27 June 2012, p. 16)
> *Besingafunwa isizwe sakwaNdlovu* (The Ndlovu nation was not liked). (*Ilanga* 6–8 August 2012, p. 11)
> *Abengochwepheshe bensimbi amaChunu* (The Chunus were iron experts). (*Ilanga* 2–4 July 2012, p. 16)

Abezitika ngabantu amabhele (The Bheles ate other people). (*Ilanga* 23–25 July 2012, p. 11)

Asilwele isizwe sawo amaMbatha (The Mbathas fought for their nation). (*Ilanga* 8–10 October 2012, p. 11)

Other historical articles published by Eric Ndiyane related to the role played by certain *amaKhosi* in the history of the Zulu nation; for example, the following titles appeared in *Ilanga* newspaper:

INkosi uDingiswayo ibushintshile ubukhosi (INkosi Dingiswayo changed the kingship). (*Ilanga* 7–9 May 2012, p. 11)

UZwide uhlasele abakwaZungu bengazelele (Zwide attacked the unsuspecting Zungus. (*Ilanga* 30 July–1 August 2012, p. 10)

Kayitshalwanga INkosi uJobe (INkosi Jobe was never buried). (*Ilanga* 17–19 September 2012, p. 10.

The *Ilanga* editors, Eric Ndiyane and Menzi Jele, not only publish historical articles, but other topics, such as:

Buyinkolo ubunyanga (Traditional healing is a belief). (*Ilanga* 16–18 July 2012, p. 11)

Zibuthwalile ubunzima iziNyunyana (The workers' unions experienced difficulties). (*Ilanga* 7–9 May 2012, p. 10)

Sibuka iqhaza likaMkabayi kaJama (We observe Mkabayi's role). (*Ilanga* 15–17 August 2011, p. 9)

Like the readers of the past *Ilanga Lase Natali* (*amakholwa*), who had formed a community on their own (*ibandla*) and engaged one another on issues through the newspaper, the current readers of *Ilanga* also engage with one another through its pages. It is evident that current readers of *Ilanga* are regular readers from the fact that their articles/letters refer to previously published articles. For example, one reader, Themba kaMpikayipheli kaNkani wakwaNgcobo, responding to a previous article, writes under the title "*Yinto eyodwa uMkhosi Woselwa noMkhosi wokweShwama*" [the Marrow Plant Celebration and the Eating of First Fruits Celebration are the same thing]. The following is an extract from his article:

Mhleli, kangiqondi kahle uma umbhali weLanga, uZethu MaPhoswa Khumalo eLangeni langomhla zingama 20–23 kwephezulu ethi iSilo uGoodwill Zwelithini siqambe igama Elisha UMkhosi wokweShwama ngelithi wuMkhosi WoSelwa. UMkhosi wokweShwama noMkhosi WoSelwa yinto eyodwa leyo, umehluko kungaba yindlela iSilo esiwuqhuba ngayo lo Mkhosi. (*Ilanga* 30–31 December 2010, p. 10)

Editor, I do not understand when the author of *Ilanga*, Zethu MaPhoswa Khumalo in *Ilanga* edition of the 20–23 this month said King Goodwill Zwelithini re-named the *UMkhosi WoSelwa* [Marrow Plant Celebration] with the name *UMkhosi wokweShwama*. These two are the same thing; the difference may be the way the King directs how it should be done. (Translation)

Another reader writes a response, titled *"Kuhle ukuzigqaja ngolimi, kodwa ..."* (It is right to be proud of the language, but ..."), to a previously published article on isiZulu language use/misuse.

Synthesis of issues discussed

In the 19th and 20th centuries in South Africa, political changes and social transformation occurred as the result of the Western forces of colonisation and Christianisation. This means that white colonial masters imposed laws that affected Africans, and especially Christianity, where missionaries preached the gospel of alienation, divided Africans as the converts secluded themselves from their fellow non-converted Africans. However, as they experienced the new religion, *amakholwa* (the converted) could not reconcile the missionaries' preaching (of love and kindness) with the missionaries' practices of discrimination and compliance to the governments' laws that oppressed the Africans. In addition, *amakholwa* found themselves experiencing a conflicted identity where they were linked to both tradition (by their origin) and the Western cultures (by education and religion). In such a context, J. L. Dube established *Ilanga Lase Natali* newspaper in 1903 to strategically provide a space where Africans could engage among themselves on issues of origin and identity, and social, political and religious importance. He insulated the newspaper from any possible influences that could manipulate it and divert it away from its original purpose. He did this by taking control of the editorship and funding the newspaper with money from his friends abroad and subscriptions from readers. Letters from Southern Africa as well as from the local Natal readers evidenced the widespread palpable influence of the newspaper.

The *Ilanga Lase Natali* newspaper became a reflective and dialogic space where readers engaged with discourses about their origins and their identity; and it became a space for protests where they voiced their disagreements regarding the legislation imposed on them by white masters. It was also a space where they could state their history as they saw it rather than the imposed distorted and misinterpreted information publicised by the whites; J. L. Dube himself wrote an article that maintained the Zulu King Dinuzulu's innocence amidst the white's popularised view that vilified him as the cause of the *Impi Yamakhanda*. J. L. Dube also used *Ilanga* as a counterforce to the divide and rule ideology of the whites, by making *Ilanga Lase Natali* back up the idea of an "African United Front". Other prominent writers were Jordan Ngubane, who wrote in several columns of *Ilanga Lase Natali* on a wide range of topics.

Alexander (2005) argues that if one does not command the language, one is automatically excluded and disempowered. The language of *Ilanga* newspaper, isiZulu, which is understood by almost half the South African population, makes the newspaper accessible to people across the socio-economic bands of society; and thus all people across the spectrum of society are included as they can express their views. Making it an isiZulu newspaper also posed a challenge to the colonial power. Scott and Ng (1999) and Ng and Bradac (1993) argue that in colonial systems, where the use of the colonial language is imposed on the natives, language routinises power. De Kadt (1996) also reiterates that language in itself does not have power, but the language locus exercises it. Therefore, isiZulu utility as a medium for an ever-growing newspaper challenges, to some degree, the routinisation of dominance of the colonial language.

Ilanga has continued its existence and growth and is flourishing even today in the new democratic South Africa. Under the democratic system, through its *"Izindaba"* (News), and columns such as *"Ngibukela Kude"* (I Observe from a Distance), *"Ezaseziko"* (Those from the Fireplace), and others, it allows views that unearth the government's shortcomings and calls on government departments to account on issues affecting the citizens. However, Ilanga is not just a 'whining' entity aimed at discrediting the government; it constructively criticises the government with the purpose of strengthening and consolidating democracy.

A key aspect that strengthens democracy is the wide participation of ordinary citizens and, as Dutta (2011) argues, for people to participate they need to be informed about various issues. The *Ilanga* newspaper supports social development as it informs citizens about development projects taking place in the country. The government also has a space (through its SIMAMA supplement, which is inserted into the *Ilanga* newspaper) to inform citizens about government projects. The reality is that *Ilanga* reaches out to a wide range of people, many of whom are situated in places that are difficult to access.

After years of apartheid that disadvantaged the African people, many citizens are still entrenched in poverty, unemployment and underdevelopment. While the government has ongoing planned projects to address such legacies of apartheid, some people are in such dire need of help that they cannot wait their turn for redress. *Ilanga* has become a space where people can tell their stories about their situations, and on reading such stories, businesses, individuals, government municipalities and organisations intervene to help. Such interventions contribute to social uplifting but also make communities take responsibility for social advancement.

In South Africa, social transformation underpinned by Westernisation occurred in the 19th and 20th centuries, which led to the distortion and/or loss of some indigenous cultures and histories. Alexander (2005) confirms that the source of power of language is to function as a transmission mechanism of culture. Using isiZulu language, *Ilanga* newspaper leads the discussions and information sharing on culture, history and biographies. Publishing such articles in a language understood by people also enables the readers to comment, debate or even correct misinformation that might occur about culture and history. The style, language, content topics and the approach of *Ilanga* newspaper helps South Africans to rise to the challenge of democracy.

Conclusion

In this chapter, I have shown that *Ilanga* newspaper has played an important role amidst colonisation and the Christianisation periods in South Africa. Surviving the test of time because of its language (isiZulu), which is understood by many people, and its style (engaging with issues of identity, culture, history, poverty, underdevelopment), which are relevant to the citizens, it still plays a role in the democratic society. It is a dialogic space among citizens on issues of origin, identity, history and social development, and a point of connection between needs and resources available in communities to address such needs. With this approach, *Ilanga* newspaper makes major contributions to social uplifting. I therefore recommend that it continues with this approach but from time to time reflects on the content topics of the articles published to maintain its relevance.

References

Alexander, N. (2005). "Language, class and power in post-apartheid South Africa". Harold Wolpe Memorial Trust open dialogue, TH Barry Lecture Theatre, Iziko Museum, University of Cape Town, 27 October.

Bakke, O. M. (2012). Black critics of Lutheran missions in Zululand and Natal in the 1950s, with particular emphasis on socio-political issues. *Studia Historiae Ecclesiasticae*, 38(1), 75–94.

Berger, G. (1998). Press time: Black publishing then and now, South Africa's alternative press. Voices of protests and resistance 1880–1960. In L. Switzer (Ed.), Cambridge: Cambridge University Press. Review Article. *Transformation*, 36, 93–101.

De Groef, M. (2010). Institutional language policy and multilingual practice in the University of the Western Cape. The scale of faculties and departments. Master's Thesis, Ghent University.

De Kadt, E. (1996). Language and apartheid: The power of minorities. *Alternation*, 3(2), 184–194.

Dutta, S. (2011). Social responsibility of media and Indian democracy. *Global Media Journal—Indian Edition/Summer Issue—*June, 1–8.

Gasa, E. D. (1999). John L. Dube, his *Ilanga Lase Natali* and the Natal administration, 1903–1910. Doctoral Thesis, University of Zululand, Kwa-Dlangezwa.

Gillwald, A. and Madlala, C. 1988. 'A Black Coup'-Inkatha and the Sale of Ilanga. Transformation 7, 27–36. Available at: http://archive.lib.msu.edu/DMC/African%20Journals/pdfs/transformation/tran007/tran007003.pdf. Accessed 20 July 2015.

Gilmartin, M. (2004). Language, education and the new South Africa. *Tijdschrift voor Economische en Sociale Geografie*, 95(4), 405–418.

Gilmour, R. (2007). A nice derangement of epitaphs: Missionary language—nineteenth century Natal. *Journal of Southern African Studies*, 33(3), 521–538.

Gowlett, D. F. (2004). *Zulu Newspaper Reader*. Springfield, IL: Dunwoody Press.

Green, M. (2008). Translating the nation: From Plaaitjie to Mpe. *Journal of Southern African Studies*, 34(2), 325–342.

Hadebe, M. M. (2003). A contextualisation and examination of the Impi Yamakhanda (1906 uprising) as reported by J. L. Dube in *Ilanga Lase Natali*, with special focus on Dube's attitude to Dinuzulu as indicated in his reportage on the treason trial of Dinuzulu. Master's Thesis, University of Natal, Durban.

Houser, S. (2010). Puritanical and apocalyptic-minded American missionaries in Southeast Africa—a contrast with Bishop John William Colenso (Austin, Texas, USA). *Studia Historiae Ecclesiasticae*, 36(1), 15–35.

Johnson, R. W. (2012). Stealing a newspaper. *Sunday Times*, 11 November 2012. Available at www.rwjohnson.co.za/images/stories/Recent/ilanga.doc. Accessed 10 December 2013.

Kamwangamalu, N. M. (2000). *Language Policy and Mother-tongue Education in South Africa: The Case for a Market-oriented Approach*. Georgetown University Press, Digital Georgetown, and the Department of Languages and Linguistics. Available at: http://www.researchgate.net/publication/253351737_Language_policy_and_mother-tongue_education_in_South_Africa_The_case_for_a_market-oriented_approach.

Marrianhill Monastery, Pinetown, A brief history. Available at http://wiki.ulwazi.org/index.php5?title=Mariannhill_Monastery,_Pinetown#Mariannhill_Monastery.2C_Pinetown_.E2.80.93_a_brief_history Accessed 10 January 2013.

Mokoena, H. (2008). The queen's bishop: A convert's memoir of John W. Colenso. *Journal of Religion in Africa*, 38, 312–342.

Mokoena, H. (2009). An assembly of readers: Magema Fuze and his *Ilanga Lase Natali* readers. *Journal of Southern African Studies*, 35(3), 595–607.

Mokoena, H. (2010). Jacob Zuma and the evanescent legacy of nineteenth-century Zulu cosmopolitanism and nationalism. *Concerned Africa Scholars Bulletin*, 84, 46–51.

Moyo, T. (2001). The changing language policies and reversing language roles in Malawi: From colonial times (1891–1964) to the present. *Per Linguam*, 17(2), 1–11.

Ndlovu, M. (2011). The meaning of post-apartheid Zulu media. *Communication, South African Journal for Communication Theory and Research*, 37(2), 268–290.

Ng, S. H. and Bradac, J. J. (1993). *Power in Language: Verbal Communication and Social Influence*. Newbury Park, CA: Sage.

Ngefac, A. (2010). Linguistic choices in postcolonial multilingual Cameroon. *Nordic Journal of African Studies*, 19(3), 149–164.

Rogerson, J. W. (2013). On being a broad church. Beauchief Abbey lectures 2013. Given at Beauchief Abbey, Sheffield 27 February 2013. Available at http://beauchiefabbey.org.uk/index.php/component/k2/item/238-broad-church-lectures-now-available-to-watch-on-line-here-as-videos.

Scott, A. R. and Ng, S. H. (1999). Language, power, and intergroup relations. *Journal of Social Issues*, 55(1), 119–139.

Statistics South Africa (2011). Census 2011, Key results. Pretoria: Statistics South Africa. Available at www.statssa.gov.za. Accessed 10 December 2013.

Swilla, I.N. (2009). Languages of instruction in Tanzania: Contradictions between ideology, policy and implementation. *African Study Monographs*, 30(1), 1–14.

Switzer, L. and Switzer, D. (1979). *The Black Press in South Africa and Lesotho: A Descriptive Bibliographic Guide to African, Coloured and Indian Newspapers, Newsletters and Magazines, 1836–1976*. Boston: G. K. Hall & Co.

Tabata, W. F. (2006). A. W. G. Champion, Zulu nationalism and "Separate Development" in South Africa, 1965–1975. Master's Thesis, UNISA.

Tabelo, T. (2011). Zulu Newspapers thrive in South Africa. Available at http://sg.news.yahoo.com/zulu-newspapers-thrive-south-africa-20110403-212428-787.html. Accessed 10 December 2012.

4
The Return of the Local: Community Radio as Dialogic and Participatory

Brilliant Mhlanga

Introduction

XK FM, a unique community radio station for the !Xû and Khwe communities of Platfontein, in Kimberley was established in August 2000 as a protégé of the South African Broadcasting Corporation (SABC). Its broadcasting licence, issued by the Independent Communications Authority of South Africa (ICASA) and renewable after every five years states that !Xûntali, Khwedam[1] and Afrikaans are the languages of broadcasting (Mhlanga 2010a, 2010b). The first two languages belong to the 12th group of languages that are identified by the Pan-South African Language Board (PANSLAB) as the languages of the San people. However, for the San people only one radio station was established – *XK FM,* a community radio station for the !Xû and Khwe. When compared to all the other public radio stations that are owned and controlled by the SABC this radio station is strikingly unique. And in terms of its remit it is limited to serving the !Xû and Khwe communities; thus implying that this radio station remains fully answerable to a public broadcaster, SABC, while doubling as a community radio station (Mhlanga 2009, 2010a, 2010b). The Group Executive News and Current Affairs, Dr Snuki Zikalala emphasised its uniqueness by stressing that 'when studying public radio stations in South Africa it is advisable to grant considerable attention to *XK FM* in order to understand factors that led to its formation'. He added that its uniqueness is not only in its remit and general mandate but is also embedded in the histories of the two communities.[2]

As will be presented in this chapter, the establishment of *XK FM* as a development project under the auspices of the SABC was informed by the Independent Broadcasting Authority Act (IBA) (1993/4). It is unusual for a community radio station to be managed as an independent entity connected to a national public broadcaster. However, the IBA Act stated that community broadcasting should cater either for a geographic community or a community of interest. In a geographic community the station should attend to a community whose 'commonality is determined principally by their residing in a particular geographic area' (Teer-Tomaselli 2001: 234). A community of interest means that the community being served must exude an ascertainable common interest. So the notion of a common interest becomes the most important feature of community radio. *XK FM's* footprint covers a radius of between 30km and 50km and reaches 4500 !Xûntali and 2000 Khwedam speakers. The history of the two communities, in particular that of marginalisation, low literacy levels, high prevalence of health-related problems and existing in isolation as migrant communities following their migration to South Africa with the help of South African Defence Forces from Angola and Namibia in the late 1980s (Douglas 1996) presents a feature of common interest, which necessitated the establishment of a community radio station for them. The majority of !Xûntali and Khwedam speakers who did not migrate to South Africa continue to live in southern Angola, western Zambia and along the Namibian–Botswana border of the Caprivi Strip.

This chapter attempts to provoke a kind of ethos and theoretical engagement on community radio as the medium of articulation for different communities. *XK FM* as a case study will be used to present the locus of enunciation for the theory of articulation presented by Enesto Laclau (2011 [1979]) and Stuart Hall (1986). Community radio as the alternative third developmental voice with the features of independence, equality, community participation and representation will be discussed. This chapter provides an exploration of the role played by radio in a rural setting, such as the one of Platfontein (where the !Xû and Khwe are located) in Kimberley with the aim of further engaging forms of social intrigue and inclusion elicited by the community radio station as the technology of empowerment. It will also be argued that the conversational approach used by *XK FM* of mixing music and talk creates a form of 'we' feeling, which translates into notions of belonging as a form of sociological natal affiliation.

The emergence of community radio as a new paradigm in South Africa

The history of community radio in South Africa dates back to the politics of the struggle against apartheid in the 1980s. Community media at the time acted as the 'voice of the oppressed' and played a significant role in mobilising and informing communities against apartheid (Teer-Tomaselli 2001: 233). However, the history of community radio is not peculiar to that of exclusion and discrimination against one group by the other (Olorunnisola 1995).[3] Anthony Olorunnisola adds that the evolution of community radio in South Africa can be traced back to *Radio Vryheid, Radio Donkerhoek, Radio Koppies, Radio Volkstem, Radio Pretoria* and beyond. These radio stations were established in 1994 by the *Pretoria Boerekommando* and the *Afrikaner Volksfront* (AVF). They operated without licences and were labelled by the new South African government as 'pirate stations', set to oppose the government.[4] Using 500 FM transmitters linked by Intelsat satellite, the SABC controlled almost 30 radio stations by the early 1990s (Hachten and Giffard 1984). Amongst these were *Radio South Africa, Radio 5, Afrikaans Stereo, Radio Metro* and other regional stations such as *Highveld Stereo, Radio Oranje, Radio Port Natal* and *Radio Algoa* (cf. De Villiers 1993; Olorunnisola 1995). These included stations that broadcast in local African languages – for example, *Radio Sesotho, Radio Venda, Radio Swazi* and *Zulu Stereo* (cf. De Villiers 1993) – and had traits of representing communities of interest.

Furthermore, the 'Jabulani! Freedom of the Airwaves' Conference held in Netherlands in 1991, organised by *Radio Freedom* (the ANC radio in exile), contributed significantly to discussions, which resulted in the IBA Act (Teer-Tomaselli 2001: 234). The IBA removed the responsibility for broadcast policy away from the direct control of the state and the SABC. As a result the IBA Act (153), in particular, was promulgated in 1993, by the Convention for a Democratic South Africa (CODESA), charged with powers to: (a) formulate broadcasting policy; (b) create licensing procedures; (c) regulate and monitor broadcasting activities; and (d) limit cross-media ownership and the enforcement of local content quotas.[5] The IBA Act made provisions for three kinds of broadcasters: (i) public service broadcasting; (ii) community broadcasting; and (iii) commercial broadcasting. Then, under the ambit of community broadcasting, the Act provides for three types of community of interest radio stations: institutional communities; religious communities; and cultural communities. A community radio station that serves cultural communities is designed to meet the cultural needs of a defined community (Teer-Tomaselli 2001: 235). *XK FM* therefore serves two cultural communities: the !Xû and Khwe.

In 1995 and 1996 the IBA Act was amended. This led to the formation of the Independent Communications Authority of South Africa (ICASA), which was finally promulgated in 2000 and was a merger of the IBA and the South Africa Telecommunications Regulatory Authority (SATRA) (Berger 2001: 162; Teer-Tomaselli 2001). Dumisani Moyo and Siphiwe Hlongwane (2009: 279) also suggest that this merger was necessitated by the 'global hype around convergence of technologies', thus confirming the need for robust communication systems, a point that was raised by one of my respondents at ICASA. ICASA was mandated to incorporate the functions of the IBA and those published in the Telecommunications Act (1996) and the Broadcasting Act (1999) (Berger 2001). ICASA functions by way of a council, which is constituted through a board that runs the affairs of the body, with the help of the secretariat, which issues five-year licences to all broadcasters including community radio stations.[6] Responses obtained from other radio stations regarding the application process for obtaining a broadcasting licence stated that the process is usually too laborious, but *XK FM's* station management stated that the process is not usually difficult for them as the licence is often obtained for them by SABC.[7] However, questions have been raised over the years about the independence of the ICASA council, starting from its appointment, the involvement of politicians and its financing mechanisms.[8]

In 1993 the National Community Radio Forum (NCRF) was formed with the aim of addressing the imbalances many communities had in relation to access to media (Teer-Tomaselli 2001: 234). Registered as a section 21 not-for-profit company, the forum had more than 120 community radio stations as part of its membership by 2005. The normative engagement of the rise of community radio in South Africa shows that it developed out of a complex configuration of audience demographics, which attempted to cater for age, language, locality, aesthetic and musical taste. Community radio is therefore seen as anchoring itself as the expression of the target communities. However, these idealistic positions fail to explain the obvious ideology of power, which is often embedded in these structures and as part of the process of state formation as seen in South Africa. A closer analysis of *XK FM's* programming, for example, showed that more time is allocated towards news and current affairs. On enquiring, it also emerged that news and current affairs programmes are managed from SABC studios in Kimberley.

Defining community radio

Community radio is a station built by the community or for the community and is used by that particular community to serve its own interests. Emphasis is on community ownership, autonomy, participation and representation. As opposed to public broadcasting, community radio programming is supposed to be community oriented, and in most cases is produced by the community (MISA 2000: 56). The definition of community refers to a geographically defined group, or people with a specific and equally ascertainable common interest (IBA 1997). These interests can include linguistic orientation and geographical location in terms of proximity with others to the extent of sharing in a communal associational life. The interests can also include ones that are developmental in nature and many more. Furthermore, Anthony Cohen (1985) defines a community as the expression of a commonality – acknowledging the functionality of associational life through which social reproduction and the creation of a common identity take place. A community radio seen from the perspective of Cohen's definition functions as the structure on which human agency within a community pivots in the articulation of a shared identity and collective solidarity, as seen in the case of the !Xû and Khwe communities of Platfontein. In South Africa, community radio encompasses four categories: (a) it is fully controlled by a non-profit entity and has non-profitable purposes; (b) it serves a particular community; (c) it encourages members of the community it serves to participate in the selection and provision of programmes to be broadcast; and (d) it may be funded by donations, grants, sponsorships and membership fees, or by a combination of the above (Teer-Tomaselli 2001).

Descriptions of what a community radio station is remain ambiguous, slippery and tautologous. Further, they fail to answer the question of what constitutes a community (Teer-Tomaselli 2001). But in the case of South Africa the IBA Act further provides for community broadcasting to cater for either a geographic community or a community of interest. In the case of a geographic community definition, it caters for a community whose commonality can be traced to a particular location as an area of residence. A community of interest is a community with specific ascertainable common interests (Teer-Tomaselli 2001). As a result, in the case of South Africa four types of community radio stations have emerged over the years: (a) those serving a geographical area; (b) campus-based radio stations – operating in colleges and university campuses; (c) religious radio stations; and (d) cultural and ethnic community radio stations (IBA 1997; Teer-Tomaselli 2001). The case study of *XK FM*, as will be shown, falls under the category of cultural and ethnic community radio stations.

Another celebrated feature of community radio is the aspect of independence and community representation. Similarly, Lisa Taylor and

Andrew Willis (1999: 136) observe that the notion of independence remains the driving force behind the development of the community radio movement in particular as a form of community representation and empowerment. To them, independence entails not depending on the authority of another, be it the state or other external agency. This means avoiding subordination and external control. However, they acknowledge the ambivalence of the concept of independence in media. Francis Kasoma (1995) argues that the question of independence when relating to media has to be qualified by attempting to answer the question: independent from whom and what? The notion of independence in community media can be understood through Stuart Hall's (1986) cultural concept of articulation in which he says it represents enunciated autonomy of a participating community outside the parameters of the public service broadcaster (PSB) and state influence. The independence of a community radio station represents a reclamation of the 'local' from the public broadcaster (Taylor and Willis 1999: 136) or a return of the local. The returned local in the case of the !Xû and Khwe represent the silent masses whose community radio helps them to present their historical presence through different programmes.

The existence of a definitive radius as a sphere of influence for a community radio also marks the relationship between community in communication and the 'symbolic construction of a community' (Howley 2010: 64). *XK FM,* for example, enjoys a radius of around 30km to 50km within Kimberley, with Platfontein as the epicentre. Given the constitution of the *XK FM* structure, research shows that community radio serves the interests of a smaller population (Lewis 1993a: 201; McCain and Lowe 1990) and has the ability to correct the distortions inherent in the majority-controlled media. Another key definition describes community radio as neither the expression of political power, nor of capital (Derlome 1990: 3). Teer-Tomaselli (2001: 233) supports this view by suggesting that a community radio is the expression of the population, and is a third voice between the state and private commercial radio.

Significant features of community radio: an overview

Community radio redefines the communication realm as a way of re-invigorating relations between the informer and the informed. The use of simple technology enhances the possibilities that people have of intervening in the production of programmes (Council for the Development of Community Media 1977: 397). For Ntongela Masilela (1996: 107), focus is on the community radio's potential as alternative media to alter the conditions of possibility in redefining various schema that distinguish alternative community media from the public and commercial media. Alternative media can be distinguished through ownership and management structures, financing, regulation, programming, and policy stance on issues of access and participation (Masilela 1996: 108). Community radio as alternative media is commonly managed through elected representatives (a board) or directly with voluntary community participation as another factor. The major feature of alternative media is 'independence' from the mainstream media, such as the state-controlled media. The view that community radio acts as an alternative media is usually associated with the media's potential to challenge the establishment, and in giving people an independent voice, which is often perceived as alternative and free speech. In terms of programming, community radio tends to broadcast community-oriented programmes produced by community members for community members. In view of their policy stance on issues of access and participation, Majid Tehranian (1990: 108), suggests that community radio is generally responsive to targeted audiences and often uses highly targeted interactive methods.

Community radio from a critical perspective entails the delineation between two different forms of media: The first is state-run media concerned with institutional politics. This form of media struggles over the power to govern and regards receivers of messages as potential side-takers. Second, a community radio such as *XK FM* is concerned with cultural politics (the functions of which are widely disseminated symbolic forms), struggles over meaning (ideology, hegemony, encoding and decoding). The latter also regards the audience as meaning makers (Riggins 1992: 13). Masilela (1996: 107) adds that these two traditions are replicated in conceptions of the significance of alternative media for political change. The overarching broader problem therefore becomes deciphering the 'community' whose interests are being served in a community radio station. The rationale for most community radio is that deep-seated participation by beneficiaries gives impetus to the station as the mouthpiece of the local community (Teer-Tomaselli 2001). Programmes are aimed at satisfying community aspirations, thereby identifying with the interests of the local population (Boeren 1994: 144).

As seen in the case of *XK FM*, another important feature of community radio is the use of local languages to ensure effective communication. Fackson Banda (2004: 138) adds that community radio should be perceived in the following ways: (a) run and managed by the local people with financial support from the local businesses; (b) existing for the local people; (c) located in the community; and (d) not-for-profit. While these four features may apply in some situations, not all of them can be applied to our case study *XK FM*. For example, the radio station *XK FM* is owned by the SABC. Therefore, all its finances, recruitment of staff and payment of salaries is the preserve of the SABC. However, it is located within a given area, Platfontein, and functions as a non-profit organisation. According to Banda (2004: 139), three typologies of community radio further emerge: (a) community radio as a geographic imperative; (b) community radio as a socio-cultural phenomenon; (c) community radio as a developmental initiative.

Community radio as a geographic imperative deals with issues of access by members of the community and proximity to the community of interest. *XK FM* as our case study is well located within Platfontein. Access to it remains possible due to its central location. Members of the community are allowed to visit and to share their views on different issues relating to programming. Physical proximity in this instance constitutes an important element for the 'community'. Ad Boeren (1994: 144) states that the formation of local radio is based on the notion that people are encouraged to visit the studio and that the community participates in the management of the station. A radio station that is within the reach of the community ensures effective participation by the community in its management and programming.

Community radio as a socio-cultural phenomenon allows for mediation and representation of territorially bounded identities. This form of representation takes place by way of mediated social experiences. Among the !Xû and Khwe, like in most African societies, the radio station has further cemented the existence of 'virtual' or 'imagined communities' through the use of language. As a result, communities based on 'natal affiliation' emerge. *XK FM's* central location in Platfontein; in-between the two communities and next to the school, casts a symbolic gesture of institutionalised acculturation. Michael Laflin (1989: 6) warns that the legitimatisation of local languages and identities through the formation of community radio stations is sometimes destructive to national unity and integration. This view was supported by SABC's Head of News and Current Affairs, who stressed that the histories of the !Xû and Khwe necessitated the establishment of a community-centred radio station. He added that *XK FM* as their radio station continues to play the role of reinforcing their sense of identity and belonging to South Africa. This to him is managed through different current affairs programmes.[9] *XK FM* is, therefore, a product of a conscious policy to promote the expression of local opinion and to mobilise local communities, as part of social transformation.

However, Charles Husband (2000: 201) argues that within the development of democratic media theory there is a discussion on how and through what means the ruled communicate their views and wishes to the ruler. Community radio therefore plays a central dialogic role in mobilising the people, especially in light of the social complexities and need for social mobility, as seen in the case of *XK FM*. In a bid to understand the feasibility of public access and deliberation, the question of whether it is possible to create democratic practices whereby people are able to participate in community ideation as equals has to be posed. Attempting to address this question is seen as a panacea to national unity (Skogerbo 1996: 105).

Community radio is often viewed by way of the role it plays as an agent and medium of development. Boeren (1994: 140) says that many development practitioners and communications specialists have tended to consider radio as the most useful medium for development, the reason being that, compared to television, radio can be accessed by a large section of the population. This argument when assessed through the !Xû and Khwe communities enjoys *prima-facie* plausibility. *XK FM* has become an important source of information for the two communities owing to their low literacy levels. Further, Boeren (1994: 141) observes:

> Radio [...] is an excellent medium to inform people with, to make people aware, to stimulate interest and to influence opinions [...] discuss development issues, acquire relevant information and learn new techniques. The main source of information is the radio programme to which they listen collectively.

Radio remains a prestigious asset to the target communities and is quite accessible than television and newspapers in that the target groups are able to listen to the different radio programmes. *XK FM* as a community radio provides impetus for mobilising local development initiatives and projects.

Repositioning the theory of articulation and the chosen research trajectories

A combination of the case study method and southern participant action research was used. This was informed by a qualitative research paradigm and linked with the works of Robert Yin (2003) and Kurt

Lewin (1946) on case study method and action research, respectively. A more grounded form of action research emerged in the form of southern participant-action research. Two components emerge here: the fact of a type of methodology that is influenced by the tenets of action-research (Elden and Chisholm 1993), followed by the notion of qualitatively engaging with participants in their situated arrangement as a form of participation (Denzin and Lincoln 2011). These two were then located within a particular ideological context – that of belonging to the 'global south', in which the research is located; i.e., conducted in Africa, specifically, South Africa. Members of the !Xû and Khwe communities together with the station's presenters, other members of staff at *XK FM*, and some officials from SABC Headquarters at Auckland Park and in Kimberley were interviewed. The researcher was able to grasp the participants' constructions and interpretations of their world, and situated meanings thereof as forms of articulation.[10] A total of 22 respondents were interviewed.

The use of a case study method allowed me to establish the validity of *XK FM* being studied as a radio station. Thus, *XK FM* as a chosen case study helped in providing a detailed understanding of community radio as a phenomenon in South Africa (Mhlanga 2006, 2010a). As Yin (2003: 14) suggests, a case study research strategy is an all-embracing method; southern participant-action research, a form of action research, was also used. Carr and Kemmis (1986: 162) described action research as simply a form of self-reflective enquiry undertaken by participants in social situations, aimed at improving the rationality of their own practices, their understanding of these practices and of the situations in which these practices are carried out. Similarly, Peter Reason and Hilary Bradbury (2001) posit that action research can be defined as follows:

> A participatory, democratic process concerned with developing practical knowing in the pursuit of worthwhile human purposes, grounded in a participatory worldview which we believe is emerging at this historical moment. It seeks to bring together action and reflection, theory and practice, in participation with others, in the pursuit of practical solutions to issues of pressing concern to people, and more generally the flourishing of individual persons and their communities (2001: 1).

Action research when linked with the case study method enabled me to explore and gain a detailed understanding of a situated research problem: *XK FM* as a community radio. A qualitative engagement of social reality was aided through the use of interviews and by participating in a number of social activities, such as being involved in a football tournament organised by the social community league representing the !Xû and Khwe (Mhlanga 2006, 2010a). A qualitative approach that analyses a 'bounded context', such as a community radio, rejects a 'value-free' scientific approach to research. As a qualitative study, southern participant-action research entails engaging with the respondents' beliefs, values and categories embodying fundamental ideological positions. This type of research enacts, confirms, legitimates and engages relations of power and domination in society. By presenting *XK FM* as a case study of a community radio station with its establishment deeply embedded in the discursive nature of the social structure of a newly resettled community in 2000, then an emancipatory project emerges within the broader project of social transformation as part of the on-going process of state formation. Max Weber's concept of *Verstenhen* (i.e., understanding facts by interpreting their meanings in the light of relevant social modes of reproduction, social goals and values) was applied (Firscher 2003: 50).

Further, Enersto Laclau (2011 [1979]: 10) adds that the challenges facing the theory of articulation are that theoretical practice and the engagement of research have been greatly hindered by two obstacles: the 'connotative articulation of concepts at the level of common sense and their rationalist articulation into essentialist paradigms'. This research embraced the influence of social structure and existing forms of social interaction though community radio. Thus, the relationship between scholarship and society in action research is often marked by bold lines of convergence, acknowledging the socio-politically situated nature of discourses and social reflections. With a hermeneutical assessment of *XK FM* as a community radio in South Africa, a form of social action that relates its goals and purposes to a situated interpretivist position of the !Xû and Khwe communities emerges.

Enersto Laclau (2011 [1979]) is the major proponent of the theory of articulation. His engagement of it stems from philosophy, in which he says articulation entails that a, 'discourse or *doxa*[11] may or may not be represented by a system of misleading concepts that do not appear linked by inherent logical relations, but are bound together simply by connotative or evocative links which custom and opinion have established between them' (Laclau 2011 [1979]: 07). In Enersto Laclau's philosophical work, articulation is represented through Plato's allegory of slaves being kept in a dark cave whose darkness they end up being accustomed to; but when one slave manages to break free and is exposed to light, another process of being accustomed to the sunlight takes place. Through this newly discovered moment of being accustomed, or moment of realisation, a kind of rupture between the knowledge of the past and the present takes place. As a result, a new form of knowledge emerges. To Laclau this realisation, which manifests itself in a form of knowledge, presupposes, then, an operation of rupture. The latter can also be further understood as 'a disarticulation of ideas from those connotative domains to which they appear linked in the form of a misleading necessity, which enables us subsequently to reconstruct their true articulations' (Laclau 2011 [1979]: 08); that is, making a clear connection between the past and the present. So a new form of articulation emerges. It is this form of articulation that in this chapter is referred to as the 'return' of the local or the process by which the !Xû and Khwe realise their humanity and peoplehood as they bond into a community championed by their community radio station *(XK FM)*.

Stuart Hall's appropriation of the theory of articulation into cultural studies takes a political route. It emerges at the critical juncture when the silent majorities who are often assumed not to think finally realise the moment of being the 'subject-authors' of their narratives, through community radio. This to him is a moment of enunciation, i.e., the point at which the historical presence of the masses interrupts history. It marks the beginning of community participation and empowerment of those considered to be the silent majorities. However, it remains noteworthy to avoid taking a reductionist position. Stuart Hall says the theory of articulation is:

> the form of connection that can make a unity of two different elements, under certain conditions. It is a linkage, which is not necessary, determined, absolute and essential for all time. You have to ask, under what circumstances can a connection be forged or made? So the so-called 'unity' of a discourse is really the articulation of different, distinct elements which can be re-articulated in different ways because they have no necessary 'belongingness.' The 'unity' which matters is a linkage between that articulated discourse and the social forces with which it can, under certain historical conditions, but need not necessarily, be connected. (Hall 1986: 53)

From the perspective given above, we note that the 'theory of articulation is both a way of understanding how ideological elements come, under certain conditions, to cohere together within a discourse [...] at specific conjectures to certain political subjects' (Hall 1986: 53). So the theory of articulation according to Hall 'asks how an ideology discovers its subject rather than how the subject thinks the necessary and inevitable thoughts which belong to it' by enabling us to think about how an ideology empowers people. It is here that community radio as new technology within a bounded context and given its proximity to a particular community acts as the fulcrum on which members of a community re-narrate their history and empower themselves (Mhlanga 2012). Laclau perceives this development as marking the existence of a community with locally materialised conditions of recapturing their past and linking it with the present and future. A form of articulation also emerges when members of these two communities are empowered through *XK FM*, which helps them to shape their future; thus a form of linkage now exists between the past, present and the future.

The establishment of *XK FM* as a community radio has brought a marked sense of social organisation among the !Xû and Khwe. Observations showed that the station has six presenters, of which three are !Xû and the other three are Khwe. The Acting station manager (Regina Beregho) is Khwe and the deputy station manager (Malton) is !Xû. This arrangement was agreed on by the Communal Property Association (CPA) in an effort to balance ethnic representation in all their activities so as to avoid conflict.

Furthermore, it emerged that this social arrangement was informed by the violent ethnic conflicts that marred these two communities following their settlement in South Africa in 1989. Most respondents stated that ethnic clashes were a common feature in their community up to around 2003/4. They also added that the establishment of *XK FM* as a community radio station and the continuous churning out of different programmes and information about their social problems had led to the two communities working together. One community leader from the Khwe community acknowledged:

> for the first in our history we have managed to work together and even share solutions to our problems even if we are two different communities.[12]

He added that the presenters as role models have taught them lessons on how feasible it is for the two communities to work together and shape their future. Given that these are two different communities with mutually unintelligible languages, the establishment of *XK FM* has caused the emergence of a third community; by bringing these two communities together, different radio programmes allow for dialogue on different issues, such as their ethnic differences, intermarriages and how they have toiled together ever since their days in Angola, Namibia and now in South Africa. Community radio, therefore, is part of the discursive formation, in which 'relations of power structure, the inter-discursivity, or the intertextuality, of the field of knowledge' takes place (Hall 1986). These two communities have a history of not interacting in their countries of origin. Observations revealed that the Khwe tend to despise the !Xû. Hence the use of derogative names like 'n#hã' used by the !Xû when referring to the Khwe, while the Khwe call the !Xû, 'n!hae'.[13] The crisis of ethnic relations was also exacerbated by the selective treatment they received from the South African Defence Forces (SADF), which favoured the Khwe at the expense of the !Xû. The SADF always offered more educational opportunities to the Khwe than the !Xû (cf. Douglas 1996).[14] *XK FM* as a case study can therefore be concep-tualised as the transformation of 'different regimes of truth in the social formation' (Hall 1986). Through different radio programmes, histories of the !Xû and Khwe are narrated, thereby enhancing the memories of their peoplehood and causing a convergence of their narratives of mar-ginalisation and suffering.

The return of the local: The !Xû and Khwe, and *XK FM* as the case study

In this section, two key concepts will be raised: the first captured by the word 'return' and the second captured by the word 'local'. However, it stands to reason that a closer analysis of these two concepts shows that they are closely linked. However, it would be ideal to put the concept of 'return' into its proper historical context from African philosophy – in particular as a form of sociological reproduction and representation of knowledge about Black Africa, nationalist discourse and those in dias-pora (cf. Césaire 1939). Its usage here follows a deconstructivist perspec-tive, which derives its roots from the subaltern's quest for control of their identity and destiny. As Aimé Césaire (1939) trenchantly contends, this quest by the subaltern marks a 'return to the native land'. In the inven-tion of his neologue on negritude, Césaire linked the concept of 'return' with the retention, re-articulation and representation of 'dignity, the personhood or humanity, of black people' (Masolo 1994: 1). To Dismas Masolo (1994) the idea of 'return' is tightly imbued with meanings of a particular group of people's historicity; that 'turns it into a consciousness or awareness, as a form of management of power relations and a "histori-cal commitment" to a "movement".' Similarly, the NCRF adds:

Community media emerged as the voice of the oppressed and played a significant role in informing and mobilizing communities, at grass-roots level, against apartheid (1999: 2).

From the observation above, two meanings of the concept of 'return' emerge; first, one relating to 'repatriation to a geographical or perceptual space', as seen in the case of the relocation of the Angolan-based !Xû and Khwe, who had been recruited into the SADF to Schmidtsdrift in South Africa at the end of the war (1976–1990) (cf. Douglas 1996; Lee and Hitchcock 2001: 13; Chamberlain 2003).[15] This is closely tied to the establishment of *XK FM* as the realisation and ultimate articulation of the two communities' sense of belonging, identity and peoplehood. Therefore, the radio station as a perceptual space stands as a direct symbolic representation of the two ethnic groups' connection with their past. The second meaning of the idea of 'return' relates to metaphorical regaining of the 'conceptual space in which culture is both field and process' (Masolo 1994: 2) – this points to the moment of articulation or connection for the !Xû and Khwe. *XK FM* as a community radio station occupies this conceptual space in which a sense of unified commonality emerges through different programmes that offer a re-narration of their history and sense of origin and identity in a transformed South Africa.

XK FM functions as a space for self-redefining for the two ethnic groups. As Kevin Howley (2010: 65) suggests, *XK FM* shows the 'pivotal role human action plays in articulating, and [...] rearticulating, any social formation'. To the !Xû and Khwe *XK FM* as a *community* radio station also stands as a space for resistance and protest against their perceived alienation and domination within the broader South African society in Kimberley. The !Xû and Khwe consider their settlement at Platfontein as a sign of victory by the !Xû and Khwe Trust (Lee and Hitchcock 2001), which was established by the two communities in 1993, and was instrumental in obtaining land for their displaced communities. Most interviewees from these two ethnic groups highlighted the abuse they often receive from government officials who deny them access to social services because they consider them as migrants and outsiders. They cited incidents where the youths and elders are denied national identity cards and passports by government officials at the registry offices in Kimberley. The !Xû and Khwe argue that historically they originated from South Africa and only migrated to Angola and Namibia during the *iMfecane* period.[16]

The !Xû and Kwe migrants were caught between the old regime and the new government in South Africa. Their linguistic and cultural distinctiveness worsened their situation in that neither of the two dominant groups, black or white, was prepared to absorb them. This forced them to remain in Schmidtsdrift, where they lived in temporary military bivouacs until 1999 (Lee and Hitchcock 2001). While stationed at the Schmidtsdrift tent camp, they were divided into separate residential sections (cf. Voster 1994). They lived in tents and were promised proper housing by the SADF and the National Party (NP) government after 1990. Their move to South Africa fulfilled two major objectives: (a) the promise by the SADF of safeguarding the two communities in a country governed by their previous enemies; and (b) protection from liberation governments in Angola and Namibia. The two communities were immediately granted citizenship on arrival in South Africa (Douglas 1996: 8). However, in 1999 the base was returned to its legal owners (the Tswana and Griqua people) following a successful land restitution case, leading to the relocation of the !Xû and Khwe to Platfontein, 10km out of Kimberley.

The Khwe are socially mobile and are better educated than their !Xû counterparts, a stratification that aggravates inter-group conflict (Archer 1995; Douglas 1996). Khwedam is a Khoe dialect and is related to a cluster of languages that include Naro and Khoekhoegowap (Voster 1994: 70). !Xûntali belongs to the Zhu language family. These languages are not mutually intelligible and are mainly spoken in military bases outside Kimberley, Platfontein and some parts of the Northern Cape (Voster 1994). A sizable number of !Xûntali-speaking homes also use Khwedam as a second language. However, this relationship is not reciprocal, since Khwedam is linguistically dominant. Most Khwedam speakers are multilingual: they speak Afrikaans, English, Portuguese, Mbukushu, Otjiwambo and Silozi, but not !Xûntali (cf. Archer 1995).

The location of *XK FM* as a cultural community radio station for the !Xû and Khwe sought to capture and articulate the history of these two ethnic groups. Its policy requires two simultaneous presenters for each language as a balancing act.[17] Broadcasting begins at six o'clock in the morning and ends at nine in the evening, and is characterised by a myriad of programmes. Where only one presenter is available, Afrikaans becomes the language of broadcasting. During weekdays, from Monday to Friday, programmes are divided into five segments: (a) *Û Kxam I'am* (Breakfast Show) – 06:00am to 10:00am; (b) Late Drive Show – 10:00am to 12noon; (c) *Ã java I'am* (What the San Must Know) – 12noon to 1:00pm; (d) *Ngewo I'am* (Youth Programme) – 2:00pm to 3:00pm; (e) Storytime for the Children – 4:00pm to 6:00pm. Other unaccounted for programmes in-between those stated above emerge as very key programmes that seek to address specific issues, such as the programme called *So Onthou Ons* (In the Past – What We Can Remember). This is a programme in which story tellers, historians and community elders are invited to present on the history of the two communities. Then there are other programmes that are normally broadcast on different days, such as the one on Mondays between 11:00am and 12noon, which touches on HIV/AIDS and other health-related issues, *Gxakhwe/dame* Journal (On Women's Empowerment), etc. On Thursdays, for example, from 11:00am to 12noon there is a programme on 'Uplifting of the San people'. Through these programmes, discourses of cultural/linguistic survival and development are articulated. These discourses are linked with the objectives of the National Khoisan Consultative Council's (NKCC) work across the San communities. As a social movement, the Council's work deals with shared activities and beliefs directed towards the demand for change in some aspects of the social order.

On participation and empowerment – community radio as the rediscovery of the oppressed

Development as a process of change set in motion principles whose objective is to eradicate poverty, injustice and exploitation. Its pursuit, together with the participation of various players, therefore becomes the central pillar upon which policies are anchored. But the concept of participatory communication as a development initiative lacks a definition capable of enabling understanding of the processes and outcomes involved. As Dagron Gumucio (2001: 01) observes, the most interesting work of a participatory nature often defies the written word. Similarly, Shirley White (1994: 08) adds that the word participation is 'kaleidoscopic'; it changes its colour and shape at the will of the hands in which it is held. Neither the absence of an accurate means of capturing the essence of participatory communication nor the fluid nature of participation has reduced the realisation that its differing forms appear to have gained usefulness in given contexts in tandem with histories of exclusion and discrimination. But to Olorunnisola (1995),[18] participation and communication are often bedfellows in the movement towards engaging the previously disenfranchised populations in social dialogue. As will be presented in this section, community radio plays a big role in giving voice to the previously disenfranchised. Its emergence in South Africa marks a new era of community empowerment as part of the state's emancipatory projects. But Last Moyo (2012: 484) cautions:

> Participation is not always positive, as it can be top-down, mediated, regulated, and therefore exclusive and undemocratic. It can serve as a regime of endorsement and disapproval for political, economic and cultural power. (2012: 484)

As a result, what remains to be seen is how community radio as part of a broader developmental paradigm aids the course of democratisation.

However, two fundamental questions appear in this notion of participatory communication as it relates to community radio. First, in what ways do the roles and association between political actors, the mass media and the public change in a participatory communication environment? Second, what are the notable dividends of participatory communication? McKee (1996: 218) observes:

> Community participation is a very vague and open concept and is used to mean very different things. It often subsumes other concepts and approaches (such as 'self-help', 'self-reliance', 'user-choice', 'community involvement' and 'participatory planning and development', which are themselves ill defined. In connection with community participation people will often talk of 'felt needs', 'local perceptions', 'bottom-up planning', 'motivation', 'latent development potential', 'catalytic development inputs,' 'integrated development at the village level' [...] Yet all these concepts are highly complex and diffuse and their meaning in any particular context is often obscure.

Scholarly consensus on the nature and extent of community participation and the participatory environment on community radio is lacking. The role played by community radio as a service to society but within a given context presents another feature of alternative communication. To Chris Atton (2002: 25) alternative media's purpose is to 'enable wider social participation in the creation, production, and dissemination of content'. Bailey *et al.* (2008: 11) add that 'participation in the media and through the media sees the communicative process not as a series of practices that are often restrictively controlled by media professionals, but as a human right that cuts across societies'. Community radio further compounds the fact that genuine dialogue with locals can be compatible with extending to them technical expertise. But it is imperative to further explore the cohesive nature and consensual realities created by this development project in bringing two often conflicting communities together, as seen in the case of the !Xû and Khwe.

There may be different approaches towards understanding community radio and, in particular, the notion of community participation as a central feature. Also of importance to scholarship now should not be the confines of epistemological location of the donors but its ontological imaginations, in particular, its sociological positioning in a country like South Africa; i.e., a country riddled with inequalities inherited and, to some extent, newly generated forms of inequalities. Views by Moyo (2012) and Bailey *et al.* (2008) that participation is highly interwoven with the right to communicate are plausible. In emphasising the role played by community radio in empowering communities and as part of the politics of inclusion, Moyo adds that 'scholars have variously defined alternative media as "participatory media", "grassroots media", or "small-scale media".'

Community radio as part of the state's emancipatory project plays an important role in South Africa's social transformation process by seeking to involve different communities as key players in programme auditing and production. As seen in the case of *XK FM*, presenters are also drawn from the two communities. For the !Xû and Khwe communities, radio broadcasts in their languages, thereby enabling them to develop a sociological natal affiliation, which according to most respondents creates a sense of belonging, ownership and empowerment (Mhlanga 2012). This return of the local and the location of *XK FM* as a community radio station marks the birth of a new approach to nation-building in which different ethnic groups and their languages occupy centre stage, i.e., with Xûntali and Khwedam as the core languages of broadcasting. Language broadcasts helps in generating a particular kind of social intrigue, which causes the !Xû and Khwe communities to perceive the radio station as their voice of empowerment. Even their minimal involvement in programme production, as it emerged, is perceived as participation, thus creating a kind of 'we feeling'. *XK FM* has become the platform on which social narratives; cultural signifiers and symbols are represented through different radio programmes following the stencil of social conversations. Radio therefore plays an important role in most African societies, in capturing the old traditional mindset and in managing communicative action within the African associational life (Mhlanga 2012).

XK FM in this case stands as a symbol and voice of empowerment for the !Xû and Khwe, and is perceived by most presenters and station staff as part of the broader emancipatory project. However, it remains to be seen whether the two communities actually have much say in the affairs of the station, given that its ownership structure and the licence clearly states that the SABC has sole ownership of the station. But to them, belonging, as captured in the sociology of language, through different broadcasts creates meaning, a sense of duty, territoriality and social responsibility, and is carried in different socially constructed symbols (Mhlanga 2012). Michel Foucault (1982: 297) trenchantly observes that 'language forms the locus of tradition, of the unspoken habits of thought, of what lies hidden in a people's mind; it accumulates an ineluctable memory which does not even know itself as memory'.

By broadcasting in Xûntali and Khwedam, *XK FM* has created a new sense of community among the !Xû and Khwe. This emergence of a new community is closely tied to notions of empowerment and community participation. When radio communicates in a particular language, creating cultural symbols and meanings, eschatologies of voice as empowerment and form of emancipatory project emerge. As James Carey (2009: 109ff) aptly captures it in his tribute to Harold Innis, through modern technology communities with spiritual conditions of permanence are formed. While the notion of a 'community' in a community radio may be 'notoriously difficult to pin down' as Ruth Teer-Tomaselli (2001: 232) argues, we also note that particularised language broadcasts tend to create virtual or imagined communities that emerge out of a shared sense of belonging, common culture and shared history. Moyo (2012: 488) adds that 'the community, defined in both spatial and nonspatial terms, suggests a close-knit collectivity that shares a common culture and history'. As seen in the case of *XK FM* and, in particular, how their CPA has been able to manage other development projects, the radio station, apart from its geographic location confirms the existence of a community of interest. The discernment of what a community is can be gleaned from a geographical and a sociological sense, implying that a community is a basic unit for 'horizontal social organisation' (Teer-Tomaselli 2001: 232).

The creation of community radio as a local development project seeks to tackle paternalism, social control and non-reciprocity, as found in the old 'mass media' order and in transmitting communication models (cf. White 1990; IBA 1997; UNESCO 1997; Teer-Tomaselli 2001). Community radio enables people to be involved in the task of codifying reality into signification, which generates critical consciousness and empowers them to seek to alter their social relations. Given the !Xû and Khwe's histories of being oppressed and marginalised, which dates back to their times in Angola and Namibia, *XK FM* as their community radio has been able to function as the translocal institution that attends to and represents their community interests (Moyo 2012). Also, the radio station's location in Platfontein as a bounded community with its community-centred programmes creates a sense of 'people sharing a common condition or problem' (Popple 1995: 4).

Community radio attempts to redefine relations between informer and the informed and to enhance, through the acquisition of simple technology, the feasibility of people intervening in the process of information production (Masilela 1996: 107). The success of *XK FM* in this regard hinges on ownership, management structures, financing, regulation, programming, and its policy and practice on issues of access and participation.

Conclusion

From the foregoing it can be concluded that there is need for a deep-seated engagement with community radio within African scholarship. There is need for research that attempts to theorise the history of the communitarian nature of African associational life and its different historical community-based communication systems. Community radio offers us a new paradigm, and has been able to receive scholarly attention, albeit with a view to understanding how it impacts on the future and as a progressive shift towards participatory development and empowerment. To this end, there is a need for understanding how communities have been able, at a moment's notice, to embrace community radio as new technologies of communication and also how these new technologies have exploited the traditional contours of communication. The issue of difference, equality, representation, autonomy and independence were highlighted as underlying features of community radio. The discussion of *XK FM* as a case study, using the theory of articulation and the 'return of the local', provided a theoretical locus on which our understanding of community radio stations can be grounded. Key features of community radio were discussed; these included that the station should fulfil the following criteria: be a non-profit organisation; exist for the local people; and be owned, controlled and managed by the local people with the help of a board set up and composed of the local people. However, as seen in the case of *XK FM*, which is managed and owned by the SABC, these key features remain normative and idealistic. But it was noted that community radio bears the picture and emblem of the community, and becomes the community's source of identity, with their hopes and aspirations captured through local language broadcasts. It also emerged that community media function as the alternative voice to the communities concerned and celebrate independence as the main feature.

Notes

1. !Xû is the name given to the speakers; the language they speak is called !Xûntali. Khwe refers to the speakers, whereas the language is called Khwedam.
2. This follows a series of interviews with Dr Zikalala in March 2010. Another interview was conducted in August of the same year.
3. From Olorunnisola's (1995) *Community radio as participatory communication in post apartheid South Africa,* http://www.comminit.com/evaluations/eval2006/evaluations-195.html
4. For more information on these Afrikaans-languages stations see: http://www.radionetherlands.nl/features/media/dossiers/hateradioafricame.html.
5. For more information on the IBA of South Africa see: http://www.info.gov.za/acts/1993/a153-93.pdf.
6. For more information on the Act refer to the ICASA website: http://www.icasa.org.za/Documents.aspx? Please see page 69.
7. This follows interviews held with different heads of radio stations at SABC Headquarters in 2010.
8. This information was obtained from one of my interviewees from the Media Development and Diversity Agency (MDDA) in 2010.
9. This emerged from the interview I had with Dr Snuki Zikalala at SABC in March 2010. A wide range of issues were raised about the management, ownership and control of this radio station. However, Dr Zikalala emphasized XK FM's uniqueness as a radio station dealing with a particular group of the San communities.
10. Officials interviewed at Auckland Park, SABC Headquarters in Johannesburg included people such as Mapule Mbalathi (the then Head of Radio News and Current Affairs), a Tsonga and the former station manager of Munghana Lonene FM. Mapule Mbalathi is also credited with transforming Munghana Lonene FM from the vestiges of apartheid, as Radio Tsonga FM, into the radio station that it is now.
11. *Doxa* is a Greek word meaning 'common belief' or 'popular opinion'; it can also be translated to mean 'custom' or 'being accustomed to something'.
12. These were the views of one member of the CPA, a community structure created to address issues obtaining in their communities. This structure is blended with members from the two communities and operates like a secretariat with offices located 5km into the farms owned by the two communities. The views were expressed during my interaction with the CPA in the offices in August 2006.
13. Information on the use of derogative names was obtained from the interviews I had with Erasmus Matesta, one of my research assistants from the side of the !Xû. He gave this information while emphasising ethnic differences among the two communities. These terms can be pronounced in the following way: '*n!hae*', used by the Khwe to depict the !Xû can be pronounced as '*ngcaye*'. It means 'people who come from the bush'. The name '*n#hã*', given to the Khwe by the !Xû, can be pronounced as '*nca*'. When probed on the meaning, they said it has no meaning but depicts the way the Khwe speak.

14. This information is also based on my discussions with people in the field. It, too, depicts ethnic cleavages that still exist in the community.
15. The war was between South Africa and the liberation armies of Angola and the South West African People's Liberation Army, Namibia's Liberation movement.
16. This argument was first presented to me by the different groups of elders who were interviewed from both the !Xû and Khwe. A number of these elders constituted the CPA. Their historical narrative was corroborated by historians I interviewed at McGregor Museum in Kimberley in 2006, 2009, and 2010.
17. Information was obtained from Regina Beregho, the station manager.
18. For more information on this scholar and the evolution of community radio in South Africa, visit the following website: http://www.personal.psu.edu/faculty/a/x/axo8/Joburg/manuscript.htm.

References

Archer, F. (1995) 'Participatory Research and Planning: Report to the Minister of Land Affairs'. Unpublished Report on Schmidtsdrift Commissioned by the Department of Land Affairs.

Atton, C. (2002) *Alternative Media*. London: Sage.

Bailey, O. G. *et al.* (2008) *Understanding Alternative Media*. Maidenhead: Open University Press.

Banda, F. (2004) 'Community Radio Broadcasting in Zambia: A Policy Perspective'. PhD Thesis, available at http://hdl.handle.net/10500/1833.

Berger, G. (2001) 'De-Racialization, Democracy, and Development: Transformation of the South African Media 1994–2000'. In K. G. Tomaselli, & H. Dunn (Eds) *Critical Studies on African Media and Culture: Media, Democracy and Renewal in South Africa, New Approaches to Political Economy*. Colorado Springs: International Academic Publishers Ltd.

Boeren, A. (1994) *In Other Words: The Cultural Dimension of Communication for Development*. CESO paperback Number 19. Hague: CESO Publication.

Carey, J. (2009) *Communication as Culture: Essays on Media and Society* (Rev. Ed.). New York and London: Routledge.

Carr, W. and Kemmis, S. (1986) *Becoming Critical: Education, Knowledge and Action Research*. Lewes: Falmer.

Césaire, A. (1939 [1969]) *Return to my Native Land*. Baltimore: Penguin Books.

Chamberlain, J. E. (2003) *If This is Your Land, Where are Your Stories? Finding Common Ground*. Toronto: Vantage Canada Publications.

Cohen, A. (1985) *The Symbolic Construction of Community*. Cambridge: Tavistock.

Council for the Development of Community Media (1977) 'Community Media and the Ideology of Participation'. In A. Matterlart and S. Siegelaub (Eds) *Communication and Class Struggle, Vol. 2*. New York: International General Publishers.

Denzin, N. K. and Lincoln, Y. S. (2011) *The Sage Handbook of Qualitative Research*. Thousand Oak: Sage.

Derlome, M. (1990) 'The Right to Communicate'. Presidential Address at the Fourth AMARC: Dublin.

De Villiers, C. (1993) 'Radio: Chameleon of the other'. In A. S. De Beer, (Ed.). *Mass Media for the 90s: The South African Handbook of Mass Communication.* Pretoria: Van-Schaik.

Douglas, S. S. (1996) 'Attractions and Artillerymen, Curiosities and Commandos: An Ethnographic Study of Elites and the Politics of Cultural Distinction'. Unpublished Thesis, University of Cape-Town, Cape-Town.

Elden, M. and Chisholm, R. F. (1993) 'Emerging Varieties of Action Research: Introduction to the Special Issue'. *Human Relations, 46 (2): pp, 121 – 142.*

Firscher, F. (2003) *Reframing Public Policy: Discursive Politics and Deliberative Practices.* Oxford: Oxford University Press.

Foucault, M. (1982) *The Order of Things: An Archaeology of the Human Sciences.* London: Tavistock Publications.

Gumucio, D. A. (2001) *Making Waves: Stories of Participatory Communication for Social Change.* New York: The Rockefeller Foundation.

Hachten, W. and Giffard, C.A. (1984) *Total Onslaught: The South African Press Under Attack.* Johannesburg: MacMillan.

Hall, S. (1986) 'On Postmodernism and Articulation: An Interview with Stuart Hall'. *Journal of Communication Inquiry, 10 (2): pp. 45–60.*

Howley, K. (2010) 'Notes on a Theory of Community Radio'. In K. Howley, (Ed.). *Understanding Community Media.* Los Angeles/London: Sage.

Husband, C. (2000) 'Media and the Public Sphere in Multi-ethnic Societies'. In S. Cottle, (Ed.). *Issues in Cultural and Media Studies: Ethnic Minorities and the Media.* Buckingham: Open University Press.

Independent Broadcasting Authority (1997) *Position Paper on Four Year Licences for Community Sound Broadcasting Services.* Johannesburg: IBA

Kasoma, F. (1995) 'The Role of the Independent Media in Africa's Change to Democracy'. *Media, Culture and Society, 17(4): pp. 537–535.*

Laclau, E. (2011 [1979]) *Politics and Ideology in Marxist Theory: Capitalism, Fascism and Populism.* London/New York: Verso.

Laflin, M. (1989) 'Hard Questions About Local Radio Stations'. *Agriculture Information Development Bulletin, Issue, 11(4): pp. 6–7.*

Lee, R. B. and Hitchcock, R. K. (2001) 'African Hunter-Gatherers: Survival, History and the Politics of Identity'. *In African Study Monograph, (Supplement 26): pp. 257–228*

Lewin, K. (1946) 'Action Research and Minority Problems'. *Journal of Social Issues, 2: pp. 34–46.*

Lewis, P. (1993a) *Alternative Media: Linking the Global and Local.* London: UNESCO.

McCain, T. A. and Lowe, G. F. (1990) 'Localism in Western European Radio broadcasting: Untangling the wireless'. *Journal of Communication, 40(1): pp. 86–101.*

Masilela, T. S. B. (1996) 'Alternative media and political schemes for assessing significance and potential'. *Africa Media Review, 10(1): pp. 92–114.*

Masolo, D. A. (1994) *African Philosophy in Search of Identity.* Bloomington & Indianapolis: Indiana University Press.

McKee, N. (1996) *Social Mobilisation and Social Marketing in Developing Communities: Lessons For Communicators.* Penang: Southbound.

Media Institute of Southern Africa (MISA) (2000) *Community Level Baseline Research into Community Media Attitudes and Needs in Zambia and Namibia.* Windhoek: MISA.

Mhlanga, B. (2006) 'Community Radio as Dialogic and Participatory: A Critical Analysis of Governance, Control and Community Participation: A Case Study of XK FM Radion'. Unpublished, Centre for Culture, Communication and Media Studies, University of KwaZulu-Natal.

Mhlanga, B. (2009) 'The Community in Community Radio: A Case Study of XK FM, Interrogating Issues of Community Participation, Governance, and Control'. *Ecquid Novi: African Journalism Studies, 30 (1): pp. 58–72.*

Mhlanga, B. (2010a) 'The Ethnic Imperative: Community Radio as Dialogic and Participatory and the Case Study of XK FM'. In N. Hyde-Clarke (Ed.) *The Citizen in Communication: Revisiting Traditional, New and Community Media Practices in South Africa.* Claremont: JUTA, pp. 155–178.

Mhlanga, B. (2010b) 'The Politics of Ethnic Minority Radio in South Africa', unpublished Ph.D. thesis, Communications and Media Research Institute, University of Westminster, UK.

Mhlanga, B. (2012) 'Sociologies of Voice and Language – Radio Broadcasting and the Ethnic Imperative'. *Journal of African Media Studies, 4 (2): pp. 209–226.*

Moyo, D. and Hlongwane, S. (2009) 'Regulatory Independence and the Public Interest: The Case of South Africa's ICASA'. *Journal of African Media Studies, 1(2): pp. 279–294.*

Moyo, L. (2012) 'Participation, Citizenship, and Pirate Radio as Empowerment: The Case of Radio Dialogue in Zimbabwe'. *International Journal of Communication 6: pp. 484–500.*

National Community Radio Forum (NCRF) (1999) *The Future of Community Radio: 'the vision'.* Unpublished, Johannesburg: NCRF.

Olorunnisola, A. (1995) Community Radio as Participatory Communication in Post-Apartheid South Africa. Found in: http://www.personal.psu.edu/faculty/a/x/axo8/Joburg/manuscript.htm (accessed 30 August 2012).

Popple, K. (1995) *Analysing Community Work.* Buckingham: Open University Press.

Reason, P. and Bradbury, H. (Eds) (2001) *Handbook of Action Research: Participative Inquiry and Practice.* London: Sage Publications.

Riggins, S. H. (1992) 'The Media Imperative: Ethnic Minority Survival in the Age of Mass Communication'. In S. H. Riggins, (Ed.) *Ethnic Minority Media: An International Perspective.* London: Sage.

Skogerbo, E. (1996) 'Privatising the Public Interest, Conflicts and Compromises in Norwegian Media Politics (1980–1993)'. Unpublished PhD Thesis, Department of Media and Communication, University of Oslo.

Taylor, L. and Willis, A. (1999) *Media Studies: Texts, Institutions and Media Audiences.* Oxford: Blackwell Publishers.

Teer-Tomaselli, R. (2001) 'Who is a Community in a Community Radio: A Case Study of Community Radio Stations in Durban, KwaZulu-Natal'. In K. Tomaselli and H. Dunn, (Eds). *Media, Democracy and Renewal in Southern Africa.* Colorado Springs: International Academic Publishers Ltd.

Tehranian, M. (1990) *Technologies of Power: Information Machines and Democratic prospects.* Norwood, NJ: Ablex.

UNESCO (1997) *World Communication Report: The Challenge Posed by Globalisation and the 'New Technologies'.* Paris: UNESCO.

Voster, L. (1994) '*Towery by die !Xû van Schmidtsdrift: 'n Verklaring'.* South African Journal of Ethnology, 17(3): pp. 69–82.*

White, R. (1990) 'Community Radio as an Alternative to Traditional Broadcasting'. *Media Development, 4(6): pp. 04–1.*

White, S. A. (1994) *Participatory Communication: Working for Change and Development.* London: Sage

Yin, R. K. (2003) *Case Study Research, Design and Methods: Applied Social Research Method Series, Volume 5, 3rd Edition.* London: Sage.

5

"Englishisation" of the World Wide Web: Implications for Indigenous Languages in Nigeria

Chimaobi Dick Onwukwe and Uzoma Chukwuemeka Okugo

Introduction/conceptual framework

The internet and indeed the World Wide Web are fast becoming the media with the highest penetration in Nigeria. They are essentially information technology (IT) resources. Urua (2006) states that the internet is a flexible, computer-based, global information system with many interconnected computer networks, enabling thousands of computers to share information. With the internet, it is now possible for people, businesses and governments throughout the world to communicate quickly and inexpensively. It has a wide range of uses including research, teaching, taxation (in form of filling in tax returns online) and shopping.

Urua (2006) further holds that the web consists of programs running on many computers and permits a user to find and display multimedia documents, i.e. documents with a combination of text, photographs, graphics, audio and video.

Globalisation no doubt is producing new ways of using and thinking about language. Linguists are expected to be concerned with not only the role played in globalisation processes of language, but also the effects of the globalisation process on language. The growing awareness of the challenges that globalisation poses to language has caused scholars to ask many questions from a sociolinguistic point of view. One such question is whether globalisation now means "Englishisation", considering the overwhelming influences of the English language and indeed culture in all spheres of life. The word "Englishisation" is a coinage used here to suggest the process, weight and overbearing influence of the English language and its usage to the detriment or at the expense of other European, African and indeed other languages of the world on the web/internet.

113

Nigeria has well over 400 languages (Emenanjo 1990) which are used across the nation. Some of the languages are well developed in terms of orthography and sound systems. Some are also standardised. Notable among these are the three acclaimed major languages – Hausa, Igbo and Yoruba among others. A language develops over time and through a conscious attempt to encourage its usage at different frontiers of communication. Its usage should span the language of primary socialisation, instruction and even media participation. Urua (2006) observes:

> Languages spoken in Nigeria can be classified into two different groups according to different criteria. Endoglossic and exoglossic. The endoglossic languages are those considered indigenous to Nigeria and they include over 500 languages listed in Grimes (2000). The exoglossic are those that have been introduced from other countries into Nigeria over years (Arabic, English, and French).

Hence, it could be said that Nigerian indigenous languages are still grappling with the rigours of development. One of the veritable ways of encouraging the growth or development of the languages is through expanding frontiers of usage to the most popular and most highly penetrated information technology resources like the internet and World Wide Web.

Statement of the problem

A language develops when, among other things, it is standardised. The standardisation guarantees the usage across formal settings and considerations for a place in language planning. Regrettably, a large percentage of indigenous languages in Nigeria have not been codified in any sense – they have no orthographies, dictionaries or grammars and are therefore not standardised or codified in any way. Hudson (1980) and other sociolinguists agree that for a language to be considered developed, it should be standardised with an orthography, literary works and reference materials. It should be used as language of instruction and of the media. The three major languages in Nigeria – Hausa, Igbo and Yoruba – are said to be standardised. Does that not guarantee them a place as languages of the web or internet? In addition, for the majority of developing languages in Nigeria; could the web and internet not encourage their development? These proposals are all with a view to expanding the frontiers of usage of the indigenous languages in Nigeria.

Wilson (2010) holds that Nigeria enjoys the highest penetration of the mobile and internet market across Africa and this is encouraged by her large population of young people. Considering the much-complained-about nonchalant attitude of the majority of Nigerian youths to their languages, could the web or internet not serve as a means of encouraging the younger generation to embrace the languages giving their flare (giving their high penetration of) for the net or web?

Again, considering, Hudson's (1980) observation that a language/languages are considered developed if it/they are standardised with an orthography, literary works, reference materials, used as <u>language of instruction and of the media</u> etc (underlining is mine), could the so-called standardised and non-standardised indigenous languages in Nigeria serve as languages of the media, in this case of the internet and the web, at least to their immediate speakers?

What possible drawbacks could the indigenous languages in Nigeria encounter should they be used as language(s) of the internet and World Wide Web? This chapter discusses the problems involved.

Study objectives

1. To examine the expansion of the frontiers of usage of indigenous languages in Nigeria through the internet or web.
2. To account for the internet or web encouraging younger generations to embrace and appreciate the indigenous languages in Nigeria.
3. To account for the internet or web avoiding the overbearing influence of foreign languages, especially English, on indigenous languages in Nigeria.
4. To examine possible setbacks in the appreciation and improvement of usage and development of indigenous languages in Nigeria using the web or internet.

Methodology

A qualitative research methodology was adopted with oral interviews conducted on 50 academic staff of Abia State University, Uturu, Nigeria. On-line data bases, textbooks, journals and library research works were also adopted as instrumentation and they guided the analysis. The academic staff are believed to have the requisite knowledge on the subject matter and hence are most relevant in eliciting data for the study.

Discussion of findings

Analysis here reveals that 45 (90%) of the respondents agreed that the internet and the World Wide Web could expand the frontiers of usage of indigenous languages in Nigeria. Again, 90% of the respondents agreed that the "Englishisation" of the internet or web, especially within the Nigerian circle, does not encourage the maximum utilisation of the internet or web in promoting Nigerian languages. On the overbearing influence of foreign languages, especially English, on Nigerian youth, 95% of the respondents agreed that the internet could encourage young people's appreciation of the indigenous languages.

Based on these findings, it is pertinent to state that the internet and World Wide Web are veritable tools for the expansion of frontiers of usage of developing languages. According to Emenajo (2004), the majority of the indigenous languages in Nigeria are classified as developing. The three major languages, however, could be said to be developed languages because they are standardised in terms of orthography, dictionaries, grammar, etc.

Udoh(Urua) (2006) contends that apart from Dr Uwe Seibert's website on Nigerian languages, there has been no conscious attempt at using any or some of the indigenous languages in Nigeria in major internet sites or on the World Wide Web. He further opines that such attempts, if any, are still evolving and scarce. For instance, major national dailies like the *Daily Sun*, *Daily Thrust*, the *Vanguard* and the *Guardian*, *Tell*, etc. have not deemed it wise to have an indigenous language version of their websites at least to serve the needs of their immediate audiences, which form the greater part of their reading audience.

Again, no federal or state parastatal, ministry or agency has indigenous language versions of their websites, when in fact these websites are primarily meant for people who use these languages. This invariably results in a total alienation of most of the people for whom the websites exist. It remains a fact that these parastatals, agencies and ministries, as well as the print/electronic media, have their websites in the English language, which of course is the official language of Nigeria. However, the conjecture here is that introducing some of the indigenous languages to their websites is an expansion of the frontiers of usage of these languages and serves to encourage their development.

Wilson (2010) observes that the level of internet usage is gradually increasing, especially among the younger generation. The level of addiction to the internet, particularly among Nigerian youth, makes the internet a veritable tool for encouraging these young people to embrace and appreciate their indigenous languages. It is generally believed that the younger generation has an unhealthy apathy towards the indigenous languages of Nigeria. This apathy is partly because there has been no conscious attempt by society to encourage the appreciation of Nigerian languages.

In the same vein, the unhealthy apathy of the younger generation in Nigeria towards their language(s) encourages the ever-increasing, overbearing influence of foreign languages, especially English on Nigerian youth. Nwulue (2009) opines that the majority of Nigerian youth see Westernisation as civilisation. There is a strong pattern of change in terms of dress, attire, social behaviour, social concepts and beliefs leaning towards Western culture. The media, however, have not helped matters in this regard, considering their pivotal roles in educating, informing and entertaining the people. It has been argued that media content and presentation, rather than promoting indigenous languages and, by extension, cultures, take a Western slant which encourages media acculturation. Onwukwe (2010) observes that the internet and indeed the World Wide Web are among the media yet to be utilised for the promotion and development of indigenous languages in Nigeria. The following observations give credence to the above analysis.

Fishman (1991) observes that lack of frequent use of indigenous languages in the domestic and formal settings has been identified as one area that militates against the development of these languages. The situation can be reversed if the members of a speech community are sensitised to the importance of their language. In relation to this, government programmes can be translated into the local languages to make them have more impact on the community. This comes into the area of cyber information dissemination.

Urua (2006:6) observes that India has a project that uses IT resources to facilitate the use and development of its languages. The SIMPUTER project provides information in local languages to local communities at a rate affordable to their members. The SIMPUTER is a low cost portable alternative to PCs, by which the benefits of IT can reach the common man. An interesting aspect of this project is that it is within what Crystal (2000:142) calls giving a "public profile" to language or making the language more visible. This project has beefed up the level of usage of indigenous languages in India and indeed their appreciation. In addition, in Kenya, rural farmers and artisans are informed of new price tags for goods and fertilisers, as well as receiving other agriculture-based information through the SMS in their indigenous language (www.bulletinafrica.com). Nigeria could borrow a leaf out of the book of these nations.

Again, as a measure to reinforce its "information for all" initiative, UNESCO makes a number of recommendations, which include the need to put in place the necessary machinery to alleviate language barriers regarding access to cultural and scientific information and to ensure the creation of national and multilingual websites (underlining is mine). UNESCO further recommends the maintenance and promotion of an internal collaboration on-line observatory on the different existing policies and regulations relating to multilingualism and multilingual resources and applications (UNESCO 2000).

The above recommendations of UNESCO underscore the place of the web and/or internet in the appreciation, development and general usage of a language/languages or even indigenous language(s). Similarly, some studies have shown that there is a strong correlation between the use of languages on the web and how such languages can be used as languages of instruction at all levels of education (Braid 1998). Hence, the web and internet could serve as a veritable tool of expanding the frontiers of usage of Nigerian indigenous languages, provide a substitute to the English-dominated web or internet and, by extension, lead to the appreciation of the indigenous languages at least by the immediate speakers. These are ways of developing the languages. However, the problem of the development of Nigerian languages will have to be given more attention if the languages are to be used for information dissemination and communication through the web.

Possible setbacks to the use of indigenous languages in Nigeria for information communication on the web/internet

Looking closely at the recommendations of UNESCO as a measure to reinforce its information-for-all initiative, notable among which is ensuring the "creation of national and multilingual websites" (UNESCO, 2000), the challenges ahead are enormous. Linguists are among the primary human resources required for dealing with these challenges, especially in the area of providing specialised skills for transforming linguistic data for the web. Hence, from the human perspective, the intellectual skills for transforming linguistic data for the web are seemingly absent.

Again, Tadadjeu and Chiatoh (2002) have raised the issue of technological requirements. Most of the web and internet/computer hardware and software are configured to process data in English. This, obviously, is a major impediment and it will be necessary to create the software and hardware to process data on an optional basis, depending on the language selected by the user.

Funding remains another challenge to the use of indigenous languages in Nigeria for information and communication on the web/internet. Extra money is needed to establish local/indigenous language versions of a website/page. Even China's SIMPUTER and Kenya's SMS project are capital-intensive. Nigeria would need to invest massively in this area. It is obvious that such financial investment appears to be an albatross in Nigeria.

Conclusion and recommendations

It has been identified that the predominant use of the English language for information and communication on the web within Nigeria has some negative implications in the move towards the development of over 400 languages in Nigeria (Emenanjo and Bleambo 1999). Urua (2006) identified that the web and indeed the internet are veritable avenues for the improvement of indigenous languages in Nigeria. Hence, the predominant use of English does not allow for maximum utilisation of the web for the development of Nigerian languages. The chapter concludes that the web can expand the frontiers of the usage of Nigerian languages and encourage the large numbers of young Nigerians who are nonchalant towards their languages to appreciate them. However, the paper further observes that in line with UNESCO recommendations, notable among which is "ensuring the creation of national and multilingual websites", the indigenous languages in Nigeria can receive a boost when there is a concerted effort towards implementing the recommendations.

The chapter therefore recommends that considering the great deal of responsibility on linguists for achieving this project, Nigeria's linguists should strive to provide specialised skills for transforming linguistic data for the web as it concerns Nigerian languages so as to blend them with hardware and software configurations.

Again, the Nigerian government needs to enact a policy that will accommodate indigenous languages in Nigeria for information and communication on the web. Nigeria could borrow India's SIMPUTER idea. Government parastatals, ministries, agencies etc. should establish a computer-based or internet-based way of reaching citizens in their indigenous languages. Very importantly, the UNESCO recommendations in line with its "information for all" initiative should be implemented in Nigeria.

References

Braid, F. R. (1998). Digitization of languages. In *The Scout Report for Social Sciences.* 2(1) pp. 31–45.

Crystal, D. (2000) *English as a Global Language.* Cambridge: Cambridge university press.

Emenanjo, E. N. (Ed.) (1990) *Multilingualism, Minority Languages and Language Policy in Nigeria.* Agbor: Central Books.

Emenanjo, E.N. (2004). Nigerian Languages and the Challenge of Globalisation. A paper presented at the 12th conference on Igbo language and culture. November, 30th.

Emenanjo, E. N and Bleambo, P. K. (Eds) (1999) *Language Endangerment and Language Empowerment in Nigeria.* Aba: National Institute of Nigeria Languages.

Fishman, J. (1991) *Reversing Language Shift.* Clevedon: Multilingual Matters.

Grimes, B. (2000) Ethnologue. Vol 1. *Languages of the World.* 14th edition. Dallas: Texas Sil.

Hudson, R. (1980) *Sociolinguistics.* Cambridge: Cambridge University Press.

"Information and communication technologies" in OZO-Mekuri, N. (Ed.) *In the Linguistic Paradise, a Festschrift for E. Nolue Emenanyo.* Aba: National Institute for National Languages.

Nwulue, B. (2009) "The impact of violent home movies on the behavior of Youths in Abia State". M.A. thesis, Department of Mass Communication, Abia State University, Uturu, Nigeria.

Okwudishu, A. U. (2006) "Globalization, multilingualism and the New "Information and communication technologies" in OZO-Mekuri, N. (Ed.) *In the Linguistic Paradise, a Festschrift for E. Nolue Emenanyo.* Aba: National Institute for National Languages.

Onwukwe, D. C. (2010) "The influence of televised Western movies on tattooing and sagging among tertiary students in Abia State". M.A thesis, Department of Mass Communication, Abia State University, Uturu, Nigeria.

Tadadjeu, M. and Chiatoh, B. (2002) "The challenge of satellite communication in African languages". *African Journal of Applied Linguistics* 3(15). pp. 45–60.

UNESCO (2000). *Report on world languages' development.* Vol 2, No.2.

Urua, E. A. (2006) "Exploiting Information Technology Resources in the Development of Nigerian Languages", in OZO-Mekuri, N. (Ed.) *Languages and Culture in Nigeria: A Festschrift for Okon Essein.* Aba: National institute of Nigerian Languages. pp. 1–10.

Wilson, J. (2010) "ICTs and development in Kenya", in Wilson, D. (Ed.) *Perspectives in Communication and Culture.* Uyo: BSM Resources. pp. 31–49.

6
Indigenous Language Broadcasting in Ghana: Retrospect and Prospect

Ufuoma Akpojivi and Modestus Fosu

Introduction

This chapter discusses indigenous radio broadcasting in Ghana with the focus on the role played by indigenous languages in empowering various social groups in the society within the democratic arrangement of the country. This contribution is an attempt to awaken research interest in various aspects of indigenous broadcasting in Ghana and other emerging democracies with similar socio-political and media developments. A literature search shows few studies that have examined the role or place of indigenous languages in the media and political democratisation process in emerging democracies like Ghana or Africa as a whole. While most studies are either focused on the positive developments that have characterised emerging democracies following the embrace of deregulation, the few available studies on the use of local language in the media are mainly from East European and Asian perspectives (Blankson, 2005). The deregulation of the broadcasting sphere in Ghana during the late 1990s and the various policies that were formulated later to make broadcasting beneficial not only to media organisations but also to the various sections of society make an evaluation of some aspects of the enterprise worthwhile.

The deregulation of the broadcast industry in Ghana has led to a shift from government controlled broadcasting to the inclusion of private participation in a now pluralist media industry. The early stages of deregulation in the early 2000 saw most media houses using English language as the primary mode for communication, with the majority of broadcast content in the English language. The domination of English in the media at that time was made nearly complete by the fact that there were practically no local dialect newspapers; almost all newspapers were published in English. Therefore, the uneducated or people who did not understand English were alienated from the English-oriented media sphere and political debates. The situation becomes dire as one moves from the urban centres towards the rural areas. Statistics from the UNESCO 2007 report shows that the majority of Ghanaians reside in rural areas and have a literacy rate of 49%. In addition, Kafewo (2006, p. 5) noted that most Ghanaians are not fluent in the English language and feel more comfortable using their local dialects in communication. Consequently, Blankson (2005) argued that the 'overwhelming dependence' of the media on the use of the English language reflects the insensitivity of the media to the majority of the people who are prevented from participating in media debates.

Such practice raises fundamental questions about the rights of citizens to access information from the media and to communicate or participate in media debates. These questions embody the global debate on the need for universal access to the media in order to bridge the information gap between the 'information rich' and 'information poor' (Cave and Prosperetti, 2001), a gap created by cultural, socio-political and economic factors. Using the radio in Ghana as a case study, this chapter will examine the relationship between the use of indigenous language in radio broadcasting and citizens' participation in the democratisation process of emerging democracies like Ghana. Firstly, drawing from the policy perspective, the chapter examines the extent to which media policies –Guidelines for Local Language Broadcasting of 2009 –have impacted on the broadcasting industry and the degree to which they have empowered the once neglected peasants to participate in both the media and political spheres. Secondly, the challenges confronting radio stations with regard to the use of local language in broadcasting will be examined. Finally, this chapter makes recommendations that will show policymakers and broadcasters how indigenous languages can effectively be utilised in the broadcasting industry and the implications this has for the media's growth and development, and democratic sustenance.

By way of structure, this Chapter begins with definitional issues pertaining to indigenous broadcasting and continues with a discussion on some matters relating to the linguistics of Ghana. This should provide the background needed to help contextualise subsequent discussions in an illuminating manner. There follows a discussion on the need for local language broadcasting in Ghana, after which various policy interventions in indigenous broadcasting receive attention. Towards the end of the chapter the challenges and prospects of indigenous language broadcasting are discussed, concluding with some recommendations for improving indigenous broadcasting in Ghana.

Ghana: a brief geo-political profile

Ghana, previously Gold Coast, is a West African country with Togo, Burkina Faso and Côte d'Ivoire bordering it on the east, north and west, respectively. The country has the Gulf of Guinea providing a coast line along its southern border, with a current population of 24,658,823.[1] The people of Ghana are scattered across ten administrative regions, with slightly more than half (55%) constituting the rural population. The literacy level stands at 51%, and this refers to people aged five years and above who are literate in English or a local language (Ghana Statistical Service (GSS), 2008).

Without going into the myths and other accounts of how the various people of Ghana came to settle in their present location, this synopsis traces the history from the 19thcentury. This reference point should serve the purpose of the study since by the beginning of the 19th century, the various groups of people forming present-day Ghana had settled in their current locations (Adu Boahen, 1975). Scholars such as Adu Boahen (1975) and Anokwa (1997) generally agree that the pre-Gold Coast settlers were made up of two language subfamilies: the Gur and the Kwa, who were settled in the northern and southern parts of the Volta River, respectively. Adu Boahen (1975) notes that these two major linguistic subfamilies, who reflected the dominant ethnic groups in the area, were further subdivided. For example, the Kwa 'mother' language, which happens to be the source of the majority of languages in West Africa, had three subcategories: the Akan, the Ga-Adangbe and the Ewe, each with further sub-ethnic and -dialect units. And the Gur to the north also had three major linguistic subgroups: the Gurma, Grusi and Mole Dagbani. These settlements and linguistic patterns have remained up to contemporary times, details of which will be discussed shortly, especially how they relate to mass media in the country.

Ghana's socio-political history is strongly linked with the country's contact with Western Europe, which dates back to the 15thcentury when Portuguese traders landed in Elmina in 1471 (Anokwa, 1997). This arrival opened the shores of the area to other Dutch, English, Swedish and Danish traders (in gold and slaves) and eventually led to the colonisation of the area by the British. After subjugating the indigenous people, the British took control over the area (i.e. modern Ghana minus the trans-Volta Togoland) and called it Gold Coast. The capital of the Gold Coast colonial administration, headed by a governor, was initially established in Cape Coast but was later transferred to Accra. Using the local government system involving town councils and native administration under the largely 'indirect rule' approach, the colonial government took steps to lay the foundations of a modern nation through the construction of 'infrastructure and physical systems' in the colony (Anokwa, 1997). This background informs the social and political situation of Ghana today.

Ghana became a sovereign state from 1957 when it gained independence from British colonial rule. This happened through persistent political agitations by the local people, led by a number of Western-educated Ghanaian elites and a series of political events. The most important of these was indigenous political activism, which began in earnest from the mid-1940s, leading to the formation of the first indigenous political party in 1947, the United Gold Coast Convention (UGCC). Another party emerged when one of the executives of the UGCC, Kwame Nkrumah, broke away and formed his own political party, the Convention People's Party (CPP). This party eventually led the Gold Coast into independence on 6 March 1957. The newly independent state assumed the name Ghana with Nkrumah as the Head of State. In 1960, Ghana became a republic under the First Republican Constitution, with Nkrumah as the Executive President.

The political situation of Ghana from independence may be divided into two periods: the first, from independence to 1992, is characterised by political instability; the second, from 1993 to current times, is politically stable. The period of political instability began with the overthrow of Nkrumah's government in 1966 through a coup d'état. After Nkrumah's removal from office, the country saw two democratically elected and five military governments. The democratic governments were led by Kofi Abrefa Busia (1969–1972) and Hilla Limann (1979–1981). None of these governments finished their first term of four years before they were also removed by military coups, which abolished the Constitution and replaced it with their own laws and decrees. These regimes were headed by Joseph Ankrah and Akwasi Afrifa (1966–1969), Kutu Acheampong (1972–1978), Fred Akuffo (1978–1979) and Jerry Rawlings (1979; 1981–1992). The re-democratisation period from 1993 to current times has seen a progressively liberal social and political environment (Gyimah-Boadi, 2009) in which Ghana has had alternating governments of two political parties. During the 23 years from 1993 to 2013, the National Democratic Congress (NDC) has held power for the majority of the time – that is, 13 years (1993–2000 and 2009–date) – while the NPP has held power for eight years (2001–2008). The various political regimes of the country since independence are presented in Table 6.1.

Table 6.1 The political regimes of Ghana from independence to date

Period	Regime	Leader(s)	Type of regime
2012 to date	National Democratic Congress (NDC)	John Dramani Mahama	Democratic/ Civilian
2009–2012	National Democratic Congress (NDC)	John Evans Attah Mills	Democratic/ Civilian
2005–2008	New Patriotic Party (NPP)	John Kufuor	Democratic/ Civilian
2001–2004	New Patriotic Party (NPP)	John Kufuor	Democratic/ Civilian
1997–2000	National Democratic Congress (NDC)	Flt. Lt. Jerry John Rawlings	Democratic/ Civilian
1993–1996	National Democratic Congress (NDC)	Flt. Lt. Jerry John Rawlings	Democratic/ Civilian
1981–1992	Provisional National Defence Council (PNDC)	Flt. Lt. Jerry John Rawlings	Military/ Authoritarian
1979–1981	People National Party (PNP)	Dr. Hilla Limann	Democratic/ Civilian
June 1979–September 1979	Armed Forces Revolutionary Council (AFRC)	Flt. Lt. Jerry John Rawlings	Military/ Authoritarian
1978–1978	Supreme Military Council II (SMCII)	Gen. Fred Akuffo	Military/ Authoritarian
1972–1978	National Redemption Council (NRC) Supreme Military Council I (SMCI)	Gen. Kutu Acheampong	Military/ Authoritarian
1969–1972	Progress Party (PP)	Dr. Kofi Busia	Democratic/ Civilian
1966–1969	National Liberation Council (NLC)	Gen. Joseph Ankrah Gen. Akwasi Afrifa	Military/ Police Autocratic
1957–1966	Convention People's Party (CPP)	Dr Kwame Nkrumah	Democratic/ Civilian

The political history of Ghana, as presented above, has little direct bearing on indigenous language broadcasting; instead, it has had a great influence on the development of the country's mass media and their practices as a whole. The various political governments came with varied legal and liberal environments, resulting in a chequered experience for the media. As shown in Table 6.1, Ghana had just brief spells of civilian rule before 1993. While the civilian regimes provided the media relative freedom, for many years authoritarian governments controlled the state media and oppressed the private ones through licensing laws, harassment of journalists, arbitrary imprisonment, banning of media organisations, etc. for expressing views that ran counter to the political order of the day (Gadzekpo, 1997; Karikari, 1998). With this state of affairs, media development was much hampered until the mid-1990s. As we will discuss later, the new democratic dispensation that began in 1993 paved the way for media independence and pluralism, resulting in the establishment of private newspaper, radio and television outlets. The first private radio station, *Joy FM*, was established in the late 1990s and subsequently there has been a flurry of radio and television units in the country. It is within this context that we discuss the impact of indigenous radio and our focus is on how local language in the media is enhancing democratic inclusiveness.

Linguistic diversity and language attitudes in Ghana

Ghana is a multi-ethnic and linguistically diverse country with over 50 ethnic groups and dialects originating from the Gur and Kwa subfamilies of languages of the northern and southern parts of the country, respectively. *Linguistic diversity* refers to 'the use or existence of multiple languages or linguistic forms' in a society (Ansah, 2008, p. 2). While the country's linguistic diversity is not in doubt, there seems to be no consensus on the exact number of languages spoken in the country as scholars have given figures ranging from 50 to 90 (see Anokwa, 1997; Ansah, 2008; Blankson, 2005; Guerini, n.d.). In addition to these scholars, some interviewees in this study alleged that there are over 50 local dialects and that the most widely spoken of these are Akan and Ewe. The difficulty in determining the exact number of languages stems from the splintered, and therefore complex, ethnic profile of the country. For instance, it has been linguistically problematic classifying communities, such as Nzema and Akan, with different or mutually unintelligible languages but belonging to the same cultures. The issue is that the people of Nzema are part of the Akan ethnic block, but they speak the Nzema language, which is different to the Akan language (Obeng, 1997). Hence, some researchers classify the Nzema language as Akan while others do not. Confronted with this scenario, it is fair to put the number of languages at over 50 in a country of 24,791,073 people (latest census figures, see Ghana Demographics Profile, 2011).

Nine of the indigenous languages enjoy government sponsorship, which privileges them over the others. The sponsorship comes in various forms such as 'budget allocations for the development of these languages (teacher training, curriculum development and publications' (Ansah, 2008, p. 2). These privileged languages include Akan, Dagaare, Dagbane, Ewe, Dangbe, Ga, Kasem, Gonja and Nzema. Some of these languages, such as Akan, Ewe and Dagbani, are studied in higher education and have sometimes been used as the medium of instruction in formal education at the lower primary levels. Additionally, these languages feature in public communication, particularly on radio and television, where they are used to broadcast news and give announcements (alongside English). There is no sustaining government policy to justify the selective development of some languages in the country apart from the notion that these languages have the majority of speakers.

Ghana is hence a typical multilingual society with varied speaker composition. Many Ghanaians can speak at least two indigenous languages: their native language and one or more other language(s). Five of the languages (synonymous with the ethnic groups) with the most speakers in Ghana are Akan, Mole-Dagbani, Ewe, Ga-Adangbe and Guan. Each of these languages has many other sublanguages spoken by distinct communities with their own traditional governance structure. Native speakers of Akan constitute almost half the nation's population at 49.1% (Ansah, 2008; Guerini, n.d.), leaving the remaining half to account for the many other languages spoken in the country. The other native speakers are composed of Mole-Dagbani 16.5%, Ewe, 12.7%, Ga-Adangbe 8% and Guan 4.4% (Ansah, 2008; Guerini, n.d).

Therefore, Akan is clearly the dominant indigenous language in Ghana in terms of both the number of speakers and the amount of written output (see Obeng, 1997). Additionally, 60% of Ghanaians speak this language as a second language (Obeng, 1997), meaning that the majority of Ghanaians speak it. In fact, Akan serves as the lingua franca[2] among the majority of Ghanaians across the country (see Guerini, n.d.). The dominance of Akan, as we will see later, is also reflected in its use in public communication and the media, particularly electronic media (both formal and popular). Certain other languages also enjoy some measure of privilege, providing them with more opportunities to develop, to the detriment of the many other languages that are neglected.

In spite of the immense influence of the sponsored languages, particularly Akan, Ghana has not been able to establish an indigenous language as a national or official language. This is not to say that the issue has not been raised for public debate. On the contrary, since independence the idea of having an indigenous language as a national and/or official language has come up for public discussion on a number of occasions. However, like Nigeria, the debate has always proceeded from perspectives charged with emotional attachment to ethnic and linguistic ties that threatened the cohesion and peace of the nation (see Eribo, 1997). English thus fits opportunely into the role (official and/or national language) as a compromise language, and the situation could remain so for a long time to come.

The advent of colonialism ensured that the English language took root and it is now a thriving language in Ghana. Functionally the official language, it has strategic educational and communication implications. It is a prestige norm used by educated Ghanaians[3] representing about 39% of the national population (see the GSS, 2008). Guerini (n.d., pp. 4–5) emphasises the significance of English in Ghana thus:

> Like most African countries, in Ghana the ability to speak English remains the prerogative of a minority of the population, although a certain degree of competence is an indispensable requisite for holding any public office (unlike the ability to speak a nationwide vehicular language, such as Akan) and for participating in many aspects of national life.

The above in part explains why language attitudes among Ghanaians largely favour English over the indigenous languages (Guerini, n.d.).

Language attitudes in Ghana

Ghanaians have high regard for language and its use, especially in the spoken medium. This underscores the fact that the majority of the people like to be told things in a language they understand, their language and 'good' language as well. From the traditional olden days until the present time, Ghanaian societies have accorded high social status to language, for example, the chief's linguists and traditional storytellers. Linguists (known as *Okyame* in Akan and some other languages) are people skilled in language use who speak on behalf of a chief or king in public, while the traditional storytellers told (and still do) stories that captured the culture and other information of their people as a form of entertainment. The respect for people with such linguistic skills stems from the society's consciousness of the place of language in the entire cultural production and reproduction in Ghanaian society. Hasty (2005) notes that Ghanaians have a high regard for oratory and equate brilliance or intelligence with impressive fluency in language. Hence, it is a fact that Ghanaians, whether educated or not, generally enjoy listening to speakers in a language they understand, especially on matters that concern them and their society. That radio continues to be the mass medium with by far the highest audience in the country (Kafewo, 2006) reinforces the important interplay among language, speaking and listening in public communication in Ghana. As we discuss later, this accounts for the proliferation and success of radio broadcasting from the mid-2000s. In recent times, particularly in the mornings, it is common to hear loud and interactive radio broadcasts on topical social and political issues in buses, bus stations, offices, shops and homes, almost all over the country.

While it is the case that language attitudes largely favour English because of its place in education, commerce, the courts, etc., as well as the opportunities it offers, the effective use of indigenous languages in Ghanaian societies also accords people high status and attracts audiences. For example, in Ghana, most of the radio and television panellists on indigenous language programmes are accorded social recognition because of their use of indigenous languages in the discussions. Therefore, the linguistic situation and language attitudes of Ghanaians have implications for indigenous language radio as an important component of public communication within the Ghanaian media.

The need for indigenous language in broadcasting

Human language is one of the most important characteristics that sets human beings apart from other creatures. This is in the sense that language represents the tool, content and structure of thought, such that knowledge is possible through language (Riley, 2007). Language has a definite purpose, the primary function being to enable people to communicate among themselves by expressing, defining and sharing their feelings, opinions, values, experiences, dislikes, etc. with one another. In this study, we argue that language is a crucial element that constitutes the culture of a society. This centrality of language is reflected in Schudson's definition of culture. According to him, 'the way of life of a society, brings individuals and families of varying circumstances and background together in a collectivity with which people may strongly identify, take primary meanings from, and find emotional satisfaction [in]' (1994, p.64). The above definition identified language as the common factor or bond that keeps individuals and family together in order to achieve common goals or objectives. In other words, language is a pertinent value of society as without language society will disintegrate (see Blankson, 2005).

Various experts have argued for indigenous languages to be used in public communication in the media. Benedict Anderson (2006) in his book 'Imagined Communities' argued that local languages play a significant role in the development of society that is characterised by large cultural systems. Schudson (1994) also posited that language is a vital element of communication, i.e. from interpersonal to mass communication; thus, broadcasting systems should reflect or use the indigenous language(s) of the society in which they find themselves (see also Ugboajah,1985). These scholars share the view that not using the indigenous languages will contribute to the concentration of vital information with a few people in society, thereby hindering the socio-economic, cultural and political development of that society. Bourgault (1995) argued that African society was built around the oral tradition of speech –communication in local languages –and this is a sacred and powerful means of communication. This oral tradition of speech 'is more trusted than written words' (de Sola Pool, 1963, p. 247) and this distinguishes African society from the Western world, where emphasis is placed on the written word. The above conceptualisation emphasises that people's interests are best served when they are addressed in their own language – a language they identify with as the bearer of their cultural destiny.

However, with the introduction of mass media in Africa by the colonial masters, the English language has been propped up as the dominant mode of communication, which antagonises the already established oral tradition of speech, i.e. the local dialects of the people. According to Des Wilson (1987, p.88) the oral tradition of speech 'remains what essentially sustains the information needs of the rural people who represent over 70% of the national populations of most Third World states'. And with the introduction of English as the means of communication, most people are prevented from understanding the message and are vulnerable to foreign cultures reflected in the media.

Therefore, Ugboajah (1985) posited that the media systems of nation states should be structured to reflect the culture and traditions of the people, as the cultural, political and economic factors of society impact on the structure of broadcasting (see McQuail, 1993). Ugboajah's argument is based on the need to protect local languages and address the marginalisation of the rural, illiterate populace who are left behind in the communication flow. To this end, countries have started formulating and implementing language and media policies that will help protect and integrate the society by bridging the information gap that exists within it. For instance, South Africa adopted the multilingual language policy in order to 'promote the status of the nine African languages by, among other things, using them as media of learning' (Kamwangamalu, 2002, p. 119). Similarly, Musau (2003) argued that there are various charters and declarations in Kenya that are geared towards protecting and promoting the use of Kiswahili and other mother tongues in the country.

The flourishing of the Ghanaian media, particularly the broadcast industry, by the late 2000s, called for some rethinking in the direction of policy and regulation. There was a realisation that it was necessary to guide the industry and make it more responsive to the needs and expectations of the majority of audiences nationwide. The key issue was the medium through which information from radio broadcasting reached audiences. However, it was not until 2009 that Ghana formulated and implemented the first policy, titled 'Guidelines for Local Language Broadcasting', which seeks to promote the use of local languages in the media through the help of the United Nations Development Programme (UNDP). Although there were other policies such as the National Media Policy (2000), and Ghana ICT for Accelerated Development (ICT4AD) Policy (2003), which charged the media 'to use local dialects in broadcasting and increase production in local content, so as to reach the marginalised public' (Akpojivi, 2012b, p. 151), it was the *Guidelines of Local Language Broadcasting* that actually served as a framework for indigenous language use in the media. However, scholars like Blankson (2005) and Musau (2003) argue that the presence of language and cultural policies with regard to broadcasting in society does not guarantee that the utmost objective(s) of the policies will be realised, as most policies are 'woefully inadequate' and their implementation problematic. Therefore, this chapter will examine the extent to which language and cultural policies in Ghana have been integrated into radio broadcasting and the degree to which this has empowered the public in participating in both the media and political spheres.

Indigenous language radio broadcasting in Ghana

The purpose of this section is not to give a comprehensive account of radio broadcasting in Ghana but to highlight the transition and practices that occurred from the colonial era when radio broadcasting started in Ghana until now. Broadcasting started in Ghana in 1935 when the then colonial governor, Arnold Hudson, established relay stations to distribute news items from London to Accra (Bourgault, 1995).

As time went by, more relay stations were opened in other towns, such as Kumasi, Korofidua and Sekondi, in order to serve the information needs of the public by giving them administrative information (ibid). However, Ansah (1985) argued that the introduction of broadcasting in Ghana by the colonial master (from the United Kingdom) was not to meet the information needs of the public but to provide a propaganda tool for educating the public about policies and events happening in the British Empire (cited in Alhassan, 2005, p. 212). This rationale for the introduction of radio in the country implies that radio is an effective tool for education, especially if the messages get to the people being targeted.

The first relay station, later known as *Radio Zoy*, was replicated across the country to broadcast programmes mainly produced by the British Broadcasting Corporation (BBC). After the Second World War, the British colonial government saw the need to introduce major structural and fundamental changes, which included the training of indigenes in broadcasting techniques and encouraging them to participate in broadcasting. For instance, by 1956 there were 'over 445 radio technicians and 163 radio managers' who were trained through the BBC (Tudesq, 1983, p. 23). Furthermore, *Radio Zoy* started broadcasting in indigenous languages such as Hause, Akan, Ewe, Ta and Dagbani (Jones-Quartey, 1960). According to Blankson, this shift from English to indigenous language broadcasting was due to the fact that the 'British administrators soon realised that radio broadcasting in Ghana must use vernacular languages if its programmes were to be understood by the native' (2005, p. 6). Ansah (1985) shared a similar view and argued that with the use of indigenous languages in broadcasting, the colonial government was able to reach more of the public with their messages, as by 1945 the subscribers of radio had increased to 5850 (cited in Alhassan, 2005, p. 212).

By 1953, *Radio Zoy* was renamed *Gold Coast Broadcasting Service* (GCBS), and after independence it was renamed Ghana Broadcasting Corporation (GBC) by Nkrumah, head of the CPP. The trend of indigenous language broadcasting continued and the early leaders of independent Ghana (e.g. Kwame Nkrumah) further encouraged the use of indigenous language in broadcasting. This, according to Ansah (1979), was to enable the government to reach out to the rural peasants and inform them about government policies. Some scholars have criticised this move as 'government propaganda to politically sensitize the rural people' (cited in Blankson, 2005, p. 7) rather than to empower them.

However, the deregulation of the broadcasting industry in 1995, following the adoption of a liberal constitution in 1992 that called for 'media freedom', witnessed the movement of radio broadcasting from indigenous languages back to English. According to Blankson (2005), such a move is attributed to the proliferation of private radio stations following deregulation, whose programmes were tailored to Western style. Indeed, the majority of the radio stations that were established during the early years of deregulation –for example, *Joy FM, Choice FM, Citi FM, Radio Gold, Uniiq FM* among others – broadcast predominantly in English. To this end, most radio programmes were entertainment (music), with the presenters speaking like radio present-ers in the United Kingdom, United States, etc. Hence, a former Deputy Minister of Communication described Ghana's radio as 'foreignisation' of radio broadcasting (Commander Griffith, 1999, cited in Blankson, 2005, p. 11).

Following public outcry and the implementation of the language and cultural policy in broadcasting, such as the National Media Policy and Guidelines for Local Language Broadcasting, there has been a sys-tematic move back to the use of indigenous languages in broadcasting. For instance, *Peace FM* and *Radio Gold* began to air their news in two native languages, Twi and Ewe, as well as in English; likewise, other radio stations such as *Adom FM, Nhyira, Kasapa FM* and *Asempa FM* started broadcasting their programmes in Akan language, also known as 'Twi-Fante'. Nevertheless, the success of such initiatives are debat-able; while some scholars argue that there has been significant progress in the use of local languages in broadcasting, other feel the use of local languages has been downplayed. The following section will examine this trend and argue that to a large extent the use of local languages in radio broadcasting has empowered the illiterate and peasant population in participating in the media and political sphere. As Bodomo et al. (2009, p. 12) have argued, the usage of Ghanaian indigenous languages has 'given opportunities to voices which were marginalised because of their inability to speak English to express their views[...]through the use of the indigenous languages in the mass media, large segments of the population who were otherwise excluded from the communication process can now participate in the democratic process', thus bridging the information gap that once existed in the society and helping the democratisation process.

Indigenous language in broadcasting: from the policy perspective

The Ghanaian media sphere is governed by many policies and Acts that serve as the framework for the operation of the mass media. However, for the purpose of this study the policies that are specifically related to local language broadcasting will be examined. These are the 1992 Constitution of the Republic of Ghana, National Media Policy (2000), the ICT4AD(2003) and the Guidelines for Local Language Broadcasting (2009). First, it is necessary to review the rationale behind each policy; this is germane to providing a framework for understanding the impact of the use of local languages in the media.

The 1992 constitution of the Republic of Ghana

Following the re-democratisation process from the early 1990s, the 1992 Constitution was formulated as part of the reform process. Heath (1999, p. 512) regarded the Constitution as the 'definitive voice of broadcasting policy' in Ghana because of its explicit provision with regard to the freedom of the media, which has consequently influenced the framing of other media policies in Ghana. Article 162 of the 1992 Constitution guarantees absolute freedom and independence to the mass media, devoid of interference and censorship. The purpose of this absolute freedom is to facilitate 'socio-political, economic and cultural development of the society in order to achieve the Millennium Development Goals (MDGs)' (Akpojivi, 2012b, p. 104). As a policymaker confirmed, the central objective of the Constitution is to guarantee the freedom of every citizen to participate in both the media environment and the political arena (Anonymous, Interview, Accra, 29 July 2010).

Other sections of the Constitutions lend support to the above provision. Article 34 of the Constitution vividly entails the directive principles of state policy, which charged the state to ensure the integration of the state, meaning that every Ghanaian should have access to public facilities and participate in public discourse. This provision is significant because the integration of society can only take place when the public are empowered. The use of indigenous languages in broadcasting is one of the major means by which this empowerment can occur since it grants radio access to the people who have been discriminated against and prohibited from taking part in civil, political and economic activities because of a language barrier.

National media policy (2000)

This is the first policy in the Ghana media environment that actually spells out the framework for the operation of the media after years of confusion about what is required of the mass media (see Buckley et al., 2005). The findings of the policy came out of other policy documents, such as the 1996 film policy seminar, and consultation with media practitioners and media experts (National Media Policy, 2000). Like the 1992 Constitution, the central objective of the National Media Policy is to 'promote and ensure a free, independent, dynamic and public spirited media that will provide access for all, and not only some of our people to participate freely, fully and creatively at the community, national and global level' (National Media Policy, 2000). To this end, the policy considered all media as a public trust whose objective is to reflect the interest of the general public irrespective of ownership structure (ibid). This policy position is relevant to the debate of local language usage in radio broadcasting because, if the people are to access the media and participate in the discourse at both community and national level, they should be able to understand the content of radio broadcast. According to the policy, the use of local languages in broadcasting is vital in order to include the people excluded from such participation because of their inability to understand English language (ibid). It is noteworthy that this idea of the use of local language in broadcasting was influenced by the need to improve accessibility to the mass media in order to achieve universal access to the media, which was also a central policy goal.

Ghana information communication technology for accelerated development (2003)

Although this policy is more related to improving the socio-economic and political development of the Ghanaian state using information communication technology (Buckley et al., 2005; see also Jebuni and Oduro, 1998), the policy goal of facilitating universal access to the media makes it relevant to this discussion. In relation to broadcasting, the policy states that there is a need to enhance universal access to the media due to the high illiteracy rate of about 40%, coupled with the fact that 51% of Ghanaians reside in the rural areas with limited or no basic amenities and communication infrastructure. Therefore, the policy calls for the establishment of three tiers of broadcasting, i.e. public broadcasting, commercial broadcasting and community broadcasting, as a way of increasing communication infrastructure. In addition, the policy charges the mass media, whether public, commercial or community, to use local dialects in broadcasting and to increase production in local content, in order to meet the information needs of the neglected 40% illiterate and 51% rural population. According to Coleman et al., the inclusion of these marginalised people in the communication process is pivotal to the consolidation of democracy (2011).[4]

Guidelines for local language broadcasting (2009)

This is the first media policy to set out the framework for the use of local language in broadcasting. This policy was formulated with the aid of the United Nations Development Programme (UNDP). The National Media Commission,[5] in a bid to encourage the use of indigenous language in broadcasting in order to preserve culture, formulated this policy to guide the broadcasters. Prior to the formulation of this policy, most broadcasters used the indigenous languages in broadcasting but were often criticised for over-exaggerating news stories during the translation process from English to the indigenous languages.

Therefore, this policy not only seeks to address such professional shortfalls but also to establish a framework by which the use of indigenous languages in broadcasting will be regulated. According to the policy, all broadcasts in indigenous languages should abide by the core values or principles of journalism, i.e. accuracy, objectivity, fairness and comprehensiveness, amongst others (Guidelines for Local Language Broadcasting, 2009, p. 1). To this end, the defining values for indigenous language broadcasting include 'the need to engender dialogue for equitable development, the provision of voice and empowerment to the people, and the need to affirm and strengthen cultural expression by leveraging indigenous knowledge through the application of core journalistic values and principles' (ibid, p. 11).

To realise the above objective, the policy makes some recommendations, and especially to media organisations. The policy tells all indigenous language broadcasters to ensure that their 'reporters, news readers and presenters speak and write the local language in which they broadcast with high proficiency' (ibid, p.7). This is to ensure that there are no linguistic problems with broadcasting or broadcast content. It is also to avoid, or drastically reduce, instances of news being misunderstood by the public. The policy further calls on all broadcasters to produce programmes that will educate the public and promote positive cultural values, especially those that are unique to Ghanaians (ibid).

Local language in radio broadcasting and citizens' participation

The above policies provide insights into the thinking of the policy formulators regarding indigenous broadcasting in the country. It could be argued that the primary objective of the policies is to facilitate universal access to the media through the use of indigenous languages, which is one of the veritable tools for speeding up development and encouraging citizens' participation. According to a Senior Media Executive and Board Member of Graphic Communications, Professor Kwame Karikari, 'the improvement in accessibility depends on the use of our mother tongues; the more we use them (mother tongues), the more we empower people to be able to communicate properly and effectively[...] if we don't encourage the use of our mother tongues in communication, the issue of the *right to communicate and participate in society will seriously be limited'* (Interview, Accra, 13 August 2010, emphasis added). The quote clearly underscores the importance of indigenous languages in the empowerment of the people through enhancing understanding and participation in societal activities. If people are to participate in debates and perform their civil duties, they should have information and understand such information. As Kuma Drah, Senior Editor of the state broadcaster GBC puts it, 'democracy flourishes when the people have access to information to be able to hold governments accountable and also know what their governments are doing. This can only happen when such information can easily be understood by the people in terms of them being proficient in the language used in passing the information across' (Interview, Accra, 3 August 2010).

Various writers share the above position. For instance, Ugboajah (1985, 1986) and Des Wilson (1987) argued that communication and information should be in the indigenous languages of the people and that structures and mechanisms should be built to encourage and facilitate media communication in the indigenous languages. According to Professor Kwame Karikari, the structures and mechanisms could only be built when societies 'demand from government laws and policies like a national language policy, a policy that will encourage the development, education and use of our mother tongues. And the re-organisation of the media, i.e. public service broadcasters and commercial broadcasters to accommodate all ethnic identities in terms of language, culture, content in their broadcast' (Interview, Accra, 13 August 2010). The above view indicates that some individuals in Ghanaian society also acknowledge the need for government and regulatory agencies in the media industry to provide direction for media consciousness and action that strive to reach the local people through their own language. Although, there is no national language policy in Ghana, the introduction of the various policies discussed early has given impetus to indigenous language broadcasting in Ghana.

Consequently, most radio stations (and also television) have started broadcasting some of their programmes – for example, news and talk shows– in the indigenous languages in order to reach out to the marginalised people. For example, programmes like Kokrokoo, Asemsebe, Mamafos Nkomo, Kanawu and Asenta are aired in the indigenous languages of Twi, Ga and Akan (see Prah, 2005). Similarly, most radio stations carry out newspaper reviews in the morning and this is often done using indigenous languages such as Akan, Twi and Ga. Although most of the private radio stations use the dominant languages of Akan and Ewe in their broadcasts (Kafewo, 2006), the state-owned radio stations broadcast in the seven major Ghanaian languages of Dagbani, Ewe, Nzem, Akan, Ga, Hausa and English. According to a regional coordinator at GBC, Peggy Ama Donkor, 'because of the public service status of GBC, it is mandatory that we broadcast some of our programmes in seven major languages in Ghana, i.e. Dagbani, Ewe, Nzem, Akan, Ga, Hausa and English, in order to reach out to the wider public and empower them politically, economically and culturally' (Interview, Accra, 7 September 2010). PuyeFranz (1998, p.3), while upholding this opinion, stated that Radio Ghana, which broadcast on two service networks(i.e. Radio One and Radio Two), 'broadcasts on average 250 hours per week in six Ghanaian languages and English', even though equal time was not allocated to all languages in broadcasting(more time was allocated to the dominant languages Akan and Ewe). See Table 6.2 below for a list of some radio stations[6] in Ghana and their medium of communication.

Observing the media sphere in contemporary times, we argue that the guidelines on indigenous broadcasting have motivated many radio stations in the use of indigenous languages in broadcasting as indicated in Table 6.1. *Peace FM*, a private commercial radio station, serves as a typical example of stations that have tailored most of their programmes to help the political, economic and cultural emancipation of the people using indigenous languages. Content analysis conducted on *Peace FM* programmes revealed that the total broadcasting time of all their programmes in a week aired in the Akan language is 166.1 hours, with 4.9% of the broadcast time devoted to news. Religious programmes like Peace Time (12.8%), Gospel Hour (9.3%) and Gospel Show (0.78%) have the most broadcasting time. Entertainment programmes like Working Time (6.02%), Ekwan so Brebre (10.9%) and Omo Tuo Special (2.4%) come second in broadcasting time. In addition, social programmes like Wo Haw ne Sen, Mpom te Sen and Asomdwoe each take up 1.2% of the broadcast time, and sport constitutes 6.83%.

Table 6.2 List of some radio stations that broadcast in indigenous languages in Ghana

Name of radio stations	Medium of communication	Location
Peace FM	Akan	Accra
Adom FM	Akan	Tema
Meridian FM	Akan	Tema
Happy FM	Akan	Accra
Top Radio	Akan	Accra
Hits FM	Akan	Accra
Great FM	Akan	Accra
Sena	Akan, Ga, Ewe	Tema
Hot FM	Akan	Accra
Asempa FM	Akan	Accra
Obonu FM	Ga	Accra
Fox FM	Akan	Kumasi
Hello FM	Akan	Kumasi
Radio Mercury	Akan	Kumasi
Capital FM	Akan	Kumasi
Nhyira	Akan	Kumasi
Max FM	Akan	Enchie
Oman FM	Akan	Accra
Volta Star Radio	Ewe	Aflao
Radio BAR	Akan	Sunyani
Eastern FM	Akan	Koforidua
Rock FM	Akan	Takoradi
Eagle FM	Akan	Cape Coast
Kasapa FM	Akan	London, UK
Ahomka	Akan, English	Elmina
Fontomfrom FM	Akan	Kumasi
Radio Savannah FM	Dagbane	Tamale
URA Radio FM	Dagaare	Wa
Radio Upper West FM	Gurenne	Bolgatanga

Source: Bodomo et al. (2009).

Also worth a special mention is the current affairs programme Kokrokoo (a morning show on *Peace FM*), which constitutes 3.1% of the broadcast time. The programme's popularity is due to the range of topical issues covered (politics, economics, culture and other burning national issues) and the fact that the hosts, panellists and audiences all contribute to the discussion. See Table 6.3 for the *Peace FM* programme schedule.

Table 6.3 *Peace FM programme schedule*

PEACE PROGRAMME SCHEDULE

TIME/DAY	MONDAY	TUESDAY	WEDNESDAY	THURSDAY	FRIDAY	WEEKENDS	SATURDAY	SUNDAY
4.00am – 6.00am	GOSPEL HOUR	GOSPEL HOUR	GOSPEL HOUR	GOSPEL HOUR	GOSPEL HOUR	4.00am – 6.00am	GOSPEL HOUR	GOSPEL HOUR
6.00am – 6.25am	AKAN NEWS	AKAN NEWS	AKAN NEWS	AKAN NEWS	AKAN NEWS	6.00am – 6.15am	AKAN NEWS	AKAN NEWS
6.30am – 10.00am	KOKROKOO	KOKROKOO	KOKROKOO	KOKROKOO	KOKROKOO	6.15am – 8.00am	KOKROKOO	GOSPEL HOUR
10.00am – 10.10am	WORKING TIME	WORKING TIME	WORKING TIME	WORKING TIME	WORKING TIME	8.00am – 9.00am	SATURDAY SPECIAL	OMO TUO SPECIAL
10.00am – 11.00am	WORKING TIME	WORKING TIME	WORKING TIME	WORKING TIME	WORKING TIME	9.00am – 10.00am	SPORTS	OMO TUO SPECIAL
11.00am – 11.05am	WORKING TIME	WORKING TIME	WORKING TIME	WORKING TIME	WORKING TIME	10.00am – 11.00am	SPORTS	OMO TUO SPECIAL
11.05am – 12.00noon	WORKING TIME	WORKING TIME	WORKING TIME	WORKING TIME	WORKING TIME	11.00am – 12.00pm	WEEKEND JIVE	OMO TUO SPECIAL
12.00noon – 12.25pm	AKAN NEWS	AKAN NEWS	AKAN NEWS	AKAN NEWS	AKAN NEWS	12.00pm – 12.15pm	AKAN NEWS	AKAN NEWS
12.30pm – 2.00pm	SPORTS	SPORTS	SPORTS	SPORTS	SPORTS	12.15pm – 3.00pm	ENTERTAINMENT REVIEW	SUNDAY RENDEZVOUS
2.00pm – 2.05pm	ASOMDWE NKOMO	AFTERNOON SPEICAL	WO HAW NE SEN	ENTERTAINMENT REVIEW	MPOM TE SEN	3.00pm – 3.30pm	ENTERTAINMENT REVIEW	SPORTS
2.00pm – 4.00pm	ASOMDWOE NKOMO	3.00 – 4.00 AFTERNOON SPEICAL	WO HAW NE SEN	3.00 – 4.00 ENTERTAINMENT REVIEW	MPOM TE SEN	3.30pm – 4.00pm	ENTERTAINMENT REVIEW	SPORTS
4.00pm						4.00pm – 4.05pm		
4.00pm – 4.05pm	EKWANSO BREBRE	EKWANSO BREBRE	EKWANSO BREBRE	EKWANSO BREBRE	EKWANSO BREBRE		ADADAM	SPORTS

4.05pm – 6.00pm	EKWAN SO BREBRE	EKWAN SO BREBRE	EKWAN SO BREBRE	EKWAN SO BREBRE	EKWANSO BREBRE
6.00pm – 6.20pm	AKAN NEWS	AKAN NEWS	AKAN NEWS	AKAN NEWS	AKAN NEWS
6.20pm – 7.00pm	EKWAN SO BREBRE	EKWAN SO BREBRE	EKWAN SO BREBRE	EKWAN SO BREBRE	EKWAN SO BREBRE
7.00pm – 8.00pm	EKWAN SO BREBRE	EKWAN SO BREBRE	EKWAN SO BREBRE	EKWAN SO BREBRE	EKWAN SO BREBRE
8.00pm – 8.10pm	AKAN NEWS	AKAN NEWS	AKAN NEWS	AKAN NEWS	AKAN NEWS
8.10pm – 9.00pm	THE PLATFORTM	ETUO MU YE SUM	THE PLATFOR	HOME AGAIN	OLD SKUUL
9.00pm – 10.00pm	ADADAM	ETUO MU YE SUM	MUSIC FILL UP	HOME AGAIN	OLD SKUUL
10.00pm – 12.00am	NIGHTLINE CRUIZE	PEACE LANE	PEACE LANE	WO BA ADA ANAA	PEACE LANE
12.00am – 4.00am	NIGHTLINE CRUIZE	PEACE LANE	PEACE LANE	PEACE LANE	PEACE LANE

Time	ADADAM	SPORTS
5.00pm – 6.00pm	ADADAM	SPORTS
6.00pm – 6.15pm	AKAN NEWS	AKAN NEWS
6.15pm – 7.00pm	P. PARTY MIX	EBE
7.00pm – 9.00pm	P. PARTY MIX	WOGYIDIE NE
9.00pm – 10.00pm	P. PARTY MIX	GOSPEL SHOW
10.00pm – 10.30pm	PEACE LANE	GOSPEL SHOW
10.30pm – 12.00am	PEACE LANE	PEACE LANE
12.00am – 4.00am	PEACE LANE	PEACE LANE

Source: Peace FM.

On the other hand, an analysis of the programmes of *Adom FM*, which also broadcasts in the Akan language, revealed that the station broadcast for 152.8 hours in a week, with programmes such as Adom Ahengua constituting 13.7% of the broadcast time. In addition, Dwaso Nsem/ Sport represents 11.9% and Adom Kaseibo 10.6%. Programmes such as Sponsored Gospel Show accounted for 9.8% of the broadcast time, Dwaso Nsem 6.5%, Work and Happiness 6.5%, Ofie Kwanso 6.5%, and Gospel Music 2.68% of the broadcast time. Programmes such as Announcements made up 1.4% of the broadcast time, Live Worship 6.7%, Adom Sport Nite 3.27%, Adom Sport 1.4%, Times with Bishop James 1.5% and Naasem University 1.3%. There are other programmes on various radio stations in which local languages are used as the broadcasting medium. For example, Drive Time and Wo Hau Ne S3n (a health talk show meaning 'What's your problem?') are aired at different times of the day.

Other radio stations also broadcast in indigenous languages. For example, according to Blankson, *Radio Gold* developed 'an Akan programme that discussed Akan culture and traditions[...]and later began to air their news in English and the two native languages of Twi and Ga' (2005, p. 12).

One significant aspect of the programme (such as kokrokoo, drive time amongst others) is the opportunity for the public to contribute to the discussion either through phone-ins, or through social media platforms like Facebook and Twitter. Such programmes have enabled the educated, uneducated and peasants in Ghanaian society to participate in media debates, thereby giving them a sense of belonging (Fosu and Akpojivi, 2013). As one news editor, Edward Nyarko, puts it, 'I think it is a good idea that stations are beginning to produce programmes in the local languages of the people[...]such interactive programmes in the local languages give the people the chance to speak on issues that are partaking to their lives and a platform to voice their concerns' (Interview, Accra, 30 July 2010). Similarly, a Senior Media Executive posited that 'stations that use local languages in their broadcast contribute significantly to the development of the society and people at large. Because first and foremost, their concern will be on the welfare of their host community or locality; this will endear the people to the station, thus [there will be] the improvement in the lives of the local residents and that of the station' (Anonymous, Interview, Accra, 13 August 2010).

Additionally, nearly all of the radio stations have taken advantage of the Guidelines for Local Language Broadcasting this policy to engage in comprehensive news analysis, and newspaper reviews in the indigenous language of the people (Akpojivi, 2012b). For example, most hosts of

Table 6.4 Programmes aired in indigenous languages and most likely to be listened to

Programmes	Language	Percentage
Newspapers Review	Twi	7
Asomdwe Nkomo	Twi	4
Mamafos Nkomo	Twi	3
Kokrokoo	Twi/English	10
Wohe te sen	Twi	7
News	Twi	4
Mma Nkomo	Twi	1
Political Issues	Gonja/Dagbani/Eng	1
Asenta	Ga	1
Education	Gonja/Dagbani/Eng	1
Agoro	Twi	1
Debates	Ga	1
Efie Kwanso	Twi	1

Source: Prah (2005).

these programmes read out some of the major stories or headlines from the newspapers in the indigenous languages before engaging their panellists on the programme. This therefore affords members of the public, who have limited opportunities to buy and read the newspapers, to have first-hand information on what is happening in the country as reported in the dailies. This, according to Kafewo, has changed the face of broadcasting in Ghana, as it has increased the audience reach and encouraged them to participate in debates primarily because of the use of indigenous languages in broadcasting (2006, p. 7). Prah (2005) in his study on the impact of indigenous language radio in Ghana, Mali and Senegal, was of the opinion that the majority of the public are most likely to listen to programmes aired in indigenous languages. See Table 6.4 for some of the programmes most likely to the listened to by the public.

Challenges and prospects

There have been challenges confronting the use of indigenous languages in radio broadcasting. The dominant challenge is the issue of majority and minority languages. As stated earlier, most of the radio broadcasts are in the two widely spoken languages, i.e. Akan and Ewe, with a few stations, such as the state-owned radio station, broadcasting in the seven languages of Akan, Ewe, Hausa, Nzem, Ga, Dagbani and English. Since Ghana is a multi-ethnic country with over 50 ethnic groups and languages, broadcasting in two or seven local languages raises the issue of majority and minority languages where those languages that are not used to broadcast news become the minority (Akpojivi, 2012a). This means the rights of the minority are being abused and this needs to be protected as documented in the UNESCO Universal Declaration on Cultural Diversity Policy 2001. It also means that only a few privileged languages are being developed with the support of the state and media institutions. As one journalist described it: 'We have over 50 dialects in the country, but most media broadcast in the dominate dialects. Do we assume that everybody speaks or understands these dominant dialects? Some groups of people have definitely been left out, and they will continue to be left out until something is done.' (Anonymous, Interview, 3 August 2010.) Similarly, another News Editor added: 'When you listen to most radio stations we have in Ghana, yes, you will realise that Akan language is becoming the dominant language used in broadcasting[...] one needs to be mindful of this, because some minority groups might think that they are being marginalised because Akan seems to be dominant in the society.' (Anonymous, Interview, Accra, 30 July 2010.)

This problem is further compounded by the inability of the various policies (already discussed) to identify and create different levels of indigenous broadcasting, i.e. national, regional and local. The National Telecommunication Policy (2005) and the National Media Policy (2000) only classified the media into public media, commercial media and community media (see Akpojivi, 2012b). To this end, the different types of media (public, commercial and community) tend to broadcast some of their programmes in indigenous languages, predominantly Akan and Ewe. However, it worth noting that community radio stations in Ghana broadcast in the indigenous languages of their host communities; nevertheless, there is no clear-cut dichotomy between community radio stations and commercial radio stations that broadcast in indigenous languages (Akpojivi, 2012a).

Going by the above, it is obvious that Ghanaian society, including its media, is still not meeting the challenge of promoting and protecting the rights of all minority groups in Ghana. The systematic use of only the dominant languages in broadcasting not only excludes some people from the communication and political processes but also poses a threat to the sustenance of democracy in Ghana since ethnicity plays a crucial role in the political configuration of the state.[7] Article 6 of the UNESCO Universal Declaration on Cultural Diversity Policy 2001, while calling for the protecting and promotion of minority rights, held that:

> While ensuring the free flow of ideas by word and image care should be exercised so that all cultures can express themselves and make

themselves known. Freedom of expression, media pluralism, multilingualism, equal access to art and to scientific and technological knowledge, including in digital form, and the possibility for all cultures to have access to the means of expression and dissemination are the guarantees of cultural diversity.

The continuation of broadcasting only in the dominant languages shows the shortfalls in realising the objectives of the media policies that target attaining universal access through the use of local languages in broadcasting.

It has to be said that the socio-cultural realities of Ghana make it practically impossible to attain the policy guidelines in their fine details. For example, radio stations cannot possibly broadcast or produce contents in all the different languages. It is in part to offset this difficulty that the guidelines have segregated the radio broadcast industry into public, commercial and community stations. The idea is that the community radio outlets produce programmes and content of and for their localities. However, although there are at least six radio stations in each of the ten regions of Ghana,[8] each region is still highly linguistically diverse and the media houses lack the financial resources and manpower to fulfil the requirements of the guidelines to the letter (Akpojivi, 2012b). As one policymaker described it, 'most owners of these private radio stations do not have the financial capabilities to produce programmes in the different dialects; in fact, none of the radio stations in Ghana can produce programmes in the different dialects because of the huge financial responsibilities involved with production and distribution' (Anonymous, Interview, 16 September 2010). Studies from scholars like Nyamnjoh (2005), Bourgault (1995) and Hasty (2005), amongst others, have discussed media production constraints in general from the African perspective. Thus, though using about seven languages appears to be reasonable, especially if those languages are understood by other speakers belonging to the minority language group, the lack of expansion into some of these minority languages beyond the seven leaves much to be desired in the context of our discussion.

Furthermore, the issue of accuracy of expressions and translation of news items in indigenous language broadcasting has posed another challenge. According to Fosu and Akpojivi (2013), there is a tendency during translation to embellish the indigenous language with 'entertaining techniques such as proverbs, witty coinages, anecdotes and allusions', which might lead to misrepresentation of words or context and affect the essence of the broadcast. This happens, although the *Guidelines for Local Language Broadcasting* provide a framework to inform such broadcasting and translations; the guidelines charge news translators to be 'faithful to the denotation and context of the original utilisation' and say that translators should avoid literal translation in order to retain meaning (2009, p. 9). However, because of the linguistic issues –most broadcasters were trained in the English language –this problem still persists. Therefore, there is a need for journalist training institutions to train journalists in indigenous language broadcasting and incorporate the use of indigenous language in the actual training of journalists. This should be complemented by an effective national language policy in general education so that indigenous language teaching and learning is taken more seriously at all levels of the educational structure than has been the case over the years. Achieving this would help satisfy the demand of the *Guidelines of Local Language Broadcasting* that charge broadcast stations to 'ensure that at all times their reporters, news readers and presenters speak and write the local language in which they broadcast with high proficiency' (2009, p. 7). This will, to a large extent, address translation problems and avoid the public's misunderstanding of the content of radio broadcasts.

Despite the challenges, there is hope with regard to the use of indigenous language broadcasting in Ghana. Because most broadcasts are still in the dominant languages of Akan and Ewe, which have significant speakers across the other ethnic groups in the country, there is the opportunity for radio stations to reach out to other minority languages excluded in the communication process. Thus, broadcasting in other local dialects will not only increase the reach of the radio station but will further facilitate the emancipation of the people by giving them the opportunity to participate in both the media and political spheres. Early research on the impact of citizens' participation on society reveals that not only is it a cornerstone for democracy but it will help 'redistribute power that enables the have-not citizens, presently excluded from the political and economic processes, to be deliberately included in the future' (Arnstein, 1969, p. 216).

Conclusion and recommendations

Citizens' participation is central to the consolidation of democracy, and one way of increasing participation in a country like Ghana characterised by a high illiteracy rate and low access to the media is through the use of indigenous languages in broadcasting. Since the introduction of the various media policies that facilitated the subsequent use of indigenous language in broadcasting, most radio stations in Ghana have started broadcasting the majority of their programmes in the dominant local languages. This has created a platform and opportunity for the marginalised and local peasants to participate and contribute towards media and political debates, as most people 'feel more comfortable participating in programmes that are broadcast in their native languages' (Blankson, 2005, p. 16). This can be seen in the popularity of programmes like Kokrokoo and Drive Time, amongst others.

Although radio broadcasts are still in the dominant languages of Akan and Ewe, this has, however, changed the broadcasting trend in Ghana from 'foreignisation of broadcasting' as argued by Blankson (2005) into the current wave of indigenous language broadcasting that has changed the face of broadcasting in Ghana (Kafewo, 2006). The use of indigenous languages in broadcasting has helped promote the local languages in Ghana and encouraged the public into participating in radio debates, which was once impossible due to the use of the English language. Nevertheless, the radio stations could still strive to expand their language beyond the few languages that have been used so far as the medium of broadcasting. This would include more citizens in the democratic discourse in the country.

This chapter recommends that policymakers should formulate a national language policy that will help promote and encourage the use of indigenous languages in Ghanaian society. This policy should recognise all the different languages and dialects in Ghana and encourage the mass media to produce programmes to meet the needs of the different ethnic groups and dialects. To this end, funding or grants should be made available to radio stations that seek to broadcast beyond the dominant dialects but are hindered by a lack of finances or human resources. These funds will to a large extent address the financial and human resources issues identified by broadcasters for the continued and consistent continuous broadcasting in Ewe and Akan, thereby addressing the issue of minority rights and protecting such rights according to international standards. In addition, journalists and broadcasters should be retrained in the use of indigenous language as this will help to address the problem of translation errors.

Notes

A total of 19 interviews were conducted with policymakers, media practitioners and non-governmental organisations (NGOs). However, because of ethical issues, the identities of some of the interviewees are not revealed in the study.

1. From the latest census results of 2010 (Ghana Statistical Service, 2012).
2. 'Lingua franca', in this sense, is a variety of language used by speakers without a common native language in order to communicate (Guerini, n.d.).

3. Scholars have generally used 'educated Ghanaian' to refer to those who have had at least ten years of formal education.
4. Scholars like Voltmer (2008), Coleman et al. (2011) and Diamond have all argued that consolidation of democracy in emerging democracies is centred on the ability of the citizens to have access to information in order to make an informed decision. But the exclusion of certain marginalised people from the communication process will to a large extent endanger democracy.
5. The National Media Commission is the regulatory body established by the 1992 Constitution to regulate and oversee the activities of the mass media in Ghana.
6. There are more than130 radio stations in Ghana; Table 6.1 is just a snapshot of some of them and their medium of communication.
7. Most studies on Ghana have suggested that ethnicity plays a significant role in the political and socio-economic development of the state. This is reflected in the two major political parties (NDC and NPP) in Ghana, which are structured along ethnic lines. While the NDC is seen as a political party for the Ewe people, the NPP is seen as a political party for the Ashanti people (see Akpojivi, 2012a).
8. Recent figures from the Ghana Communications Authority (GCA, the regulatory body in charge of broadcasts), indicate that the least number of radio stations a region has is six while the highest is as many as 37.

References

Adu Boahen, A. (1975) *Ghana: Evolution and Change in the Nineteenth and Twentieth Centuries.* London: Longman.

Akpojivi, U. (2012a) 'Community Radio Regulation and Its Challenges in Ghana'. *Journal of African Media Studies*, 4(2), pp. 193–207.

Akpojivi, U. (2012b) 'Media Freedom and Media Policy in New Democracies: An Analysis of the Nexus between Policy Formulation and Normative Conceptions in Ghana and Nigeria'. PhD Thesis, University of Leeds, UK.

Alhassan, A. (2005) 'Market Valorisation in Broadcasting Policy in Ghana: Abandoning the Quest for Media Democratisation'. *Media Culture and Society*, 27(2), pp. 211–228.

Anderson, B. (2006) *Imagined Communities* (New Edition). London: Verso.

Anokwa, K. (1997) "Press Performance Under Civilian and Military Regimes in Ghana". In F. Eribo and J. Ebot (Eds.). *Press Freedom and Communication in Africa*. Asmara: African World Press, pp. 3–28.

Ansah, G.N. (2008) 'Linguistic Diversity in the Modern World: Practicalities and Paradoxes'. *The International Journal of Language Society and Culture* [Online] [Accessed on 14 May 2011] issue 26. Available from: www.educ.utas.edu.au/users/tle/JOURNAL/.

Arnstein, S. (1969) 'A Ladder of Citizen Participation'. *Journal of the American Institute of Planners*, 35(4), pp. 216–224.

Blankson, I.A. (2005) 'Negotiating the Use of Native Languages in Emerging Pluralistic and Independent Broadcasting Systems in Africa'. *Africa Media Review*, 13(1), pp. 1–22.

Bodomo, A., Anderson, J. and Dzahene-Quarshie, J. (2009)'A Kente of Many Colours: Multilingualism as a Complex Ecology of Language Shift in Ghana'. *Sociolinguistic Studies*[Online][Accessed 6 September 2013]. Available from: http://www.equinoxjournals.com/ojs/index.php/SS/index.

Bourgault, L. (1995) *Mass Media in Sub-Saharan Africa*. Bloomington: Indiana University Press.

Buckley, S., Apenteng, B., Bathily, A. and Mtimde, L. (2005) 'Ghana Broadcasting Study: A Report for the Government of Ghana and the World Bank'. [Online] [Accessed 1 January 2006]. Available from: siteresources.worldbank.org.

Cave, M. and Prosperetti, L. (2001) 'The Liberalisation of European Telecommunications', in M. Cave and R. Crandall (Eds) *Telecommunications Liberalisation on Two Sides of the Atlantic*. Washington, DC: AEI-Brooking Joint Center for Regulatory Studies.

Coleman, S., Blumler, J., Dutton, W., Shipley, A., Steibel, F. and Thelwall, M. (2011) *Leaders in the Living Room: The Prime Ministerial Debate of 2010: Evidence, Evaluation and Some Recommendations*. Oxford: Reuters Institute for the Study of Journalism, University of Oxford.

De Sola Pool, I. (1963) 'Mass Media and the Politics in the Modernisation Process', in L. Pye (Ed.) *Communications and the Political Development*. Princeton: Princeton University Press.

Eribo, F. (1997) "Internal and External Factors affecting Press Freedom in Nigeria", in F. Erobo and J. Ebot, (Eds.). *Press Freedom and Communication in Africa*. Asmara: African World Press, pp. 51–74.

Fosu, M. and Akpojivi, U. (2013) 'Convergence, Citizens Engagement and Democratic Sustainability in Emerging Democracies: The Case of Ghana and Nigeria'. *Journal of Mass Communication and Journalism*, 3(1), pp. 1–5.

Gadzekpo, A. (1997) 'Communication Policies in Civilian and Military Regimes: The Case of Ghana'. *African Media Review*, 11(2), pp. 31–50.

Ghana Demographics Profile (2011). [Online]. [Accessed on 15 May 2011]. Available from: www.indexmundi.com/ghana/demographics_profile.html.

Ghana Statistical Service (2008) *Ghana Living Standards Survey: Report of the Fifth Round*. [Online] [Accessed on 17 May 2011]. Available from: http://www. statsghana,gov.gh/docfiles/glss5_reports.pdf.

Guerini, F. (n.d.) 'Multilingualism and Language Attitude in Ghana: A Preliminary Survey'.[Online] [Accessed on 18 January 2011]. Available from: http://www. ethnorema.it/pdf/numero%204/03%20Articolo%20Guerini.pdf, pp. 1–33.

Hasty, J. (2005) *The Press and Political Culture in Ghana*. Indiana: Indiana University Press.

Heath, C. (1999) 'Negotiating Broadcasting Policy: Civil Society and Civic Discourse in Ghana'. *Gazette*, 61(6), pp. 511–521.

Jebuni, C. and Oduro, A. (1998) 'Structural Adjustment Programme and the Transition to Democracy', in K. Ninsin (Ed.) *Ghana: Transition to Democracy*. Dakar: CODESRIA.

Jones-Quartey, K. (1960) 'The Ghana Press', in *Committee on Inter-African Relations, Report on the Press in West Africa*, prepared for the International Seminar on Press and Progress in West Africa, University of Dakar, Senegal.

Kafewo, S. (2006) *Ghana: Research Findings and Conclusions: African Media Development Initiative*. London: BBC World Service Trust.

Kamwangamalu, N. (2002) 'Language Policy and Mother-Tongue Education in South Africa: The Case for a Market-Oriented Approach', in J. Alatis, H. Hamilton and A. Tan (Eds) *Roundtable on Languages and Linguistics 2000*. Washington, DC: Georgetown University Press, pp. 119–134.

Karikari, K. (1998) 'The Press and the Transition to Multi-Party Democracy in Ghana', in K.A. Ninsin (Ed.) *Ghana: Transition to Democracy*. Dakar: CODESRIA, pp. 189–210.

McQuail, D. (1993) *Media Performance: Mass Communication and the Public Interest*. Newbury Park: Sage Publication.

Musau, P. (2003) 'Linguistic Human Rights in Africa: Challenges and Prospects for Indigenous Languages in Kenya'. *Language, Culture and Curriculum*, 16(2), pp. 155–164.

National Media Commission (2000) *Ghana National Media Policy*. Accra: NMC.

National Media Commission (2009) *Guidelines for Local Language Broadcasting*. Accra: National Media Commission.

Nyamnjoh, F. (2005) *Africa's Media, Democracy and the Politics of Belonging*. London: Zed Books.

Obeng, S.G. (1997) 'An Analysis of the Linguistic Situation in Ghana'. *African Languages and Culture*, 10(1), pp. 63–81.

Prah, K. (2005) 'Speaking African on the Radio: Impact Assessment Survey of FM/Community Radios Using African Languages in Ghana, Mali and Senegal'. [Online]. [Accessed on 6 September 2013]. Available from portal.unesco.org/ci/en/file_download.php/250d3e9ec5315169f9d32fOae27159c3Africa+langua ges+impact+study.pdf.

PuyeFranz, V. (1998) 'Media and the Preservation of Culture in Africa'. [Online] [Accessed on 6 September 2013].Available from www.culturalsurvival.org/ ourpublcations/csq/article/media-and-preservation-culture-africa.

Republic of Ghana (1992) *The Constitution of the Republic of Ghana 1992*. Accra: Government Printers.

Republic of Ghana (2003) *The Ghana ICT for Accelerated Development (ICT4AD) Policy*. Accra: Government Printer.

Riley, P. (2007). *Language, Culture and Identity: An Ethnolinguistic Perspective*. London: Continuum.

Schudson, M. (1994) 'Culture and the Integration of National Societies', in D. Crane (Ed.)*The Sociology of Culture*. Oxford: Blackwell Books, pp. 63–81.

Tudesq, A. (1983) *La Radio en Afrique Noire*. Paris: Editions A. Pedone.

Ugboajah, F. (1985) *Mass Communication, Culture and Society in West Africa*. Munich: Hans Zell.

Ugboajah, F. (1986) 'Communication as Technology in Africa Rural Development'. *Africa Media Review*, 1(1).

UNESCO, Universal Declaration on Cultural Diversity (2001). [Online] [Accessed 9 January 2013]. Available from: portal.unesco.org/en/ev.php-URL_DO=DO_ TOPIC&URL_SECTION=201.HTML.

UNESCO (2007) 'UIS Statistics in Brief Ghana'. [Online] [Accessed on 1 August 2009]. Available from http://stats.uis.unesco.org.

Voltmer, K. (2008) "Comparing Media Systems in New Democracies: East Meets South Meets West", *Central European Journal of Communication*, 1 pp. 23–40.

Wilson, D. (1987) 'Traditional Systems of Communication in Modern African Development: An Analytical Viewpoint'. *Africa Media Review*, 1(2), pp. 87–104.

Part III
The Indigenous Language Media in Political and Cultural Expression in Africa

7

Indigenous Language Radio in Kenya and the Negotiation of Inter-Group Relations during Conflict Processes

Philip Oburu

Introduction

Over the years, Kenya gave the impression of a relatively stable nation-state in sub-Saharan Africa and became one of the beacons of hope within the war-ridden *Great Lakes Region of Africa* (Anderson, 2005; Anderson, and Lochery, 2008; Lonsdale, 2008). However, the highly disputed elections in 2007/2008 and their aftermath, which led the International Criminal Court (ICC) to confirm charges against Uhuru Kenyatta, William Ruto and Joshua Sang, rejuvenated debates on Kenya's political stability in the wake of global insecurity (Baretta, 2013; Onguny, 2012a; Onguny, 2012b). In addition, the contestation of the March 2013 presidential election results at the Supreme Court of Kenya, declaring Uhuru Kenyatta and William Ruto as winners, also adds to the growing uncertainty around Kenya's political future, as the two princi-pals face serious charges of crimes against humanity (Sharma, 2012).

Despite the growing trend in sub-Saharan Africa whereby multi-party elections often culminate in violence, a confluence of factors may explain why the 2007 elections in Kenya were more violent than those conducted in March 2013. Many reports have indicated that the 2007/08 conflicts stemmed from mere distrust of the then Electoral Commission of Kenya (ECK) when Kibaki, the former president, decided to appoint 19 out of 22 members of the ECK without consulting the opposition (Brown, 2009; Lynch, 2008). Posing credibility concerns, the appointments seemed to have reinforced the beliefs previously held by the opposition that plans were underway to manipulate the results of the 2007 general elections. As a result, violence erupted along the lines of the two major party loyalties, those affiliated to Odinga's *Orange*

Democratic Movement (ODM) and those allied to the Kibaki-led Party of National Unity (PNU).

Several studies have indicated that the tensions between the two political camps encouraged different groups to cling to their supposed "ethnic territories" while forcing "enemies" out of these regions, some of which were now reclaimed as stolen "ancestral lands" (Lynch, 2008; Zuckerman, 2009). Also, the move by Kibaki's government to impose a temporary ban on all live media in the midst of the 2007/08 crisis, under the umbrella of public order and safety, strengthened the view that the government was masking the brutal attacks carried out on civilians by the state police (Anderson and Lochery, 2008). From this perspective, some have suggested that the fear of a media crackdown encouraged the use of alternative means of news dissemination, such as social media platforms (Makinen and Kuira, 2008; Okoth, 2011). This underscores the significance of media narratives in nurturing political processes, whether from a critical or descriptive perspective.

Also at the heart of the 2007/08 conflicts was the international community's intervention through the norm of "Responsibility to Protect" (R2P), as the government was considered incapable of protecting civilians from serious crimes against humanity (Sharma, 2012). Although it helped to reduce the magnitude of violence across the country, the intervention was also received with mixed feelings. On the one hand, there were nationalist sentiments that appeared to create the perception that the "West" was tampering with Kenya's sovereignty, once engulfed in colonial creed (Harrington and Manji, 2013; Rutten and Owuor, 2009). On the other hand, various humanitarian groups applauded the intervention as a relief since it provided room for dialogue between the two belligerents and their loyalists, leading to the re-establishment of social order (Baretta, 2013; Brown, 2009; Lonsdale, 2008).

Comparatively speaking, the elections in March 2013 were conducted in a different atmosphere. First, the ongoing ICC cases seemed to have had a significant influence on the manner in which politicians conducted campaigns across the country, including their choice of language. Nonetheless, the cases also realigned political alliances ahead of the 2013 elections with Kenyatta and Ruto, foes in the 2007 elections, teaming up under the banner of Jubilee Alliance. Their central message to voters was that they were both victims of a Western plot and they cast Raila Odinga, their major opponent, as part of the larger scheme in their indictment by the Rome Statute. The second issue, related to the first, was the indictment of Joshua Sang, a radio journalist broadcasting in Kalenjin, for war crimes alongside Kenyatta and Ruto. Sang is mainly accused of facilitating inter-group hatred on air. His indictment by the Court seems to have sent a strong signal to the local journalists about the insensitive collection and dissemination of messages to the public, especially in situations of violence. Thirdly, the indication by political parties that they would accept the outcome of the 2013 elections or contest the results at the High Court, trumped the concerns of violence. Lastly, the reforms that came about as a result of the power-sharing deal between Kibaki and Odinga, for instance the adoption of the new Constitution in 2010, also provided a new framework for the 2013 elections.

Among the many factors identified as possible catalysts of the 2007/08 post-election conflicts are the narratives adopted by various indigenous-language radio stations (Jamal and Deane, 2008; Makinen and Kuira, 2008; Onguny, 2012b; Zuckerman, 2009). This chapter therefore focuses on indigenous radio frames and how they shape public opinions in conflict processes. Drawing on Azar's (1990) theory of *protracted social conflicts* (PSC) and the *framing approach* (D'Angelo, 2011; Entman, 2010; Matthes, 2012), it examines the extent to which the radio stations broadcasting in Luo, Kikuyu and Kalenjin influenced inter-group relations as well as attitudinal changes prior to, during and after the 2007/08 conflicts. The study is a modest attempt to move beyond the normative approaches that reposition ethnicity and colonial legacy as the primary drivers of inter-group conflicts in African states. The central overarching question the study addresses is the following: how did indigenous-language radio negotiate inter-group political claims before, during and after the 2007/08 conflicts? The goal is to understand why and how the 2007/08 conflicts shifted from electoral discourse to embrace negative ethnicity.

The term "indigenous radio" is used to depict radio broadcasting in languages spoken by specific ethno-linguistic groups, which live within a multi-ethnic society where the politics of cultural hybridism is weakened by inter-ethnic interests and/or claims of ethnic essentialism (Onguny, 2012b). Often, indigenous radio stations broadcast in non-official languages, although some societies are gradually recognizing local dialects as part of the official languages. The main particularity of indigenous radio stations is that they are likely to appropriate and customize news story lines to slant towards the specificities of the groups they serve (Arnold and Schneider, 2007; Neyazi, 2010; Shi, 2009).

The main limitation of this study revolved around the sensitivity of the topic. For instance, radio hosts in the target locations declined to comment on their programming and/or editorial strategies, as the ICC investigations were still underway. The study therefore relied on the accounts provided by radio listeners in the target locations as well as the perspectives provided by policymakers in the region. This explains why the discussion does not reflect on how external forces such as advertising, ownership, and regulations may have affected radio programming during these conflicts. Equally, the study was conducted entirely in English. While this may have limited some people from participating, the use of English was regarded necessary to avoid translated materials that may not have reflected the views of respondents in a genuine manner.

Protracted Social Conflicts (PSC): An overview

The PSC model posits that the understanding of intractable conflicts stretches beyond internal and external dichotomies that have emphasized overt conflicts over covert ones, a trend that has, according to Azar, clouded over the underlying forces characterizing such conflicts. According to Azar, protracted conflicts are not only sporadic, but they also present unique properties whose manifestations strike at the centre of developmental needs, thus becoming the main challenge for national cohesion in developing countries since the end of the Second World War and Cold War. He writes,

Many conflicts currently active in the underdeveloped parts of the world are characterized by a blurred demarcation between internal and external sources and actors. Moreover, there are multiple causal factors and dynamics, reflected in changing goals, actors and targets. Finally, these conflicts do not show clear starting and terminating points [...] [As such] protracted social conflicts occur when communities are deprived of satisfaction of their basic needs on the basis of the communal identity. However, the deprivation is the result of a complex causal chain involving the role of the state and the pattern of international linkages. Furthermore, initial conditions (colonial legacy, domestic historical setting, and the multi-communal nature of the society) play important roles in shaping the genesis of protracted social conflict. (Azar, 1990: 6–12)

In this way, Azar's perception of conflicts contrasts the realist notion of conflict as a comparative advantage between states and their capacity. In other words, the author considers social conflicts as a process without well-defined beginnings and endings. As a process, Azar infers that there are sets of conditions that inform conflict situations: those responsible for transforming peaceful situations into conflictual ones; those that activate violence; and those relative to conflict outcomes. Given these characteristics, Azar argues for a four-cluster theory of intractable social conflicts, which are: communal content; deprivation of human needs; governance and the state's role; and international linkages.

Communal content is based on the premise that protracted conflicts are commonly identity-based (ethnicity, race, culture, religion etc.) and that the "disarticulation between the state and society as a whole" explains the rigid correlation between the state and identity groups, especially in multi-communal societies where, according to him, colonial legacy has created a problematic relationship between the state machinery (controlled by a small identity/ethnic group or a coalition of group identities) and other social groups whose needs have been neglected by the state machinery. In this way, the degree of cultural heterogeneity in a society is likely to influence the manner in which different identity groups accommodate each other, especially in the redistribution of state power.

Deprivation of human needs, according to Azar (1990), underscores the fact that protracted conflicts are fanned by need deprivation and the failure, by the incumbent authority, to address these grievances in a responsive manner. In this view, the author infers that need deprivation fosters collective action, for they are "non-negotiable" (where needs are not limited to political access, economic development and cultural recognition). He argues that the ideological apparatus manipulated by political interests and antagonistic group relationships embedded in historic realities may generate mistrust between different communities and thus lead to attacks and counter attacks. This cluster seems to be grounded on the human need theory assumptions highlighting the centrality of material and non-material satisfactions.

With regard to governance and the state's role, Azar (1990) perceives them as key elements of contentment or discontentment of individual and communal demands. That is, the state is considered as a body with the mandate to protect, cater to, lead and govern all groups peacefully or by force. As such, states that fail to provide their citizens with structures deemed necessary for individual and collective emancipation (for reasons not limited to corruption, authoritarianism and ineffectiveness) are likely to face protracted conflicts. In this perspective, the author presumes that in the newly formed nation-states (mainly post-colonial states), the Western liberal leadership model has failed, and that "dominant identity groups or a coalition of hegemonic groups" have monopolized key political institutions and used the state machinery for their own political gains while leaving the needs of other groups unaddressed.

Lastly, international linkages that describe politico-economic relationships around the globe are believed to have put both the stronger and weaker states on the same level of economic competition. This relationship, according to Azar (1990), has not only created economic dependency, but also redefined military relationships and cross-border interests. Consequently, the sovereignty of weaker states has become more fragile, for their socio-political institutions are greatly influenced by the international system. This suggests that the politics of control or co-optation of various conflicts can be illuminated by looking at the international linkages, such as the global economic system.

Although the PSC has been well received in peace-building literature as a relatively comprehensive approach, the model has also been criticized on multiple levels. Cordula Reinmann,[1] a feminist scholar, argues that the model is gender-insensitive as it fails to account for family and/or power relations that may surface prior, during or after conflicts. Others have pointed out the generality of the clusters (Byman, 2002; Galtung et. al., 2002; Sandole, 1999). Equally, Galtung (1996) critiques Azar's model on the basis that conflicts are a transformational process with both positive and negative manifestations, and that social conflicts cannot be perceived solely as a negative occurrence.

In spite of the rich analytical, interpretative and prescriptive nature of Azar's PSC model and the analytical gaps already identified, still little attention is paid to the centrality of media narratives in contemporary conflicts, especially in multi-ethnic states (Onguny, 2012a). The extant literature does not explain how the perceived differences, conditions and incompatibilities that are often inherent in conflict situations transform from their latent nature to overt manifestations (and vice versa).

Rationale of integrating media framing within the PSC model

While the academic literature generally supports that contemporary conflicts are mainly intrastate and intractable (Azar, 1990; Sandole, 1999; Shinar, 2003), there are divergent accounts when it comes to the root causes of such conflicts, especially in settings that are ethnically heterogeneous. A host of literature often focuses on the salience of ethnic differentiation and how it affects inter-group relations in situations of competition (Baretta, 2013; Brooten, 2006; Gower and An, 2009; Somerville, 2009). The main question, in this regard, is what makes different groups choose to act or not according to the prompts of ethnic allegiances?[2]

Some studies emphasize the ambiguities around democratic liberties and perceptions of citizenship and nationalism as the main sources of socially intractable conflicts (Anderson, 2005; Bayer, 2010; Galtung et al., 2002), which explain conflicts in terms of the shifting perceptions of one's self-determination. Others perceive ethnicity and cultural differences as the sore point of intractable intrastate conflicts (Baretta, 2013; Blanton et al., 2001; Jenkins, 2004; Klopp and Kamungi, 2007; Roeder, 2003; Rutten and Owuor, 2009). The latter stream of research considers intrastate conflicts as "being motivated by ethnic sentiments, as being grounded in deeply-set hatreds, and as being virtually inescapable" (Fenton, 2004: 1). Cultural allegiances are thus underpinned as the most pervasive aspect of conflicts. In the "newly" formed nation-states, however, historical contingencies and colonial legacy that saw the division of various groups along the lines of territorial allegiances are often regarded as the epicentre of intrastate conflicts (Posner, 2007; Tir, 2005; Ulrich and Wolff, 2004). In this view, intrastate conflicts are essentially treated as a matter of historical grievances nurtured during colonial occupation and perpetrated by post-colonial leaders.

Despite the rich analytical frameworks advanced by many of these studies, the salience of indigenous media frames, as an essential aspect of conflict intractability, is often downplayed or neglected, yet they make a significant contribution with regard to how different groups process political information. Indeed, indigenous media, especially radio, have been at the centre of debates as polarizing agents since *Radiotélévision Libre des Milles Collines* (RTLM) was cited as one of the catalysts of Rwanda's genocide in 1994 (Frère, 2009; Thomson, 2007). This suggests that media framing is a key aspect of conflict severity and intractability. In essence, media framing can broadly be understood as a schema of interpretation socially constructed through news story lines to influence audience perception of a particular event or phenomenon (Tewksbury and Scheufele, 2009).

The salience of an occurrence, in this case, hinges on what Benford and Snow (2000) call "frame amplification", which happens when the perceived values or beliefs are idealized, embellished, clarified or invigorated, all of which make certain contents more salient than others. Recently, research on media framing has argued for an *integrative* approach to framing, implying that news frames not only disseminate persuasive angles of news interpretation, but also the reasons as to why the circulated frames are of great significance (D'Angelo, 2011; Matthes, 2012), pointing to the duality inherent in the media framing process. That is, media frames may serve as an interpretative tool or mental maps that help people make sense of different situations based on worldviews and their daily life experiences. In this way, framing provides disputants with the means to negotiate their perceived differences in a manner that reflects their collective ideals. On the other hand, media frames may embrace persuasive discourses aimed at rallying opinions towards a particular cause, whether negative or positive (Kaufman and Smith, 1999). This repositions media frames as a strategy influencing people's stances on issues, which can easily distort the image of "others" for self-serving purposes.

This suggests that the framing of conflicts by indigenous radio can serve as a strategy and mental map because "people seek information about the crisis and evaluate the cause of the event and the organizational responsibility for the crisis based on media coverage of the crisis" (Gower and An, 2009: 107). The question, therefore, is not whether the media can influence the patterns or directions of a conflict, but rather, to what extent they can lead to the escalation or de-escalation of such conflicts. Several studies have demonstrated (mainly in a negative light) how different groups have used the media to stigmatize inter-group divisions. In Asia, the case of Burma, characterized by military rule and civil wars since the country's independence from the British in 1948, is exemplary. The attempt by the opposition media to rally voices against military rule has only increased intermittent violence in the country (Brooten, 2006). In the Middle East, the wavering Palestinian–Israeli relationship has been linked to media narratives exploiting identity symbols characterizing the conflict as Arab/Islamic and Israel/Jewish ideological confrontations. As Shinar (2003: 8), notes: "since late 2000, most explanations given by media about the changes in Palestinian–Israeli relations have dealt with the failure to reconcile rather than with the deeper roots of the conflict."

In Latin America, El Salvador's *Radio Vecercemos* was accused of providing a rebel group with a "voice" to indict the Salvadorian army in the murdering of six Jesuit priests, sparking civil war. The *Frente Farabundo Martí para la Liberación Nacional* (FMLN), a rebel group, is believed to have exploited *Radio Vecercemos* to publicly accuse the Salvadorian army of murdering the priests, a claim that continues to hamper the peace process in that region (Consalvi, 2010). Europe's Yugoslav civil wars involving the Serbs, Croats and Bosnians were also related to media categorization of different groups into ethnic entities (Wimmer et al., 2004). In Africa, the 1994 genocide in Rwanda is often cited as an example, given the narratives embraced by RTLM and *Kangura* press, which led to the killings of *Tutsis* and *Hutu-moderates* (Thomson, 2007).

In DR Congo, *La Voix du Patriote* was one of the media believed to have disseminated messages that sparked inter-ethnic hatred (Frère, 2009). In Burundi, *Le Témoin-Nyabusorongo* is also believed to have contributed to the escalation of the conflicts in 1993 (Kaburahe, 2004). The civil wars in Uganda's *Acholiland* have also been attributed to media's portrayal of the Acholi groups as enemies of the state (Ogenga, 2002). The case of post-apartheid South Africa also illustrates the significance of media narratives in reinforcing reconciliatory or vengeful messages (Krabill, 2001). The temporary ban on live media imposed by the Kenyan government during the 2007/2008 conflicts, and the confirmation of charges (by the ICC) against Kass FM's radio host, Joshua A. Sang, also illustrate the significant role of the media in influencing the directions of a given conflict (Onguny, 2012b).

Given these trends, one cannot underestimate the centrality of media narratives when seeking to constructively understand the competing claims inherent in socially protracted conflicts, and even more so, in fragile multi-ethnic societies. It is within this perspective that media framing has been integrated as a fifth cluster in Azar's PSC model.

Data collection and analysis

This study was based on cross-methodology, which emphasized the following methods: documentary research, in-depth interviews with 59 respondents, observation and articulating methodology. Various factors also influenced the choice of the three research sites. With respect to the choice of research sites, Kisumu was appealing because the Luo, one of Kenya's major ethnic groups, remain the majority group. It is also close to Bondo town, home of Raila Odinga (also a Luo), who is former Prime Minister of Kenya and a presidential contender in both the contentious general elections held in December 2007 and the disputed March 2013 elections. Kisumu was also among the areas worst hit by the 2007/2008 conflicts, and is often regarded as a base for opposition politics since the split between Jomo Kenyatta, Kenya's first president, and his then vice president, Jaramogi Oginga Odinga (father to Raila Odinga), in 1966.

Eldoret was selected because it is home for the majority of the Kalenjin, also one of Kenya's largest ethnic groups. Eldoret is close to Kabarnet, home to the former head of state, Daniel T. Arap Moi (a Kalenjin), who ruled Kenya for 24 years (1978–2002), a period that saw Eldoret become one of Kenya's major economic footholds, given the creation of an international airport and a public university. Furthermore,

Eldoret town was one of the hot spots during the 2007/2008 conflicts. This is where the much-hyped footage of people burnt alive in a local church, Kenya Assemblies of God Church in Kiambaa, took place. Most recently, Eldoret North's Member of Parliament and a presidential hopeful in the coming general elections, William Ruto (also a Kalenjin), has been indicted by the ICC in alleged crimes against humanity committed during the 2007/2008 conflicts. Nyeri was regarded a suitable research site because the Kikuyu, Kenya's largest ethnic group, remain the ethnic majority living there. Nyeri is also close to Othaya, home to Mwai Kibaki , who was re-elected following the controversial elections in 2007. Kibaki hails from the Kikuyu group. The first President of Kenya, Jomo Kenyatta (also a Kikuyu), came from Gatundu, in Central Province, a constituency now represented by his son, Uhuru Kenyatta, a presidential hopeful in the next elections, who is also facing charges of crimes against humanity following the 2007/2008 conflicts.

Given the temporal disconnectedness that characterized this study, various documents such as journals, books, articles, policy briefings, official reports, online documents, websites, statistical data, research and conference reports were consulted to obtain related information. This helped to uncover underlying issues that were inherent in the conflicts before conducting the actual fieldwork of interviewing different groups. Observation was also used as a method to establish direct contact with the target populations to provide a nuanced understanding of the conflict and how this particular conflict manifested itself across distinct ethno-linguistic communities. As a method of enquiry, observation can be defined as an "involvement in the here and now of people's daily lives [...] [thereby] gaining access to phenomena that are commonly obscured from the standpoint of a non-participant."[3] Observation was useful in providing a broad description of the key features that characterized the study's target groups and their habitats.

In-depth interviews (with a total of 59 respondents, 15 per location of study) were then used as a follow-up to documentary research and observation. The main purpose for using in-depth interviews was to establish the general views of respondents in the three locations of research about the negotiation of inter-group relations via indigenous radio in the events leading to the 2007/2008 conflicts. The use of in-depth interviews was also motivated by the fact that the understanding of social conflicts requires a thorough probing process. Articulating methodology, defined here as the "process of creating connections" (Slack, 1996), was then used to tease the links between various conjectures that emerged from documentary research, observation and in-depth interviews. Articulation was used in conjunction with *inter-sectionality*, which stems from feminist and racial studies, to understand "the ways that individuals are actively involved in producing their own lives and so overcomes some of the determinism of previous ways of thinking about identities that often classified individuals into fixed categories as oppressed or oppressor" (Valentine, 2007: 14).

Findings and discussion

As already mentioned, the objective of this study was to examine the political implications of Kenya's indigenous-language radio on inter-group conflict processes. Other objectives were to: a) map out the patterns of indigenous radio listenership in the three locations of research; b) determine the dominant indigenous radio stations in the three locations of study; and lastly c) find out why indigenous radio listenership is important in the lives of those interviewed. The findings of this study suggest an irregular trend with respect to the accommodation of inter-group claims in the period leading to the 2007/2008 conflicts. This seemed to be dependent on the stage at which the conflict unfolded.

Prior to the conflicts

Prior to the 2007/08 conflicts, the interviews suggest that the negotiation of inter-group relations centred on past historical contingencies, most of which were linked to the colonial legacy that, presumably, had led to the disintegration of the local groups while creating administrative boundaries that paid little attention to the traditional bonds that held these groups together. Consequently, land ownership, political representation, and group economic emancipation appeared to be the sore points of inter-group relations.

In Kikuyu and Kalenjin radio, the concerns about inter-group relations were negotiated in terms of the land resettlement schemes that followed shortly after Kenya's independence in 1963, which are believed to have stigmatized inter-group hatred in the Rift Valley Province. In the process, *Majimbo*[4] Constitutional debates were at the centre of the stories narrated by respondents from Nyeri and Eldoret. While Kikuyu-language radio emphasized the narratives of eviction from the Rift Valley Province dominated by the Kalenjin group, Kalenjin radio, on the other hand emphasized the rhetoric of invasion, supposedly by the Kikuyu "foreign" settlers, although there are other groups such as the Luo and Luhya that settled in the Rift Valley following the same resettlement schemes.

With regard to Luo radio, the precarious inter-group relations were essentially a matter of political representation, alleging dissent over a Luo presidency and betrayal by the incumbent government. One of the respondents in Kisumu narrated this displeasure and how radio served to remind the Luo constituents of the presumed betrayal by the Kibaki government.

> There was a sense of betrayal from the Kikuyu once Kibaki became the president in 2002. When Odinga campaigned so hard for him in 2002, Kikuyu and Luos were best friends. Once they [Kikuyu] got what they wanted, they decided to turn their backs from the very people who voted for them and disregarded the reforms that Odinga and other politicians campaigned for. [...] It was normal for the Luo voters to be reminded about what had happened in 2002 so that they are not fooled again.

Despite the differences in framing, both the Luo and Kalenjin radio stations seemed to demonize the Kibaki-led PNU by strengthening the perception that the Kikuyu group was the primary beneficiary of the Kibaki government, and that another party needed to take over the leadership. Conversely, Kikuyu radio portrayed the Odinga-led ODM as an ethnic-minded party led by an arrogant Luo, Raila Odinga, who could not be entrusted with the task of governance, presumably, because he was a dictator.

Dominant frames during the (violent) conflicts

During the violent conflicts, sparked by the announcement of the official results that gave Kibaki a second term, indigenous radio narratives shifted from historical scores to inter-group mutilation. In this period, the discourses of cross-victimization and finger-pointing became particularly potent. In every location of research, it appeared that radio stations strengthened the perception that their respective groups were victims of hate, mistreatment, unfairness and opportunism. In the process, sentiments of attack and counter-attack served to bolster self-defence mechanisms, a trend that may have shifted the conflict from electoral discourse to ethnicity.

For instance, in Kisumu and Eldoret, the Kikuyu were cast negatively because they were believed to be the reason why the government "stole" the elections to further their gains and interests. Furthermore, the heavy deployment of the police force in Kisumu and Eldoret was framed as the government's move to contain dissent from the Luo and

Kalenjin groups, initially perceived as ODM's core support base. Vote-rigging, intolerance and oppression by the government became the main frames used by Kalenjin and Luo radio to justify the violence. One respondent in Eldoret had this to say about the cause of violence against PNU affiliates:

> All the opinion surveys gave Raila a strong lead over Kibaki, even during the actual tallying of the votes. A day before the release of the official results, there was confusion all over, with contradictory messages coming from different journalists. At one point, we hear that Raila had been declared the winner, the next minute we hear that it is actually Kibaki who took it. This is what sparked anger and violence against the PNU party and their Kikuyu members. Everyone went to vote in peace and they started playing around with people's will. [...] You don't expect us to keep quiet and let go our hard-earned victory. It is like stepping on a snake expecting it not to bite back.

Kikuyu radio, on the other hand, appeared to disgrace these assumptions, alleging a planned attack on their communities. As a result, narratives of self-defence and ethnic survival dominated Kikuyu radio, which culminated in retaliatory attacks by the alleged gangs of *Mungiki*,[5] an outlaw cult linked to a youthful Kikuyu group. Although vote-rigging was also central to the narratives adopted by Kikuyu radio, it was framed in a manner that cast the Kikuyu as the primary targets of planned attacks, perpetrated under the guise of vote-rigging. This negative characterization was blamed on regional politicians who, supposedly, used indigenous radio to propagate the ideologies of separation rather than inter-group cohesion. This is illustrated by a comment from a respondent in Nyeri:

> Some of these radio stations [indigenous] are mouthpieces for the local politicians who use them to spread hate while advancing their personal agendas [...]. Many Kikuyus were targeted and killed for political reasons, and some [radio stations] openly called for the eviction of our communities yet these people have lived there [Rift Valley] for decades. Where do they expect them to go? When you are attacked, you have to defend yourself. I don't see the problem with the radio telling our people to watch out for the attacks. Whether *Mungiki* was involved in the attacks or not, the point is, these were planned attacks against the Kikuyus and we had the right to protect ourselves.

During the violent conflicts, indigenous-language radio frames seemed to have heightened the irrationality of other groups by painting them as untrustworthy, hateful, vengeful and intolerant. The discourses of the power struggle between groups became the lens through which different radio stations characterized inter-group relations. As a result, every group seemed to justify the violence in terms of self-defence and group survival, often alleging misuse of power and distrust over the other groups.

Dominant frames after the (violent) conflicts

Following the vicious conflicts that claimed the lives of hundreds of innocent people and displaced hundreds of thousands, indigenous radio stations changed their narratives, this time endorsing the peace negotiations[6] that were underway. Rather than focusing on inter-group mutilation and cross-victimization, the radio stations emphasized the peace talks between Kibaki and Odinga, the two main rivals. In the process, the radio stations strengthened the perception of collective interests that cut across inter-group allegiances rather than an individual group's perceived gains or losses. The radio stations also heightened the perception of a joint nation-building process, often reminding their respective audiences of their collective pride such as tourism and the world marathon that were blackened by the images of conflict.

Although the tone varied throughout the coverage of the post-conflict transformation process, the discourses of power-sharing, nation-building, democratic governance and inter-group reconciliation were the most frequently invoked angles of news analysis, all of which reinforced the notion of collective ideals while, at the same time, consoling the victims of the conflict. For instance, a respondent from Nyeri stated:

> [...] The radio stations [indigenous] were very important because people were calling to console one another and offer their support to those who were displaced from their homes in various parts of the Rift Valley. Although many people had lost their lives at this point, people came to realize that violence was not the best way to resolve political differences. The innocent are always the ones who have to pay a higher price.

In this period, indigenous radio reinforced the perception that the governing authorities were in control of the situation, and that they were putting their differences aside for the sake of the Kenyan people.

Instead of focusing on individual group solutions to the conflict, collective solutions were encouraged, such as the need for democratic reforms, with Constitutional amendments topping the list as possible remedies for inter-group conflicts. Equally, the outcome of the conflicts was framed in terms of youth movements, which drove conflict narratives away from finger-pointing to policy-based issues such as youth unemployment. As one respondent in Eldoret noted, "Although it is true that the local [indigenous] radio stations communicated separation in the past, we should also recognize their efforts in bringing the communities together and talking about issues that really caused the conflict, such as youth unemployment."

A similar reaction came from another respondent in Kusumu who said "The radio stations [indigenous] preached peace by inviting church leaders on their talk shows rather than politicians who had personal agendas." Equally, a respondent from Nyeri noted, "Gospel songs dominated the airwaves instead of politically driven songs that caused tension between different tribes [ethnic groups] just before the elections". That is, rather than playing provocative songs as interlude or signature tunes, as was the case prior to and during the violent conflicts, religious songs were used to calm the tensions between different groups.

Patterns and significance of indigenous-language radio listenership in Kenya

Radio still has the widest geographical reach in Kenya, with about 80% of the population relying on it as a source of information. In terms of broadcast formats, drama, music, comedy, talk shows and phone-in programmes seem to be the main ways by which indigenous radio stations disseminate different kinds of information. In order to map out the patterns of indigenous radio listenership in the locations of study, respondents were asked questions relative to radio access and ownership, the frequency at which they tuned into indigenous radio, their favourite indigenous radio stations, and if they simultaneously used other media outlets.

These variables helped determine the penetration, concentration and distribution of indigenous radio in the target locations. With regard to radio access and ownership among respondents, all respondents (59) in the three locations had access to radio devices, supporting the fact that radio still remains the most accessible medium of communication in Kenya. The access was influenced by the low costs of radio devices and by the circulation of cheap radio-enabled cell phones that provided respondents with a means to access various FM stations without having to buy a radio device. Only three respondents of those interviewed did not own a radio device, but had access to radio through family, friends, colleagues, or public transportation.

In terms of the dominant indigenous radio stations in the three locations of study, Coro FM (a state-run Kikuyu-language station), Ramogi FM (a Luo-language radio owned by the Royal Media Services) and Kass FM (a private Kalenjin radio) were the radio stations that were listened to the most by those who took part in the study. In Nyeri, Coro FM seemed to appeal to many respondents compared to other indigenous radio stations broadcasting in Kikuyu such as Inooro FM, Kameme FM, KBC Central Service (in Kikuyu) or any other Kikuyu radio station. In Eldoret, the majority of respondents cited Kass FM as their favourite indigenous station compared to other Kalenjin-language radio stations such as Chamgei FM (owned by the Royal Media Services), KBC Western Services (in Kalenjin) or any other stations that broadcast in Kalenjin. In Kisumu, Ramogi FM (owned by the Royal Media Services) was the most appealing radio compared to Radio Lake Victoria, KBC Western Services (in Dholuo) and other radio stations such as Radio Maendeleo, a community radio station reaching out to Kisumu residents, mostly in Bondo District.

In relation to the frequency at which the respondents tuned in to their respective indigenous radio stations, participants were asked if they listened to indigenous radio on a daily basis, every other day, once or twice a week, or if there were other times when they would tune in to these stations. The study found that the majority of participants either listened to indigenous radio on a daily basis or tuned in to these radio stations every other day. This was a common pattern in the three locations of the study. This indicates that indigenous-language radio stations have a strong following in the regions they serve, affirming the presumptions that media audiences are likely to select and use the media that fulfil their needs or expectations (Gripsrud, 2002). This was associated with the language of broadcast and the appropriation of news content in a manner that resonated with the values and expectations of the groups served.

With regard to the simultaneous use of other media, participants were asked if they used other media outlets to supplement the information they gathered while listening to their respective indigenous radio stations. Many participants (46) indicated that they simultaneously accessed other sources of media to complement the information they garnered through indigenous radio, with all participants (59) indicating that they listened to the local official-language radio stations such as Citizen FM, Capital FM, Metro FM, Kiss FM, House of Reggae, Easy FM, Classic FM and Hope FM. The TV stations that were commonly referred to were the Kenya Television Network (KTN), Citizen TV, Nation Television (NTV), Family TV, Kenya Broadcasting Corporation (KBC), and other TV channels available through pay-per-view satellite and cable channels, mainly Multi-Choice, STV (formerly Stellavision), and Cable Television Network (CTN).

Newspaper readership was relatively low among the respondents. Only 28 of those interviewed read the press on a regular basis in order to have an in-depth understanding of the issues discussed on the radio. The most-read private newspapers included The *Daily Nation*, *The Standard*, *The People*, *East African*, and *The Star*. Some respondents also cited the state-run *Kenya Times* as one of their favourite newspapers. The Internet recorded the lowest following compared to other types of media. Out of the 59 respondents, only 12 used the Internet on a regular basis to further their understanding of the issues discussed on the radio. The study also found that the majority of respondents relied on word of mouth as a source of information.

In terms of the significance of indigenous-language radio, one of the greatest advantages of radio was linked to the fact that it can be listened to while performing other activities and moved around from one location to another. In the process, respondents were able to entertain themselves, follow news or seek information relating to what was happening around them. Further advantages of radio over other media were associated with cost, accessibility and its oral nature as a medium of communication. Respondents therefore tuned to indigenous radio for a number of reasons. As a developmental tool, indigenous radio served as a vehicle by which development-oriented information, such as farming practices, was channelled to different populations, especially to those with a poor command of English or Swahili, the two official languages in Kenya. The findings also indicate that indigenous radios reconfigure their news content in a manner that takes into account the social, economic and political characteristics of the groups served.

Culturally, indigenous radio serves to uphold Kenya's diverse languages and cultural identities. As a social forum, indigenous radio stations provide their audiences with the means to maintain their cultural particularities by focusing on a group's intrinsic values that were once passed on from community elders to the younger generation through storytelling. The majority of respondents found indigenous radio a suitable tool for communicating complex customary issues such as circumcision and cross-ethnic marriages. Indigenous radio was regarded as the proper means by which such topics could be addressed, given the language and cultural proximity that these radio stations have with the groups they serve.

The main challenge for indigenous radio content is the accommodation and negotiation of inter-group political claims in times of stiff competition or conflict. This means that the same programmes and formats discussed above can also be appropriated in a negative light to generate inter-group polarization, especially in situations of inter-group competition such as electoral processes. Consistent with earlier studies on propaganda circulation, this study found that indigenous radio messages also serve as a vehicle through which "communal" propaganda circulates to slant the group's perception of the "ethnic others" in situations of conflict. However, the same findings also suggest that the (mis) representation of the "ethnic others" changes with time when "new" ethnic alliances take shape. In other words, the narratives of inclusion and exclusion depend on the negotiation of inter-group relations.

Parameters of inter-group frames in indigenous radio during conflict situations

The findings suggest a high level of intersectionality between various clusters. This study established four broad issues around which inter-group claims were framed during the 2007/08 conflicts: *cultural allegiances, political affiliations, economic pressures* and *territorial insecurity*. If ethnicity seemed to be one of the many ways in which inter-group claims were negotiated by the Kikuyu, Luo and Kalenjin radio stations, it is because the ethno-linguistic fragmentation of the Kenyan people continues to create an environment where cultural allegiances such as language, religion, ancestry and blood kinship still serve as pathways through which power relations and social processes are vested and negotiated across communities. By associating political parties (e.g. ODM and PNU) with ethnic groups, indigenous radio narratives were strategically framed in a manner that served to generate inter-group polarization and subsequent violence.

However, such categorizations often hinge on one's level of socio-cultural consciousness, what Jenkins (2004) calls the selfhood (how you see yourself) and the personhood (how others see you). This serves to question the centrality of ethnicity *per se* as the starting point in conflict situations, especially in multi-ethnic nation-states. In other words, ethnicity is an episodic process and a form of group categorization, which exemplifies around the perceived elements of content and discontent such as land ownership, political associations, economic disturbances and the media's representation. In this way, the salience of ethnicity should be examined within the larger cultural structure explaining inter-group relations. Hall and Meeks (2007) have pointed out that ethnicity itself is a matter of signifying practices that are situational.

Although several factors contributed to the 2007/08 conflicts, patronage politics and the allegations about vote-rigging did reinforce the perception that political affiliations are a sore point of inter-group relations. Because Kenya is an ethnically diverse society (with at least 42 different groups), once clustered together by colonial authority, post-colonial governance seems unable to resist the forces driven by ethno-regional competition. Indigenous radios often exploit these forces to reinforce certain perceptions with regard to the distribution and redistribution of power between ethnic groups.

In this way, political affiliations have served as the unitary force by which "communal interests" are advanced. That is, political affiliations in post-colonial Kenya are shattered by ethno-regional struggles to control the state machinery, regarded as the means through which regional interests can be fulfilled. In the process, various groups perceive the state machinery as extraneous to their interests, and by extension, to the interests of the "under-represented" groups. This intricate power relation between groups and the fight to control the state machinery is what Fukui and Markakis (1994:6) refer to as "ethnocracy,"[7] implying that "ethnic/tribal identities are essentially political products of specific situations, socially defined and historically determined". This may explain why geographical location became one of the crucial elements in the association or dissociation with political groups, which was reduced to an ODM–PNU tussle.

The economic dimension of the 2007/08 conflicts was mainly articulated in terms of unequal resource allocation, with a persuasive discourse of regional marginalization. For instance, the claims advanced by the Luo and Kalenjin radio stations ,supposing that the Kikuyu were the sole beneficiaries of the Kibaki-led government, suggested that the economic disparity between regions and groups is a sore point of inter-group relations in Kenya. This is because regional loyalties have been politicized in a manner that evokes pre-existing deep-seated emotions of disgruntlement between different groups and their perceptions of regional economic disparity. This explains why the economic and power imbalances, often associated with past regimes, became the main frames of reference in indigenous radio. While the Luo and the Kalenjin radio stations cemented the perception that the Kibaki regime failed to promote economic development in some parts of the country with the same kind of enthusiasm as others, Kikuyu radio stations dismissed these allegations while emphasizing the 5% national economic growth under Kibaki's watch.

Economic pressures can be understood by looking back at the shifts that have characterized regional economic growth with different presidents in office. When Jomo Kenyatta became the first President of the Republic of Kenya (1963–1978), he was mainly criticized for the alleged appointments of civil servants within his entourage as well as the illegitimate land allocations to his own family and to his Kikuyu community (Lonsdale, 2008), a claim believed to have widened the economic gap between the Kikuyu and other communities. When Moi took over the presidency (1978–2002), the focus shifted from Central Province (where Kenyatta hailed from) to the Rift Valley Province (Moi's home area). Much of Moi's effort was focused on the transformation of Eldoret town into a major city, with a multi-million dollar international airport established in 1995, a project that has been since regarded as a waste given that the two major airports in Nairobi and Mombasa already operate below their capacity (Ghosh, Gabby and Siddique, 1999). Since Kibaki took over (2002 to date), there have been claims that the allocation of public service positions has shifted from the Kalenjin (that dominated during Moi's reign) back to the Kikuyu group (Anderson and Lochery, 2008). According to this view, the likelihood that adequate resources will be channelled to a given region appears to be linked to whether or not a member of that ethnic region controls the state machinery, i.e. that member is seen as a guarantor of resources.

Last but not least, territorial insecurity was articulated in terms of unclear land tenure policies, especially in the Rift Valley Province. The discourses of territorial insecurity were particularly salient on Kalenjin and Kikuyu radio, often alluding to the thorny land claims that have served to generate inter-group conflicts in the Rift Valley Province over the years. This explains why the *Majimbo Constitution* (devolved Constitution), and the manner in which it was translated into "popular language", became highly political as various ethno-regional political elites defined its contours in accordance with the responses and appeals of the groups they represented.

These claims were also interwoven with the perceptions that successive governments have proved to be incapable or unwilling to address controversial land claims, forcing Rift Valley residents to resort to violence as a means to voice their discontent. This may explain why the perceived claims transformed into personal and/or inter-group accounts, resulting in discourses of fear, violence and Internal Displacement of Persons (IDPs). In this way, the perceptions that people had on territorial belongingness were, in part, influenced by the kinds of narratives used by indigenous radio to frame them. As discussed in the previous sections, media frames are likely to influence the patterns and directions of a conflict, given their capacity to inform people's attitudes about a given occurrence.

Understanding the shifts in indigenous radio frames in conflict processes

The findings indicate some levels of discordance with regard to indigenous radio narratives, translating into attitudinal shifts as the conflicts unfolded. This is illustrated in Figure 7.1. Prior to the conflicts, historical grievances served as the defining element of contentment or discontent with regard to the pledges of the rival parties and groups. This explains why land ownership debates, emphasized by Kalenjin and Kikuyu radio stations, appeared to resonate well with residents in Eldoret and Nyeri, given the land resettlement policies adopted shortly after Kenya attained independence in 1963. The perception that the Kikuyu were the primary beneficiaries of the ill-doctored land tenure systems, was transformed into attacks and counter-attacks between the "invaders" and "evictors". Luo radio stations, on the other hand, seemed to reinforce the perception that the Kikuyu were adamant with

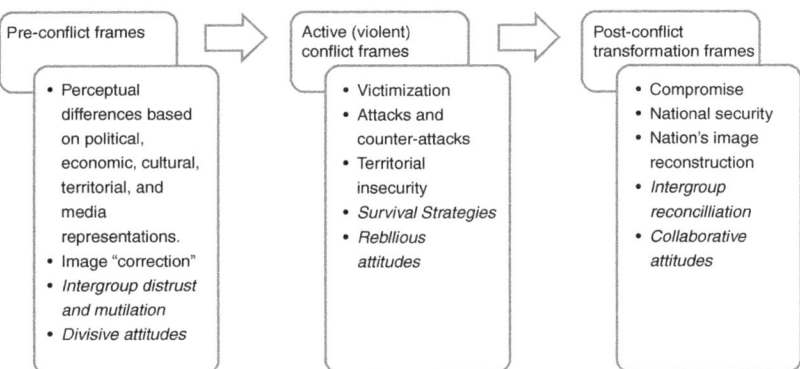

Figure 7.1　Changes in indigenous radio frames and attitudinal shifts in conflict processes

respect to a Luo presidency. From the framing perspective, this shows that negatively framed messages, with ethnic or cultural undertones, may foster sentiments of distrust and polarization along ethnic affiliations, and thus reinforce divisive attitudes amongst various groups.

Conversely, during active (violent) conflicts, the perceived areas of contention evolved into violence against the perceived "others". Every group appeared to be a victim of something and wanted to justify its course of action (violence) on the grounds of group survival and self-defence. In so doing, indigenous radio may also mobilize and rally group beliefs toward the proclaimed cause while, at the same time, demonize the other groups as the reason for their perceived suffering/discomfort. Cross-victimization remains the central discourse of indigenous radio. For instance, Luo radio emphasized the notion that the Kikuyu group had transformed the state into a "family business" where no other groups were allowed to take the top management position. This perception hinged on the narratives of vote-rigging and government mischief, and the claims that the incumbent government was using the police force to contain political dissent. For the Kikuyu radio stations, the violence was mainly a planned occurrence targeting the members of certain groups. For the Kalenjin radio stations, unfair land ownership remained the sore point of the Kikuyu–Kalenjin relationship. Active-conflict frames therefore served to maintain inter-group distrust, strengthening rebellious attitudes between different groups.

These narratives may lead to the escalation or de-escalation of conflicts depending on the actions taken by various groups. Conflicts are likely to escalate if the narratives focus on or encourage groups' defence strategies such as counter-attacks, at the expense of reconciliatory discourses. This is because violence is essentially a matter of social contracts if we consider Jean-Jacques Rousseau's perceptions. He argues, "the strongest is never strong enough to be always the master, unless he transforms strength into right, and obedience into duty. Hence the right of the strongest, which, though to all seeming meant ironically, is really laid down as a fundamental principle." This concurs with Fukui and Markakis's (1994) assumption that violence is also one of the ways in which people "test their power" and redefine relational and power boundaries. This is why active conflicts may take months, years or even decades because each disputing party seeks to establish its strengths as rights, and no party is willing to see their defeat transform into compliance. Media narratives are therefore central at this stage, as they influence the perceptions that people hold with respect to intervention strategies.

Post-conflict (violent) transformation frames were indicative of collaborative efforts for conflict resolution and inter-group reconciliation. Bound together by a belief that civil war was very plausible, indigenous radio stations diverted their frames to support power-sharing negotiations that were ongoing, often highlighting joint problem-solving. This change in the framing process bolstered collaborative attitudes between groups, paving the way for dialogue and mediation between the two party affiliates even though the outcome of the mediation process did not fully reflect the demands of both parties. Overall, post-conflict frames were fairly similar across different indigenous radio stations. This points to two things: a) differences in framing are likely to change the course of a given conflict; b) changes in the framing process also inform attitudinal shifts with regard to inter-group relations.

Although Figure 7.1 appears to suggest linearity in its sequence of frames, it should be understood that post-conflict transformation discourses can fall back to pre-conflict or active-conflict (violent) frames, depending on how the perceived differences are negotiated across time. This is why indigenous radio narratives are likely to contribute to the escalation or de-escalation of conflicts. That is, even in the de-escalation mode, if the narratives of compromise and reconciliation no longer reflect the appeals of the disputants, the conflict may regain its covert nature. In this view, "another" conflict may take shape from these latent forces, and possibly transform into an active (violent) conflict. Overall, frames highlighting the notion of collective ideals are more likely to strengthen collaborative attitudes amongst the disputants, while those emphasizing group allegiance reinforce divisive and rebellious attitudes. This can be explained in terms of *fragmented* and *concerted* framing as illustrated in Figure 7.2.

Differentiated framing underscores a form of media narrative whereby group differences are negotiated in terms of competition likely to generate inter-group polarization. One group is often perceived as susceptible to gaining at the other's expense. This kind of framing is more likely to be prevalent in pre-conflict situations (and in the early stages of active/ violent conflict) when claims of ethnic essentialism and/or ethnic self-determination become the defining characteristics of nationhood or inter-group relations. In this way, ethnicity is defined in terms of blood kinship and common ancestry explaining one's sense of belonging.

Indigenous radio stations often adopt a certain rhetoric (through programmes and music on-air) that leans towards the values or views of the groups they serve, which may negatively impact inter-group relations. Differentiated framing often reinforces exclusivity and competitive

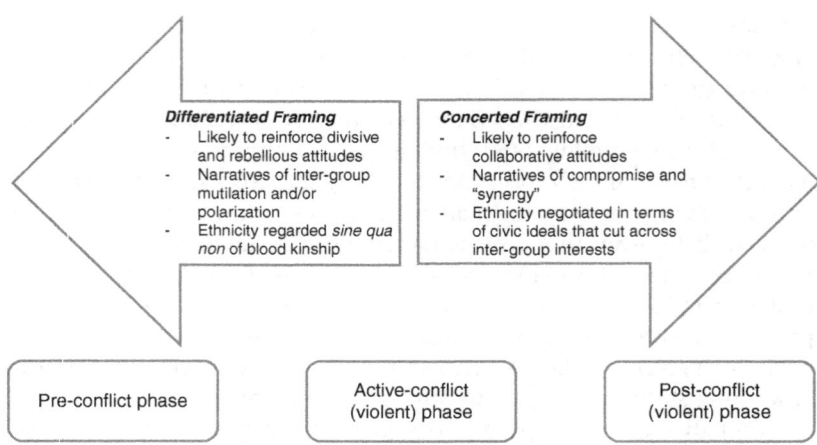

Figure 7.2   Elasticity of indigenous radio frames during conflict processes

attitudes, especially in multi-ethnic societies, thereby giving less room for constructive inter-group dialogue. Intra-group tensions may also stem from this kind of framing, especially when members of the same group are faced with fierce competition *from within*.

In contrast, *concerted* framing describes a form of media narrative that is negotiated in terms of the perceived national values that cut across inter-group interests. Ethnicity, in this regard, is not articulated as a *sine qua non* of blood kinship or common descent; rather, it is negotiated in terms of citizenship and national self-determination. In this perspective, indigenous radio may choose to embrace a rhetoric that underlines the perceived national values such as inter-group reconciliation and/or cohesion, public safety, national integrity and the rule of law, rather than focusing on group allegiance.

Concerted framing is more likely to surface in the late stages of prolonged, active conflicts and in post-conflict reconstruction phases, as radio narratives shift from inter-group competitiveness to embrace the perceived shared civic ideals, a move that may temporarily halt the violence while groups negotiate different peace initiatives. This is likely to reinforce inclusivity and collaborative attitudes among different groups, thus providing an opportunity to address the perceived differences through constructive dialogue, compromise and *synergy*.[8] At this stage, altruism seems to be the main guiding principle.

Conclusion

This study argued that the 2007/08 conflicts were a mixture of complex processes characterized by local, national and international forces that interacted recursively to influence groups' perceptions of each other. It showed that groups may differ significantly in the ways they make sense of a given conflict, a factor that questions the dominant discourse of ethnic categorization as the primary cause of violent conflicts in multi-ethnic societies. However, the study shows that indigenous radio is not the primary cause of inter-group conflicts, but is nonetheless part of the broader enabling forces that create favourable conditions for inter-group conflicts to occur.

Without overstating the prospects of indigenous radio in conflict prevention, the study found a strong correlation between indigenous radio frames and conflict transformation, whether positive or negative. The shifts are concurrent with attitudinal changes, also conditioned by the changing radio frames. Although editorial strategies, radio ownership and the place of advertisement undeniably play a crucial role in radio programming, the study indicates that indigenous radio can facilitate inter-group accommodation or appreciation even in situations of violent conflicts. In this regard, indigenous radio is likely to steer peace-building processes in multiple ways (adapted from Shinar, 2003 and Roth, 1992).

As *bridge or constituency builders*, indigenous radio narratives may strengthen or weaken relationship bonds that have existed for a long period, since they shape audiences' positioning with regard to the "cultural other". By condemning violent behaviour and promoting a positive image of other groups, they may construct positive relationships between disputants, and ultimately reduce the degrees of inter-group polarization. As *participatory tools or mediators*, indigenous radio stations may choose to embrace frames that privilege or avoid certain ways of engaging with the public.

In this way, they may provide a forum for dialogue between conflicting parties, depending on the rhetoric and position taken in these forums. As *information providers/conduits*, the analyses provided by indigenous radio, whether critically or in a distorted manner, have far-reaching implications on how radio audiences understand an ongoing conflict. Lastly, as *policy/diplomatic initiators*, certain ways of solving or mitigating conflict may be privileged or underprivileged by indigenous radio depending on the groups served. This may help in shaping the politics of intervention, thus transforming a conflict from its destructive nature into a constructive process.

Notes

1. See Cordula, Reinmann: "Why are Violent, Intra-state Conflicts Protracted? Looking at Azar's Model of Protracted Social Conflict from a Gender-sensitive Perspective." Accessed October 3, 2011. http://www.peacestudiesjournal.org.uk/dl/AZAR.pdf.
2. This question was adapted from Fenton, S. (2004) "Beyond Ethnicity: The Global Comparative Analysis of Ethnic Conflict", *International Journal of Comparative Sociology* 59(3–4), pp. 179–194.
3. See Jorgensen, D. L. (1989) *Participant Observation: Methodology for Human Studies* (Newbury, CA: Sage).
4. Majimbo is a Swahili word often used along the lines of devolutionism or regionalism. For more on Majimboism, refer to Anderson, D. M. (2005) "Yours in Struggle for Majimbo: Nationalism and the Party Politics of Decolonization in Kenya, 1955–64", *Journal of Contemporary History* 40(3), pp. 547–564.
5. For more information on the gangs of Mungiki and their roles in the 2007/08 conflicts, refer to Rasmussen, J. (2010) "Mungiki as Youth Movement: Revolution, Gender and Generational Politics in Nairobi, Kenya", *Young/ Nordic Journal of Youth Research* 18(3), pp. 301–319.
6. Given the magnitude of the 2007/08 conflicts and the inability of the Kenyan government and the African Union to provide a common ground between the proponents of ODM and PNU parties, the international community, though the former United Nations Secretary General Dr Kofi Annan, was called to intervene in order to ascertain the way forward for Kenya, as it was considered incapable of handling its internal affairs.
7. Fukui and Markakis (1994) define "ethnocracy" as the monopolization of the state machinery by some groups and the exclusion of others groups. That is, *"the ruling groups have a proprietary attitude towards the state, and what they promote as the 'national' identity is the mirror of their own ethnic ego. Consequently, the process of 'national integration' promoted by the state verges on assimilation"* (p. 8).
8. See Covey, S. (2011) The Third Alternative: Solving World's Most Difficult Problems. New York: Free Press.

References

Anderson, D. M. 2005. Yours in Struggle for Majimbo: Nationalism and the Party Politics of Decolonization in Kenya, 1955–64. *Journal of Contemporary History*, 40, no. 3: 547–564.

Anderson, D. M. and Lochery, E. 2008. Violence and Exodus in Kenya's Rift Valley, 2008: Predictable and Preventable? *Journal of Eastern African Studies*, 2, no. 2: 328–343.

Arnold, A-K. and Schneider, B. 2007. Communicating separation?: Ethnic Media and Ethnic Journalists as Institutions of Integration in Germany. *Journalism*, 8, no. 2: 115–136.

Azar, E. 1990. *The Management of Protracted Social Conflict: Theory and Cases.* Bookfield, VT: Gower.

Baretta, F. 2013. Ethnicity and Degree of Partisan Attachment in Kenyan Politics. *Journal of Asian and African Studies*, 48, no. 1: 114–125.

Bayer, S. 2010. Peaceful Transitions to Democracy. *Journal of Peace Research*, 47, no 5: 535–546.

Benford, R. D. and Snow, D. A. 2000. Framing Processes and Social Movements: An Overview and Assessment. *Annual Review of Sociology*, 26: 611–639.

Blanton, R., Mason, T. D. and Athow, B. 2001. Colonial Style and Post-colonial Ethnic Conflicts in Africa. *Journal of Peace Research*, 38, no. 4: 473–491.

Brooten, L. 2006. Political Violence and Journalism in a Multi-ethnic State: A Case Study of Burma (Myanmar). *Journal of Communication Inquiry*, 30, no. 4: 354–373.

Brown, S. 2009. Donor Responses to the 2008 Kenyan Crisis: Finally Getting it Right? *Journal of Contemporary African Studies*, 27, no. 3: 389–406.

Byman, D. L. 2002. *Keeping the Peace: Lasting Solutions to Ethnic Conflicts.* Baltimore, MD: Johns Hopkins University Press.

Consalvi, C. H. 2010. *Broadcasting the Civil War in El Salvador: A Memoir of Guerrilla Radio*. Austin, TX: University of Texas Press.

D'Angelo, P. 2011. Studying Framing in Political Communication with an Integrative Approach. *American Behavioral Scientist*, 56, no. 3: 353–364.

Entman, R. M. 2010. Media Framing Biases and Political Power: Explaining Slant in News of Campaign 2008. *Journalism*, 11, no. 4: 389–408.

Fenton, S. 2004. Beyond Ethnicity: The Global Comparative Analysis of Ethnic Conflict. *International Journal of Comparative Sociology*, 59, no. 3–4: 179–194.

Fukui, K. and Markakis, J., eds. 1994. *Ethnicity and Conflict in the Horn of Africa.* London: Currey.

Frère, M-S. 2009. After the Hate Media: Regulation in the DRC, Burundi and Rwanda. *Global Media and Communication*, 5, no. 3: 327–352.

Galtung, J. 1996. *Peace by Peaceful Means.* London: Sage.

Galtung, J., Jacobsen, C. G., and Brand-Jacobsen, K. F. 2002. *Searching for Peace. The Road to Transcend.* London: Pluto.

Ghosh, R. N., Gabby, R. and Siddique, A. 1999. *Good Governance Issues and Sustainable Development: the Indian Ocean Region.* New Delhi, IND: Atlantic Publishers & Distributors.

Gower, K. K. and An, S-K. 2009. How do the News Media Frame Crises? A Content Analysis of Crisis News Coverage. *Public Relations Review*, 35: 107–112.

Gripsrud, J. 2002. *Understanding Media Culture.* New York: Oxford University Press.

Hall, S. and Meeks, B. 2007. *Culture, Politics, Race and Diaspora: The Thought of Stuart Hall.* London: Lawrence & Wishart.

Harrington, J. and Manji, A. 2013. Satire and the Politics of Corruption in Kenya. *Social & Legal Studies*, 22, no. 1: 3–23.

Jamal, A. I. and Deane, J. 2008. The 2007 General Elections: The Role of Local Language Media. *The International Journal of Press/Politics*, 13, no. 3: 319–327.

Jenkins, R. 2004. *Social Identity*. London: Routledge.

Kaburahe, A. 2004. *La Mémoire Blessée*. Brussels: La Longue Vue.

Kaufman, S. and Smith, J. 1999. Framing and Reframing in Land Use Change Conflicts. *Journal of Architectural and Planning Research*, 16, no. 2: 164–180.

Klopp, J. and Kamungi, P. 2007. Violence and Elections: Will Kenya Collapse? *World Policy Journal*, 24: 11–18.

Krabill, R. 2001. Symbiosis: Mass Media and the Truth and Reconciliation Commission of South Africa. *Media, Culture & Society*, 23: 567–585.

Lonsdale, J. 2008. Soil, Work, Civilization and Citizenship in Kenya. *Journal of Eastern African Studies*, 2, no. 2: 305–314.

Lynch, G. 2008. Courting the Kalenjin: The Failure of Dynasticism and the Strength of the ODM Wave in Kenya's Rift Valley Province. *African Affairs*, 107, no. 429: 541–568.

Makinen, M. and Kuira, M. W. 2008. Social Media and Post-election Crisis in Kenya. *The International Journal of Press/Politics*, 13, no. 3: 328–335.

Matthes, J. 2012. Framing Politics: An Integrative Approach. *American Behavioral Scientist*, 56, no 3: 247–259.

Neyazi, T. A. 2010. Cultural Imperialism or Vernacular Modernity? Hindi Newspapers in a Globalizing India. *Media Culture Society*, 32, no. 6: 907–924.

Ogenga, O. 2002. Causes and Consequences of the War in Acholiland. In *Protracted Conflict, Elusive Peace: Initiatives to End the Violence in Northern Uganda*, ed. L. Okello. London: Conciliation Resources, 10–13.

Okoth, F. M. 2011. Immediacy and Openness in a Digital Africa: Networked-convergent Journalisms in Kenya. *Journalism*, 12, no. 6: 674–691.

Onguny, P. O. 2012a. Exploring the Dilemmas of Peace in the East African Community (E.A.C.): Implications of the 2007–08 Conflicts in Kenya. *Harvard Africa Policy Journal*, 10th Edition, Spring 2012.

Onguny, P. O. 2012b. Vernacular Radios and Conflict Framing in Africa: Perspectives on Kenya. *Global Science and Technology Forum*, December, 106–115.

Posner, D. N. 2007. Regime Change and Ethnic Cleavages in Africa. *Comparative Political Studies*, 40, no. 11: 1302–1327.

Roeder, P. G. 2003. Clash of Civilizations and Escalation of Domestic Ethnopolitical Conflicts. *Comparative Political Studies*, 36, no. 5: 509–540.

Rutten, M. and Owuor, S. 2009. Weapons of Mass Destruction: Land, Ethnicity and the 2007 Elections in Kenya. *Journal of Contemporary African Studies*, 27, no. 3: 305–324.

Roth, L. 1992. Media and the Commodification of Crisis. In Raboy, M. and Bernard, D., eds. *Media, Crisis and Democracy: Essays on Mass Communication and the Disruption of Social Order*. Sage Publication: Media, Culture and Society Book Series, 144–161.

Sandole, D. 1999. *Capturing the Complexity of Conflict: Dealing with Violent Ethnic Conflicts of the Post-Cold War Era*. London: Pinter (A Cassell Imprint).

Slack, J. D. 1996. The Theory and Method of Articulation in Cultural Studies. In *Stuart Hall: Critical Dialogues in Cultural Studies*, eds. Morley, D. and Chen, K.-H.. London: Routledge, 112–127.

Somerville, K. 2009. British Media Coverage of the Post-election Violence in Kenya, 2007–08. *Journal of Eastern African Studies*, 3, no. 3: 526–542.

Sharma, S. K. 2012. The 2007–08 Post-election Crisis in Kenya: A Success Story for the Responsibility to Protect? In *Responsibility to Protect: From Principle to Practice*, eds. Hoffmann, J. and A. Nollkaemper. Amsterdam: Amsterdam University Press, 27–38.

Shi, Y. 2009. Re-evaluating the 'Alternative' Role of Ethnic Media in the US: the Case of Chinese-language Press and Working-class Women Readers. *Media Culture and Society*, 31, no. 4: 597–616.

Shinar, D. 2003. The Peace Process in Cultural Conflict: The Role of the Media. *Conflict and Communication Online* 2, no. 1: 1–10. Retrieved August 09, 2011. http://www.cco.regener-online.de/2003_1/pdf_2003_1/shinar.pdf.

Tewksbury, D. and Scheufele, D. A. 2009. News Framing Theory and Research. In *Media Effects: Advances in Theory and Research*, eds. J. Bryant and M. B. Oliver (3rd ed.). New York: Routledge, 17–33.

Thomson, A. 2007. *Media and the Rwanda Genocide*. London: Pluto Press.

Tir, J. 2005. Dividing Countries to Promote Peace: Prospects for Long-Term Success of Partitions. *Journal of Peace Research*, 42, no. 5: 559–562.

Ulrich, S. and Wolff, S., eds. 2004. *Managing and Settling Ethnic Conflicts: Perspectives on Successes and Failures in Europe, Africa and Asia*. London: Hurst & Co.

Valentine, G. 2007. Theorizing and Researching Intersectionality: A Challenge for Feminist Geography. *Professional Geographer*, 59, no. 1: 10–21.

Wimmer, A., Goldstone, R. J., Horowitz, D. L., Joras, U. and Schetter, C., eds. 2004. *Facing ethnic conflicts: toward a new realism*. Lanham, MD: Rowman & Littlefield.

Zuckerman, E. 2009. Citizen Media and the Kenyan Electoral Crisis. In *Citizen Journalism: Global Perspectives*, eds. S. Allan and E. Thorsen. New York: Peter Lang, 190–196.

8
Mobilising Nigerians towards a National Population Census: The Role of Indigenous Language Media

Oloruntola Sunday

Introduction

Most nations of the world consider the national census exercise important because, apart from being one of the indices of modern society, a population census provides comprehensive demographic information on which to base development planning. Unfortunately, previous population censuses in Nigeria have always ended in controversy. Even the much applauded 1991 census, adjudged to have been the best so far in the country, led to 107 court cases throughout the federation.

One of the major problems facing census in Nigeria is the misconception that borders on the view of census figures as weapons of hegemony in terms of the advantages they confer on political representation and revenue allocation. Thus, some states and local governments see the census as politics by other means.

This not only presents the problem of correcting such misconceptions; there is also the need to go further and communicate the intents and purposes of the national census in order to foster acceptance and achieve the right behaviour. It is therefore appropriate to assert that for a proper understanding of the role of the census in national development, the role of the mass media, especially indigenous media, cannot be overemphasised. This is due to socio-cultural and economic factors that have ensured that even though the majority of the populace is literate in English (and pidgin English) as the major language of communication, there is still a strong emphasis on indigenous languages as a means of cultural identification in a rather tribalistic country like Nigeria (Amfani, 2009; Aziza, 2011). This chapter takes a look at the role indigenous language media can play in preparing and mobilising

Nigerians to comply and participate in future national census exercises, possibly beginning in 2016.

Theoretical underpinnings

The interpretation and social meanings given to trends and practices in society are arrived at via several means. However, the central nature of the media in all aspects of social life places them at the centre of attempts to make sense of the world we live in. This brings into focus the *agenda setting theory*. As a theory of communication, agenda setting holds that the media determine matters of social importance (Anaeto, Onabajo and Osifeso, 2008). Sunday (2012) agrees with this assertion, noting that this theory points to the power of the media to determine what is important in society. If social mobilisation is to be achieved, the issue must be considered important enough to require prompt action by the populace, and the only social apparatus that can drive this objective is the mass media, given its ability to reach a large number with "powerful" and arguably credible messages.

The credibility of the message is a function of a number of intervening variables, one of which is the extent to which it is socially, culturally and contextually relevant and resonant. This brings into play the relevance theory. Sperber and Wilson (1997) discuss communication within the context of the relevance theory, pointing out that communication is a social process, and the meanings derived from verbal communication have their roots in local lore. This clearly justifies the need for indigenous media, *oramedia*, or Western media using local languages. Through the use of traditional media of communication, or through the use of local languages, social mobilisation messages are bolstered with the advantage of resonance, which helps to make them more credible, and more effective.

Justifying the census

As stated in *The Comet* of July 12, 2001 editorial:

> The value of an accurate census is legion [sic] in a modern state. Census gives comprehensive demographical [sic] information that is depended upon to distribute developmental facilities. It shows age, generational distribution, gender spread, density of human settlement in cities, councils, states, regions as well as human spread between the urban and rural divides. Census shows labour mobility, manpower use and educational distribution among others.

In the words of a past Chairman of the Nigerian National Population Commission, Chief Samu'ila Makama:

> There are three main reasons why we conduct census. One, if these figures are reliable and since the figures are used for revenue allocation, it would enable people to get revenue that is equitable to them. Two, we can rely on population figures to enable us to delineate political constituencies so that the representatives of each community would be proportionate to their population. Lastly, if the demographic data generated is reliable, it helps to plan for sustainable development.

As observed by Ikechukwu Idegbe in *This Day,* January 30, 2005, "A population census in Nigeria, is still being given wrong connotations and interpretations, thereby making a free and accurate census a hard task". According to The Comet newspaper editorial cited above:

> above all else, because the population of a state or region also determines how much a claim can be made upon national resources and to the leadership of the polity, parts of the union called Nigeria, always engage in great struggle to be credited with higher populations than they actually have, thereby creating a false national population, favourable only to those who have the most power to manipulate the figures in-the- power that-be.

From the foregoing discussion, one can see that the elite has always viewed the census from the political point of view and its economic importance as an avenue to get a great proportion of the country's resources at the expense of the role of census in national planning. To change this negative perception of the census, publicity remains an important component of preparation and planning for the census exercise. This, as a result, will help in preparing the citizenry for an accurate and credible population and housing census.

Fadeyi (2005) points out that census publicity includes an advocacy and public sensitisation campaign to inform, educate and mobilise the population for effective participation and support. According to him, public enlightenment programmes, jingles on radio and television, and seminars should be conducted. Also, he suggests an effective rural campaign to sensitise the public about the census exercise, especially regarding the importance of census data for socio-economic planning.

However, this justification has not translated into acceptance or appropriate compliance in attempts to conduct national censuses in Nigeria, as the next segment of this chapter shows.

A timeline discourse of censuses in Nigeria from 1911 to 2006

The colonial government in 1911 conducted Nigeria's first head count, and efforts have since been made to repeat the process at ten-year intervals. The first post-independence head count in 1962/63 was controversially cancelled. Also, the 1973 Census was cancelled by the late Murtala Mohammed in 1975, while no census was conducted throughout the 1980s. However, in 1991, the Ibrahim Babangida regime conducted a census, which put the population of the country at 88 million. Though the exercise was adjudged by the military regime as the best so far in the history of census in Nigeria, as previously mentioned 107 court cases were recorded as having been brought against the National Population Commission (NPC) by those who disputed the accuracy of the head count. Therefore, it is not an overstatement to say that census has always been a subject of controversy in Nigeria.

Unfortunately, it is an exercise that no serious government can shy away from. Therefore, the Olusegun Obasanjo regime during its first term indicated plans for another census for the nation in the year 2001, which was postponed till the last quarter of 2005. Since then, efforts have been made to conduct an accurate census, one that is reliable and acceptable to Nigerians.

The 2006 census results, conducted between March 21st and 27th, 2006 were also vigorously contested, particularly in the south, especially as the census showed that Kano in the north is Nigeria's most populous state and that the north of the country as a whole accounted for more than half of Nigeria's total population of 140 million (Vesperini, 2007). This contention is clearly evidenced by the 148 petitions filed at the three census tribunals that were set up by the government in 2007 to look into cases arising from the results of the census. The biggest concern was that Lagos, purportedly with a population of more than ten million at the time, was adjudged officially to only have just above nine million people –even lower than Kano State (Amokeodo and Isah, 2011).This disputation shows the contentious nature of censuses in the country, given their economic and political implications, especially in terms of revenue allocation and power sharing.

The role and place of the mass media

The success of a census exercise, as with most other exercises of this nature, requires public cooperation and participation. Yahaya (2010) opined, in light of the response to the 2006 census, that for success to be achieved in subsequent exercises, there was a need to "promote more positive public understanding of census and its data and neutralise negative perceptions, aggressively pursue statistical enlightenment and literacy on the part of policy makers in the public and private sector, and present the census data in a less technical and more user-friendly manner". Public enlightenment is often defined as feeding the public with facts, figures and policies of the government through a series of campaigns and programmes. In 1976, the then Federal Commissioner for Information, Major General I. B. M. Haruna, stated that "the policy of the Nigerian government was to give full enlightenment to the people in order to create a dynamic society which is receptive to modern changes". Emphasising the role of information in development, he further said:

> It is the belief of this regime that changes will not take place peacefully unless those who are expected to know, know and accept the reason, the methods and the reward of the deserved changes. Therefore, unless there is effective communication between government and the governed, especially at grassroots level, our people will not respond willingly to necessary changes. Government must not content itself with merely informing people of its activities, plans and achievement. Government must help the people to understand its aims and aspirations.

Today, the above statements still hold. Nigerians, especially the people at the grassroots level, must be properly informed, educated and mobilised about the aims, objectives and aspirations of the federal government with regard to the national head count. The role of the media, therefore, cannot be overemphasised. Uyo (1987), citing Frederick Whitney, points out that the role of the media in any society is "to inform, keep up-to-date, educate, broaden and deepen one's perspective". Thus, to broaden and deepen Nigerians' perspectives about census, the mass media and especially the indigenous languages media must be utilised. This brings to the fore the need for a platform to inform, enlighten and engage the public and other stakeholders.

The mass media have a number of roles to play in society. These roles, direct and indirect fallouts of their functions, border on informing, educating, engaging, acculturating, socialising and mobilising the pub-lic (Daramola, 2005). This is the result of their ability to reach large numbers of people, as well as present them with a message, which if well prepared, can persuade and convince them to accept a line of thought or support a movement. Ojete (2008) notes that the function of the media to mobilise and engage the public revolves round "creat-ing awareness and educating the citizenry [...] to ginger, motivate and encourage them to cooperate [...] and willingly participate". Parks and Lloyd (2004:8), looking at social mobilisation, define it as the course of action of bringing together stakeholders to raise awareness, to assist in the delivery of resources and services, and to strengthen community participation for sustainability and self-reliance. Social mobilisation is an all-encompassing activity involving not only the community but key players such as heads of state and other political leaders, various ministries, district and local government authorities, community and religious leaders, businesses, environmentalists, non-governmental organisations (NGOs), service clubs, journalists, filmmakers, artists and entertainers, to name the most common examples.

It is therefore safe to say that only the mass media, working in col-laboration with other media forms, can reach these stakeholders effec-tively and achieve the objectives of such public participatory activities, one of which is the census (McQuail, 2007).

Even though a case is made for the use of media for social mobilisa-tion, studies appear to place interpersonal or group communication as the most effective front for mobilisation, especially since it is usually bottom-up (Beissinger, 2002). In the opinion of some writers (see Aziza, 2011), the "grassroots" in Nigeria (as in many developing countries) are poor and largely illiterate, and although they may be able to converse with a smattering of English, they are more comfortable in their indig-enous languages, which are not the mainstay of traditional, Western media. This may present a problem of "dis-communication", especially given that the intended audience may not be comfortable with the lan-guage of communication. This brings into focus the role of indigenous, "traditional" media as tools of mobilisation, especially for censuses in Nigeria

The case for indigenous language media

The language of communication is almost as important as the com-munication message itself. As Cline (2013) puts it: "We cannot make sense of an argument without being able to make sense of the language,

meaning, and purpose of what is being communicated in the first place."
This presupposes that language ensures that whatever message is being
communicated, it is relevant within a context, and therefore understandable; which are both crucial points if the objective is to gain acceptance
and possibly achieve persuasion, conviction and appropriate behaviour.
Olukotun (2006) maintains this position as well in identifying the
contextual imperative of language in communication and media usage
when he points out that most campaigns do not work because there is
an inability to understand English and this frustrates mobilisation objectives, thus creating a strong need for a vernacular option. Accurate esti-
mates of literacy rates in Nigeria, as with anything else, are hard to come
by, but it is true to state that those who are literate in the major Nigerian
languages far outnumber those who are literate in English, although the
two groups are not mutually exclusive. Unfortunately, government policies and programmes have always been communicated to the citizenry
more in the English language than in their indigenous languages.

A cursory look at our news-stands and the information available from
the Nigerian Press Council with regard to the number of newspapers in
the country show that publications in the English language far outnumber newspapers and magazines published in the three major languages
in Nigeria: Hausa, Ibo and Yoruba. Also, the writer observed from watching programmes on broadcast media that more time was allocated to
English language programmes to the detriment of indigenous language
programmes. Yet, this neglected majority is expected to contribute their
quota to the task of national development.

With the exception of *Gaskiya,* a Hausa language newspaper published by *New Nigerian* Newspapers Limited, no newspaper in any
Nigerian language is being published by the federal government. There
is currently no indigenous language newspaper being published by any
state government in Nigeria. Past and present efforts to publish newspapers and magazines in the indigenous languages have always been the
initiative of private individuals. In most cases, these publications have
been short-lived.

Yet, before the advent of Europeans, the people had always communicated and contributed to their society through their indigenous
languages. Even the history of the Nigerian press reveals that the first
newspaper in the country, *Iwe Iroyin*, was published in an indigenous
language. Omu (1978) shows that indigenous language newspapers in
the early history of the Nigerian press promoted literacy, provided functional knowledge and helped to promote nationalistic feelings among
the people in the second half of the (19th century). In short, *Iwe Iroyin*,

apart from its educational function, criticised the evils of slave trade, while other indigenous language newspapers that came after it helped in promoting nationalistic sentiments that eventually led to the independence of Nigeria.

Unfortunately, the progress recorded during that period waned as the English language newspapers that came later took the forefront. However, Alabi (2010) believes that indigenous language newspapers provide a potent means of mobilising people towards development. Ethusani (2005) supports this view when he says that "the development ascendancy of the countries in Asia confirms my conviction that language is a formidable tool for human development". According to him, Asian countries such as Japan, Taiwan, Malaysia, South Korea and Indonesia (and now India and China) have attained a high level of development partly because they held onto their local languages. He regrets, however, that today in Nigeria and indeed in all of Africa, except for Tanzania and one or two other Eastern African countries, official business is being conducted in French, Portuguese, Arabic or English while the indigenous languages are left underdeveloped.

The Nigerian government should learn from Sri Lanka, a former British colony like Nigeria, but in which the indigenous language press actually enjoys greater prestige and wider circulation than the English language press, especially through its National Languages Project. Newspapers with the largest circulation are in Sinhalese, the language of two-thirds of the million people. Two Sinhalese Sunday newspapers sell about 200,000 copies weekly, and the dailies have healthy circulation figures, as do the newspapers published in Tamil. While the circulation figures of the Sinhalese newspapers are rising, those of the English language press have been static or increasing at a much slower rate. Thus, the indigenous language newspapers in Sri Lanka have had a greater impact on the cultural life and political thinking of the population than their English language counterparts (Sunday, 1985).

In the United Republic of Tanzania, Swahili has been chosen as the official and national language. In 1970the ruling party, the Kenya National African Union (KANU), launched a speaking-Swahili campaign. Swahili is the African language spoken over the widest geographical area of Africa, but it was not the sole language spoken in Tanzania before its adoption as the national language. Today it has helped to cement the unity of the different tribes and races of the old Tanzania and Zanzibar and has helped to facilitate the propagation of President Nyerere's socialist ideology of Ujama. Similarly, in Sierra Leone, Krio has become the national language.

While the Federal government recognised the use of the three national languages in the National Assembly during Nigeria's Second Republic, there have been no deliberate efforts to reach the people at the grassroots through the use of indigenous language media.

The Nigerian media have played a significant role in the growth and development of the country. They helped to wrestle power from the colonial government and played a part in the exit of military rule and the enthronement of democracy. Therefore, the Nigerian media can play a significant role in the area of public enlightenment and publicity in order to change negative public perception about the census before the conduct of the next census, which is tentatively billed for 2016. As observed by one Guardian editorial:

> Conducting an effective and reasonably reliable census is not only important for a nation's internal needs. Given the imperatives of current interdependence of nations, whereby certain global governance objectives are set on the basis of universal data, it is important that a relatively high-population country like Nigeria should be able to provide sufficiently reliable demographic statistics on herself.

Ojete (2008) looks at the performance of the Nigerian press in the conduct of the 2006 national census. He points out that even though the media were used extensively via placement of adverts, jingles, commentaries, newspaper/magazine features, sponsored editorials, etc, there was little evidence that this use of media was employed for public enlightenment, and that a high level of distrust in the conduct of the census exercise was encouraged by the "several investigative features on the pages of newspapers and magazines and other analyses aired on the radios and TVs". Considering this, it is only safe to assume the reverse – if the media had published reports that had painted the census in a good light, then there would have been an increased level of acceptance of the results of the census, and a positive perception of census exercises among the populace.

However, if Nigerians are to be properly sensitised and mobilised towards the conduct of a reliable and credible national head count, that would be useful for sustainable development; the role of indigenous language media cannot be over emphasised, seeing that Western traditional media has not been that effective. In the words of Adeniyi and Bello (2005), Africa, including Nigeria, may remain underdeveloped if it continues to rely on European languages for discourse and advancement of learning. Indigenous media for the purpose of social mobilisation would help to reach the people at the grassroots level thereby eliminating the intermediary role of the opinion leaders, who may not adequately explain the motives of the government to the citizenry.

There are many reasons to advocate for indigenous media to play a more prominent role in engaging Nigerians in the build-up to the next population census, if that exercise is to be successful. Traditional/indigenous media draw their resonance from the fact that they are situated within the cultural frames that the people are comfortable with and will most likely accept. This strong association that indigenous media channels have with culture stands them in good stead to achieve enhanced audience exposure and message penetration.

There may, however, be deterrents to using traditional media. Nnabuihe and Ikwubuzo (2006) note that indigenous language media, especially newspapers, die almost immediately after they are established due to factors including a penchant for the elite (who can afford to buy and advertise in such newspapers) to prefer English newspapers. If there is no economic base for indigenous media to stand on so that they can be a platform for effective communication and engagement with the populace on such important issues as the census, then there is no point advocating for the increased use of indigenous media, as it can be argued: who reads/listens to them?

On the other hand, the success of programmes such as news broadcasts in local languages on mainstream radio and television stations, as well as the encouraging trend set by Globe Broadcasting and Communications Limited – through its inventive and interesting pidgin radio station, Wazobia FM, which has successfully grown to be one of the most preferred radio stations, even by the elite, in Lagos and other major cities in Nigeria (Kano, Abuja, Port Harcourt) – shows that there can be a strong following for indigenous language media, and this may prove to be a veritable platform to drive social mobilisation. This becomes even clearer in the wake of the report that the violence that claimed the lives of nine health workers in Kano State in February, 2013 was incited by a radio programme of Wazobia FM, which criticised polio vaccination as an attempt at reducing the Muslim population (Premium Times, 2013) – a clear indication that local media can be as much a force for good as for evil.

Recommendations

As the 2016 population census approaches, it is apparent that it is imperative to begin the process of informing, persuading, convincing and converting the Nigerian people to participate to the best of their ability to ensure the success of the exercise. The role that the media can play in the process has been clearly outlined and discussed in this paper, but in so doing, a few problem areas were identified, and thus recommendations are being proffered, so that the media (in this instance, indigenous media) can optimally play their surveillance correlation, and social mobilisation roles to great effect. The following points need to be noted:

1. The effectiveness of indigenous media hinges on the availability of an audience who are literate enough in the local language to read it or understand it when it is spoken. There is therefore a need for the government to engage actively in improving the level of literacy of the populace, urban and rural, to ensure that there is resonance.
2. Social responsibility is essential in the operation of the media, Western or indigenous. The case of Wazobia FM in Kano suggests that any irresponsible act on the part of the media in the enlightenment campaign in the run-up to the census will result in apathy and non-compliance, even violence.
3. Social media are growing stronger and stronger as platforms for advocacy and social mobilisation. The indigenisation of social media (to reflect the local language) will position them powerfully as the means to create awareness, build affinity, foster understanding, and hopefully, ensure that the right attitude to the census is achieved.
4. Clearly, there is also the need to adequately indigenise communication and advocacy content ahead of the exercise. At the moment, the 60–40 rule (60 percent communication content in English, and 40 percent indigenised or localised communication content) is not being adhered to strictly, but that can serve as a starting point; interpersonal communication efforts should also be in the local languages.
5. The efforts of local language stations such as Radio Lagos, which delivers its programmes in Yoruba, to provide local content programmes must be applauded. While efforts are being made to increase the level of local stations and communication content, the existing platforms must be harnessed optimally for advocacy through various forms of programmes in order to get Nigerians to buy into the idea of the headcount.

Conclusion

This chapter has looked at the history of census in Nigeria and the problems associated with it, especially the misconceptions surrounding it. It further highlights the importance of the mass media in sensitising and mobilising the people towards are liable and credible census in 2016. However, it is observed that although indigenous language media may contribute to effective communication and advocacy ahead of the census, it is not the only means by which that goal can be achieved. The chapter also urges that indigenous language media usage must be engaged strategically for this purpose and in keeping with contemporary trends of media innovation.

References

Adeniyi, H. and Bello, R. (2005) "Nigerian Media, Indigenous Languages and Sustainable National Development", a paper presented at the 9th Annual Conference of the African Language Teachers Association (ALTA) Yale University C.T.

Alabi, O. (2010) "The Role of Indigenous Language for Political Advertising – A Study of Ogun State 2007 Gubernatorial Election". *Communication Review*, Vol. 4, No. 24(2), August, 2010. pp. 47–55.

Amfani, A. H. (2009) "Indigenous Languages and Development in Nigeria". Retrieved Online from the Institute of Nigerian Languages, University of Nigeria (Aba Campus) at http://inlan.edu.ng/ampani.html, on 08/03/2013.

Amokeodo, T. and Isah, A. (July 1, 2011)"Census Crucial For Development – Tribunal Chairman". Retrieved Online from Leadership newspaper's online edition at http://www.leadership.ng/nga/articles/1287/2011/07/01/census_crucial_development_%E2%80%93_tribunal_chairman.html, on 08/03/2013.

Anaeto, S., Onabajo, O. and Osifeso, G. (2008) Models and Theories of Communication. Bowie, USA: African Renaissance Books Incorporated. p. 89.

Aziza, R. O. (2011) "Nigerian Languages' Teaching and Usage: Problems and Prospects". Retrieved Online from the Institute of Nigerian Languages, University of Nigeria (Aba Campus) at http://inlan.edu.ng/leadazipaper22011za.html, on 10/04/2013.

Beissinger, M. R. (2002) Nationalist Mobilization and the Collapse of the Soviet State. Cambridge: Cambridge University Press. p. 35.

Cline, A. (2013) "Language, Meaning, and Communication: The Role of Language in Constructing Arguments". Retrieved Online from http://atheism.about.com/od/critical thinking/a/language.htm, on 08/03/2013.

Daramola, I. (2005) *Mass Media and Society*. Lagos: Rothan Press Ltd. p. 62.

Ethusani, G. (2005) "Language and the Nigerian Project", a paper presented at the 2nd National Conference of the School of Language, Federal College of Education, Okene. July 20th–July 23rd, 2005.

Fadeyi, A. (2005) "Just before the Census", an article published in the Guardian May 5, 2005.

Haruna, I.B.M. (1976) "Mass Communication as Key to Peaceful Change in Society in Public Enlightenment" being a keynote address at a seminar for government information officers in Lagos, Nigeria in 1976. Lagos, Federal Ministry of Information.

Nnabuihe, C. and Ikwubuzo, I. (2006) "A Peep into News Publications and Reading Culture in Igbo Language of Nigeria" in A. Salawu (Ed.) *Indigenous*

Language Media in Africa. Lagos: Centre for Black and African Arts and Culture, (CBAAC), p. 42.

Ojete, E. (2008) "Social Mobilisation Role of the Nigerian Mass Media: A Study of the 2006 National Population Census", in F. I. A. Omu and G. E. Oboh (Eds) *Mass Media in Nigerian Democracy*. Ibadan: Stirling-Horden Publishers, p. 87.

Olukotun, A. (2006) "The Indigenous Language Press and Democratic Mobilisation in Nigeria: A Historical Structural Overview" in A. Salawu (Ed.) *Indigenous Language Media in Africa*. Lagos: Centre for Black and African Arts and Culture. p. 126.

Omu, F. (1978) Press and Politics in Nigeria (1859–1937). London: Longman, p. 67.

Parks, W. and Lloyd, L. (2004) *Planning Social Mobilization and Communication for Dengue Fever Prevention and Control: A Step-by-Step Guide*. New York: World Health Organisation.

Sperber, D. and Wilson, D. (1997) "Remarks on Relevance Theory and the Social Science". *Multilingua*, Vol. 16, pp. 145–151.

Sunday, A. O. (1985) "An Analysis of the Content, Orientation and Leadership of Irohin Yoruba", a B.Sc. Mass Communication Research Project submitted to the Department of Mass Communication, University of Lagos.

Sunday, O. (2012) *Media Usage, Personality Traits and Attitudes to HIV/AIDS: A Study of Agriculture Students in Selected Universities in South-West Nigeria*. Saarbrucken, Deutschland: Lambert Academic Publishing, pp. 15–16.

Uyo, A. (1987) Mass Media in a Nutshell. New York: Civilities International, p. 65.

Vesperini, H. (2007) "Nigeria's 2006 Census Results Resurrect North-South Rivalry". Retrieved online from http://naijanet.com/news/source/2007/jan/12/1000.html, on 08/03/2013.

Yahaya, I. (2010) "Identification and Consultation with Census Data Users: The Nigerian Experience", a paper presented at The Regional Seminar on Census Data Dissemination and Spatial Analysis, Nairobi, September 14–17, 2010.

Mc Quail, D (2007) "Mc Quail's Mass Communication Theory" (4th Edition) London: SAGE Publication Limited.

Newspapers

Premium Times (February 22, 2013) "NBC Suspends Operating License of Kano Wazobia FM". Retrieved Online from http://saharareporters.com/news-page/nbc-suspends-operating-license-kano-wazobia-fm-%E2%80%93-premium-times, on 09/03/2013.

Punch, January 11, 2005 p. 42

This Day, January. 30, 2005 p. 8

The Comet, January. 12, 2001

The Guardian, January. 5, 2001

9

The Dynamics of Language Politics in Religious Expression in African Indigenous Churches

Itohan Mercy Idumwonyi and Ijeweimen Solomon Ikhidero

Introduction

Language is never simply a neutral instrument to convey meaning, but rather a culturally subjective system reflecting peoples' worldview. The importance of speaking to a people in their own language cannot therefore be over-stressed, because language as a system of communicative symbol only receives meaning from its culture and society (Kinge'I 1999, 1). Twentieth-century Africa has produced diverse forms of Christian expression, the core of which is the emphasis on the Africanness of Christianity. Africans have rightly observed that their traditional languages, thought patterns, and worldviews can be adapted to make Christianity relevant to the African situation. How did this come about? Why did Africans turn to indigenous language in the expression of their Christian conviction? What were the main developments in this process?

Our aim in this chapter is to attempt to evince how African Independent Churches used indigenous language to creatively bring about a mutation that aided the sustenance of African Christianity; how they used language as a model to set African Christianity on a dynamic pedestal to construct a new tone for religious discourse; and how African Christians became protagonists in ways more inventive and rewarding for breaking down cultural barriers and creating a richer and more global Christianity. By employing the functional theory of language and engaging phenomenological, anthropological, historical, and critical methods, we will discuss the influence of translation on the phenomenal progression of African Christianity with particular reference to Nigeria.

Christianity in Africa, having been introduced by missionaries, was mostly founded and administered by them. The liturgy, hermeneutics, religious world view, etc. were designed according to Western thinking (Oduro 2006, 1). However, the dawning of a new era occasioned a role reversal. Christianity in Africa ceased to be the sole responsibility of missionary endeavor. For example, by March 1888, the first case of a split within a mission church took place, as some Yoruba laity led by Ladejo Stone in Nigeria withdrew from the Baptist Mission to found the Native Baptist Church (Ayegboyin 1997, 14). Scholars agree that, amongst other factors, the following necessitated this turn of events: opposition to missionary leadership; a desire for political and religious independence; the failure of missionaries to communicate using the appropriate indigenous language; the reluctance of missionaries to accept the worldview of colonized Africans; and, of course, the inability of natives to fully connect with missionary ideals because of language barriers (Oduro 2004, 26–40; Ayegboyin and Ishola 1997, 14). Thus, what became a common truism for Africans was: "If your God cannot speak to you in your own language, then He is a foreign God. For He is in every culture, He speaks and understands our indigenous language. The limits of my language mean the limits of my world" (Anonymous author).

These axioms were more than enough reason for Africans to creatively birth an advance African strand of Christianity. This observable development, which started with the first split, marked the inauguration of an unprecedented phenomenon with the African Indigenous (Initiated, Independent, and Instituted) Churches (AICs) in Nigeria and other parts of Africa (Ayegboyin and Ishola, 1997, 11). African Christians, with the creation of AICs, became the chief protagonists of cultural assertiveness and contributed largely to making African Christianity relevant and meaningfully contextual. For this, AICs earned the accolade "the signature tune of African Christianity" (Wilbert 2002, 19). For example, indigenous music became the hallmark of worship sessions in the AICs so that missionary hymns and hymnodies, which could never be sung exuberantly, were replaced. The vibrancy that natives exhibited whenever sermons were preached or songs were sang in indigenous languages, particularly in their own (mother tongue) language, suggested that they not only took pride in indigenous language but had a clearer understanding of their religious experience because of it. It was evident that Christianity never really made sense to the majority of Africans because they did not properly understood foreign – Latin or English – languages.

It is clear that, amongst the several tools imperialists used in the course of colonizing natives, language was a major scheme and tactic for domination. Concealed beneath the discursive layers of everyday language was their blueprint to "take over" and largely to define and subjectivize natives, who were openly thought of as "uncivilized" (Graham and Cole 2012, 1). In this case Africans saw in their indigenous language a radical tool to challenge and represent themselves differently and, in so doing, engaged in purposeful resistance. The usage of indigenous language in Christian liturgy in AICs became purely a struggle for the re-discovery of African religiosity and nationalism. It was for the emancipation and liberation of the Church in Africa from foreign political domination and ecclesiastical bondage. It was a struggle for an independent African Church where members could worship God in their own way and find satisfaction for their spiritual needs and aspirations.

A sketch analysis of language structure

Apart from claims of "spiritual encounter", language was a major force that propelled the growth and development of Independent Churches in Africa. It will be apt here to attempt a definition of the term "language". For a layperson, language is the coordination of comprehensible sounds, corresponding to symbolic signs, by which means a group of people wakes up to reality and interacts with itself. Linguists like Langacker see language as "a set of principles [that] relat[es] meaning [with] phonetic sequences" (1972, 1). For Catford, language is a "type of patterned human behavior" (1965, 1). What this means is that language is the science of communicating meaningful sounds. Meaning, in this regard, could be symbolically made up of semantics, syntactics, and pragmatics. If this is correct, then language acquisition becomes synonymous with access to meaning in its triple aspects: semantics, syntactics, and pragmatics. This view gains currency with Pieter Verburg when he states that "the whole sphere of language consists entirely and exclusively in the semantic dimensions of expression, effect and representation. Language is characterized by its three component functions" (1998, 1). Emmanuel Babalola usefully affirms that "communicative language is fundamentally concerned with making meaning in the language, whether by interpreting someone else's message, or by expressing one's own, or by negotiating when meaning is unclear" (2009, 45).

A language consists of a fixed collection of sentences (also called words) composed of a fixed set of letters or symbols. The inventory from which these letters are taken is called the alphabet, over which the language is defined. Language itself in oral/aural life on the lips and in the ears of its users, and writing becomes its visual symbolization. To realize that language is independent of writing, we have only to recall the many tribes, nations, and ethnic linguistic groups that scientists and anthropologists are keenly studying. These group members possess no form of writing but their languages still exist today. Leonard Bloomfield precisely substantiates this view when he asserts that "writing is not language, but merely a way of recording language by means of visible marks" (1966, 21). Thus, spoken language is common to all human beings, and all systems of writing are overtly based upon units of spoken language. Therefore, when we write the grammar of a language, we often supplement writing with special marks to indicate the stresses, pitches, and breaks of oral speech. Speech, therefore, is a primary element of language as all languages are spoken before they are written. It is common knowledge that a child speaks before he or she learns to write, and, as has been mentioned earlier, there are many languages that are yet to be written.

Linguists agree that language structures may contain any or all of the following: (i) phonology; (ii) morphology; (iii) syntax; and (iv) semantics. Phonology deals with the system of speech sounds employed by native speakers of a language; morphology deals with words and their meaningful parts; syntax treats the ways in which words are arranged to form sentences; and semantics deal with meaning (Aronoff and Fudeman 2005; Payne 2006; Shopen 2007). Our focus, here, is drawn to morphology and syntax.

Making reference to linguistic relativity in unqualified terms is thought to be a process that is inherent to the internal structure of a given language. It means that one's view of the world is dependent upon the language that one speaks; that is, the internal structure of a given language determines one's thoughts and behaviors. This notion gives credence to the axiomatic expressions stated above. It also suggests how impossible it is to translate everything from one language to another as the internal structure of one language may differ radically from another. What this means is that certain words, sounds, or signs are more difficult to express in some languages than in others. The knowledge and understanding of a language, which consequently facilitates the impulsive response of users, is, however, not devoid of some form of politicization.

The politics of the English language in Nigeria

The advent of the English (foreign) language in Nigeria is traceable to the colonial era. In contemporary Nigeria, the English language is a second language, having been acquired as a colonial legacy. It profits from being associated with a colonial power, is fixed within a different paradigmatic structure, and occupies a privileged position as a language in contact. The interference of elements in the structure of one language with those in the structure of another is the immediate result of language contact. Therefore, Nigeria is said to be bilingual as the majority of its citizens have knowledge of two or more languages. Scholars argue that the English language assumes a hegemonic position because of political, technological, cultural, administrative, educational, and economic reasons (Crystal 2004; Dollerup and Lindegaard 1994, 3).

Ignoring the fact that every language has its own peculiar narrative, the English language subsumes several languages and becomes the official language. For example, in a multilingual Nigeria, about 300 ethnic groups are presented and virtually each of these groups has at least two distinct languages. And these several language-like dialects can be said to be a replica of the Biblical Tower of Babel (Babalola 2009, 51), such that we can talk of Bini dialect, Esan dialect, Kalabari, Izon, Yoruba, Hausa, Igbo, Efik, Tiv, Isoko, etc., indicating a true reflection of a multi-dialectal community. Yet none of these, perhaps due to the pluralistic nature of Nigeria, seems to be any match for the English language – apparently they lack hegemonic power, prestige, and acceptance on a national level (Ayo, Ayo, and Thomas 1997, 36). The English language, having assumed this privileged place, holds sway over Nigerian indigenous languages. The argument advanced by some for it gaining the priority position is that it is a homogenizing tool for communicating across tribal and linguistic frontiers and has enabled the co-existence of several languages within the country (Mobolaji Adekunle 1994, 25). While this argument may be justifiable, it seems illogical. It seems to support the fact that some languages are superior or inferior to others. It is argued here that there is no single language that is either inferior or superior to another; each language is relevant and powerful within its cultural context. Languages, such as the English language, only acquire a preferred position by reason of social and political privileging. What this means is that social construction enables this general approval. We argue that if emphasis and attention is given to the teaching and learning of our mother tongue (which is considered informal and non-standard) before learning a second (English) language at school, then we will be privileged, coordinated bilinguals (Vyas and Patesh 2009, 1). This will help to check the extinction of many languages, which is already threatening several ethnic groups – even in rural and interior communities – where the English language is now being prioritized.

What is more, Randolph Quirk agrees and asserts that all human languages are equally complete and perfect as instruments of communication (1962, 44). The significance of this is that every language is as well equipped as any other to enable people to say what they want to say. It is, therefore, right to state that the essence of translation (otherwise known as vernacularization) in AICs cannot be overemphasized. Vernacularization became an apparatus for effective communication and for making sense of the day-to-day social relationship within the religious landscape. It eliminates the need for translation, which was the seal of missionary churches in Africa. This is, however, not without some complexities.

Language and the Complex Nature of Translation

The historical and cultural setting for the speakers of one language differs considerably from that of speakers of another language. It is not surprising that problems are encountered in translating a message from one language to another. M.A.K. Halliday affirms this position when he opines that the learning of a second (foreign) language is normally affected through patterns from our native language on the language one is learning (1964, 147). This is so because translation problems stem from the two-fold character of language. A language is both a cultural artifact and an instrument of cultural analysis, in the sense of the sumtotal of human activity. Just as there are definite differences between the material cultures of different human communities, so are there variations between languages. A Reverend Father, Christopher Ejizu, reiterates this fact in his narrative about a catechist in Igboland (Eastern Nigeria) who got the following answer from an old lady convert at the catechism examination for baptism: *"Uzo otu nmuo one di?"* – "How many types of spirit are there?" The old woman reportedly answered: *"Fa abakanu-abaka. Kedu ebe aga ebido-ebido guba? Aga ebido na Ulaga, m'obu Ike-udo, m'obu Ijele, mobu na Nw'-ikpo?"* – "They are legions. Where would one begin to enumerate? Would I mention *Ulaga*, or *Ike-udo*, or *Ijele*, or *Nw'ikpo*?" Obviously, the old lady misunderstood the question and answered with a list of local masquerades, which also are known as spirits in Eastern (Igboland) Nigeria.

The above analogy affirms Vyas and Patesh's position that translation problems have a dual nature – linguistic and cultural, reflecting the two-fold character of language (2009). The physico-cultural problem embraces environmental differences (such as different land and weather conditions, different flora and fauna), different items of food and clothing, as well as the non-correspondence of non-existence of certain colors, words, and moral, legal, and political matters, etc. Translation procedures such as analogies, similes, and metaphors as well as direct borrowings, often take care of these material and cultural differences. A striking example of the linguistic problem is the contrastive perception of physical action exemplified by the Anglo-Saxon and French languages. While English follows the film sequence, whereby each step of the action is documented and given equal emphasis, French focuses attention on the end result and relegates the modus operandi to secondary position. Another aspect of this phenomenon is to be found in the obligatory and optional features of language. These are not identical in every language.

Other typical linguistic problems include ambiguities due to the shared characteristics of two or more grammatical or lexical items in one language, with no corresponding ambiguities in another language where a single item has a wide range of contextual meanings. A particularly restricted meaning of an item in a language cannot similarly match with another. These and other features constitute a major problem in translation. Quite often, natural equivalents supply a ready solution, and alternative recourse may be made to the technique of loan translation. Consequently, the English ("standard") language, defined solely in syntactic terms, was meaningless to the natives until it was translated. In this sense, the point of interpretation, which assigns meaning to symbols of a formal language, provides the extension of symbols and strings of symbols of an object language.

It is therefore apparent that language is not a collection of separable and self-sufficient parts; rather, the parts are mutually dependent and mutually determined. In addition, languages vary at different degrees for individual learners, and English as a second language proved difficult for many natives. This complexity is explicitly revealed during liturgy where a foreign language is in use and several worshippers fail to respond. It was also the case that newcomers in the church spend a longer time in catechism, not because they were dull at learning but because of the complexities associated with learning a second language. This assertion is made here because visits to some mainline churches and AICs between June and July 2012 in Nigeria revealed that the response received from the same audience when an indigenous language (mother tongue) was in use was always overwhelmingly and incomparably more active than when the foreign language was in use. In a personal interview with some adherents in the mainline and African Independent churches, the consensus of opinion from respondents revealed that hearing a sermon or worshipping in an indigenous (*Nigerianized*) language provides better understanding of the message. It creates in them a feeling that they are relating with a God who knows and understands them. Some of the respondents remarked: "We can express ourselves meaningfully because we have the feeling that God is in our culture".

We observed that mainline churches like the St. Joseph (Roman Catholic) Church in Benin City, Nigeria, are involved in an acculturation project. A picture of Jesus and Mary (the mother of Jesus) depicted in the natives' attire and with the natives' skin color is an attestation to this fact. In addition to the above, the Edo Liturgical Group recently petitioned the Roman Catholic Church in Benin Archdiocese (Nigeria) to incorporate the celebration of Edo Mass in the diocese prime time, to make copies of the Edo Bible and Missal available in the church for all parishioners, and to use Edo songs at Mass. In addition, they requested that priests in the archdiocese should learn to celebrate Mass in the Edo language, and above all, that an Edo priest should be appointed as Archbishop of the Benin Metropolitan (See Simon Ebegbulem 2013). Is it therefore incorrect to suppose that the continuous use of a foreign language in liturgy was one of the concealed blueprints mapped out by missionaries to "take over" and subjectivize the natives? Without doubt, the problems associated with understanding the English language were some of the major reasons for the emergence of AICs.

The Emergence and Phenomenal Growth of African Indigenous Churches

The emergence of AICs to various degrees was characterized by a desire for African self-expression and freedom from missionary or parent-church control. This control pattern led to protest and increased attempts by natives to emancipate themselves from missionary imperialistic whims. Decisively, some indigenous people privileged the power of the Holy Spirit over and above doctrinal and dogmatic matters. This group of people had become so charismatic in nature that they needed an opportunity to fulfill their own "Zion" and drew more freely from elements found in traditional religions. Making reference to various forms of healing and revelation, they stressed the re-interpretation of Christianity in terms of the felt needs of indigenous cultures. These prophetic and charismatic figures became instrumental for the rise and growth of African Christianity as their evangelistic crusades, with the aid of indigenous media and language, proved effective for this goal (Turner 1963, 13). Notable amongst such charismatic prophets were Sophia Odunlami of the Precious Stone or Diamond Society, which originated from the St. Savior's Anglican Church, Ijebu-Ode (Ayegboyin 1978, 3), Prophets Christianah Abiodun Akinsowon and Moses Orímoládé of the Cherubim and Seraphim church in Western Nigeria, and Garrick Braids from Niger Delta in Nigeria (Ayegboyin and Ishola 1997; Fatokun 2006, 4).

While a number of the AICs prefer to be identified as "spiritual churches", others describe themselves as "messianic", while others prefer to be described as "prophetic-healing movements", solely because they are focused on the charismatic personality of a prophet who depends extensively on visions and prophecies. By this, they mirror their commitment in different activities, which by their affirmation are meant to invoke the Holy Spirit of God or are to be interpreted as a signal of His descent upon the worshippers (Baeta 1962, 1). What this means is that they claim a monopoly and appropriate the power and presence of the Holy Spirit. They feature healing, prophecies, the interpretation of prophecies and dreams, and, of course, the performance of diverse miracles as a sign of the baptism of the Holy Spirit (Adogame 2011). (The capitalistic effects of focusing on the charismatic personality of a sole prophet/founder who depends on visions and prophecies could be a subject for future study.)

The overwhelming presence of obviously unregistered churches in the streets of Nigeria confirms the phenomenal growth AICs since the first split. David Barrett, in his 1970 survey, revealed that the number of distinct denominations that were registered with the government was over 760 (1968, 78; Baur 1998, 493). It is interesting to note that these religious movements differ widely in style, organization, and attitude (Allan 2001, 107–113; Hackett 1987; Omoyajowo 1982).

They are tagged "African Churches" because they are founded in Africa by Africans and primarily for Africans. As noted earlier, one of the many factors that led to the emergence of AICs was the failure of the missionaries to take on board the culture, symbolized in language and taking sides with the doctrine of "un-translatability" of the second language into indigenous language. This presumption was, however, debunked by the AICs in the effective usage of indigenous languages to promote the growth of Christianity in Africa. Commenting on *"Ijo Orile Ede Adulawo Ti Kristi"* (National Church of Christ), founded in 1919 by the Reverend Adeniran Ake in Ibadan Nigeria, David Ogungbile asserts that such AICs pioneered the cause of African Christianity through the recognition and use of African linguistic genres in their liturgical practices and really made Christianity relevant to Africans (2001, 77). Corroborating this stance, R. C. Mitchell and Harold Turner suggest that many of these churches sprang up as a means to reform and make Christianity more relevant to the day-to-day needs of African life (1966, 45).

From the end of the 19th century and the early part of the 20th century, quite a number of indigenous (prophetic) churches emerged in Nigeria and other African countries. Besides the inability for translation, the overwhelming socio-economic, political, and "spiritual" problems that ravaged the continent also helped to raise millions of adherents for the AICs. This, however, is not the focus of the chapter.

Theorizing Language, Translation, and Culture

Language ideology is explicit or implicit representation in a social world. It helps to organize individuals and institutions and build relationships between human beings and across culture. Language explores the ways in which ideas intersect with it, and is shaped by point of view. It focuses on the way people encode their beliefs and biases in a wide range of different media, including narrative fiction, cultural and religious experiences, etc. (Simpson 1993, i).

The relationship between language and culture, and language and cultural identity were not discovered in the 20th century. For example, the model given by Roman colonial practice with regard to language was never to despise the language of the conquered, nor did they force conquered people, by all means, to use the Latin language. This practice, as Burke, Crowley and Girvin suggest, was a lesson that the English colonists applied with enthusiasm (2000, 1–2). It is thus obvious that language and culture have long been intertwined, and the link between them is based on particular theoretical suppositions that are traceable in specific historical examples.

Language has been a constitutive force in the construction of subjectivity, as well as social and cultural being. It validated sight for the colonized so that they were able to engage with the categories and forms of representation that furthered their political and cultural ends (Burke, Crowley, and Girvin 2000, 8). Amazingly, the turn to indigenous language provided a new prospect, which occasioned a major impact on the construction of cultural identity for indigenes. This is so because finding and articulating a voice was key for many previously silenced people insisting on and gaining cultural identity. It is correct to affirm that, no matter how unfashionable a culture and language might seem, the usage of indigenous languages has continued to be a priority and a major issue in Africa (Burke, Crowley, and Girvin 2000, 9).

In language and cultural theory, the problem of structure and agency revolves around the extent to which language is viewed as a structure that orders and defines social reality. These also constitute humans as social beings and map their world as a social world. For instance, some theorists suggest that language determines the ways in which we perceive the world around us. This emphasizes our potential to engage creatively with our society. Language is expression. That is, it is a vehicle for transforming ideas into words (Burke, Crowley, and Girvin 2000, 13). Expression – in this context, translation – constitutes the act of reproducing representations and the shaping of experience. It also operates in the realm of particulars, producing representations of specifics, rather than abstract concepts. It brings a unique and individual object of understanding (Burke, Crowley, and Girvin 2000, 16).

Translating is the process of rendering another language into one's own (or another) language in order to produce an enhanced understanding of a foreign language. This theory of translation is distinct and sufficiently important to merit special attention because of the innovative role it played in the formation and expansion of African Independent Churches. In the wake of the politicization that trailed the monopolization of churches by missionaries, Africans devised a means to recreate themselves. The bond of hegemonic language used by colonizers could not continue to hold sway over Africans. This radical shift occasioned a change in the course of history: Africans, in addition to the "standard" language of the missionizing colonizers, started to use indigenous languages; their voice could now be heard. Indigenous language became instrumental for showcasing AICs in the public sphere.

Functional Role of Language, Translation and its Implications for African Christianity

In this section, we shall be considering the functional role of language in these fundamental social and religious institutions. Language acquisition, simply put, is access to meaning or semanticization. And translation resolves itself into the transfer of meaning from one linguistic system to another. In this case, the act of translating stresses the role of language as a communication code through which meaning is expressed. It also necessitates some unification of the cultural context, which is an invaluable aid in reducing extreme cultural and linguistic differences. Besides, they have both established the fact that no language is completely "unmixed". For, in most cases, the lexicon of a language consists of three layers: a substratum, representing the surviving elements of an autochthonous often prehistoric language defeated by the language of the victorious invaders; then, a super-stratum, representing the language of the invaders, which disappeared in the language of the autochthonous population; and an ad-stratum, made up of the elements of a foreign language absorbed in border districts, where the population is partly mixed, and supplemented by "learned" borrowings. This means, in effect, that language partakes in varying degrees in the common heritage of humans.

Language is a part of the non-material culture and enables the construction of a society. A common language is one of the unifying tools that impose order upon human experience. It sensitizes humans to certain kinds of experience as it simplifies the complexity of experience in ways that allow us to make sense of categories, bringing peace and understanding. This is evident in the ways indigenous people (when they are outside their immediate community) respond in a very high and spirited manner whenever sermons are preached or songs are sang in an indigenous language that they understand. What this means is that indigenous people take pride in their own mother tongue, particularly during religious worship. In addition, it is easier for religious ideas and concepts to spread among people who speak related languages than with neighboring people who speak entirely different languages. This attitude, absolutely, contributed not only to the emergence but to the phenomenal growth of African Independent Churches.

Lamin Sanneh, in his groundbreaking book, *Translating the Message,* for instance, underscored the role of translation in breaking down cultural barriers and creating a richer and more global Christianity. Sanneh argued that the very act of translating the message of Christianity into the indigenous cultural context carried with it the supposition that the collective truth of Christianity could be applied to any given culture's set of traditions (2009). With this, Sanneh brought the missionaries into deep interaction with the strengths of the indigenous cultures. A foremost consequence of this interaction was that it opened a *novel vista* for indigenous people to understand that God is existent in indigenous cultures and can hear natives in their indigenous languages. This idea greatly confirms the reason for the axiomatic expressions noted above. Sanneh is insightful when he notes that translation was and continues to be a central part of cultural renewal in the face of the unrelenting assault of colonialism (Sanneh 2009). Consequently, African Christians were able to reinvent themselves in the public sphere and have since continued to remain formidable in global Christianity.

With the search for an indigenous renewal of faith and interaction of African Christianity with global Christianity, there has been an emergence of a new religiosity. Nigerians, like other Africans, no longer feel like strangers since AICs have introduced patterns that resonate with their indigenous language and cultural values. Missionary religious hymns and tunes, which have little rhythm without bodily movement, were dull and had less meaning for Africans, who were accustomed to ecstatic religious practices. These hymns are now being replaced with *"Nigerianized"* pop songs, which are often translated into the vernacular. In addition, drums, local flutes, gongs, clapping of hands and tapping of feet, etc. are appreciated and used a lot in these churches.

The methods of worship in these churches have taken on the symbolic traditions of the past (referred to as "indigenization of Christianity"). Moreover, new rites are being created, which are in harmony with the Nigerian (African) mentality. In the light of this development, a new Nigerian (African) religiosity has added several elements to Christian worship. The *Ijo Adulawo* (an AIC in Nigeria), for example, uses *"iwure"* in place of *"adura"*, as *adura* is considered an incorrect translation of "prayer". To the Ijo Adulawo, *iwure* conveys the intrinsic quality of making a strong petition and an interaction between humans and the spiritual being(s). Closely connected with *iwure* is the response to prayer that is rendered in English as "amen" and in indigenous parlance as "a*min*". For the Ijo Adulawo and the Holy *Aruosa* Church in Nigeria, *amin* (amen) lacks its literary and mystical connotations; it is *short* of conveying the affirmative implication of *"ase"* or *"ise"*, a Yoruba and Bini (Nigerian) word and traditional response to prayer.

Scholars have argued that *ase* (or *ise)* has strong elements of order, command, power, bidding, effect, consequence, and imprecations. The psychology of the Yorubas and the Binis, like most Africans, is such that a word has an inherent efficacious power, which, when uttered, certainly sanctions the request so that a compulsive and unfailing effect is guaranteed. To the Yoruba and the Bini people, *amin* seems to be less affirmative and less compulsive than *ase* and *ise*. The use of *amin* is regarded as an alteration of the Yoruba/Bini thought patterns. The insistence on the maintenance of the traditional response explains the use of *ase/ise* (Ogungbile, 73). By implication, traditions are being preserved and used in Christian worship so that Christianity is rejuvenated and accepted by tribal people (Isichei 2004, 191). Future study should highlight the privileged use of indigenous languages in the Oba of Benin Holy *Aruosa* Church.

Conclusion

In this chapter, it is argued that language is a powerful vehicle of culture. Language symbolizes the common beliefs and psychological make-up of the community from which it springs. The chapter portrays how African-oriented Christian Churches use indigenous language and culture as a medium to gain a meaningful relationship with the Divine (God), and to appeal to African emotionalism as opposed to already existing Western-oriented Christianity. Today, African Independent Churches have actualized the dynamics of the vernacular for the development and expansion of African Christianity and culture. The daunting response from religious adherents when liturgy is performed in indigenous languages confirms the fact that God really speaks to indigenous people in their own language; God is not foreign, He is, indeed, in every culture and understands indigenous language.

With the translation of Christianity into the indigenous cultural context, cultural boundaries are dismantled and a richer and more global Christianity is produced so that today African Christianity is in continuous contact with world Christianity. What this means is that the collective truth of Christianity is being applied and made meaningful to any given culture, irrespective of whether or not the language is standard. Since the primary function of language is to communicate meaning, translation further amplifies the function of language by ensuring the transmission of meaning across many linguistic barriers.

Finally, because the English language presently enjoys the status and potency that no African language enjoys, it will be an uphill task to move it aside. This is acceptable because it has some value; what is needed is the proper and continuous training of native agents who would translate the English language into indigenous languages. Native agents should be taught, when necessary, how to meet our varied cultures in their particularity as we continue to grapple with changing times.

References

Adekunle, Mobolaji. 1972. "Multilingualism and Language Function in Nigeria" in *African Studies Review*. Vol. 15(2) pp. 185–207.

Adogame, Afeosemime U. 2011. *Who is Afraid of the Holy Ghost?: Pentecostalism and Globalization in Africa and Beyond*. Religion in Contemporary Africa Series. Trenton, NJ: Africa World Press.

Anderson, Allan. 2001. Types and Butterflies: An African Initiated Churches and European Typologies. *International Bulletin of Mission Research*. http://www.amazon.com/Types-Butterflies-Typologies-International-Missionary/dp/B000815NZ6.

Aronoff, Mark, and Kirsten Fudeman. 2005. *What is Morphology?* Malden, MA: Blackwell.

Ayegboyin, Deji. 1978. *Religion, Medicine and Healing.* Lagos, Free Enterprise Publishers. Religious Studies, Vol. 12, No. 1.

Ayegboyin, Deji and Ishola, Ademola. 1997. *African Indigenous Churches:* Lagos, Nigeria: Greater Heights Publications.

Ayo, Bamgbose, Banjo Ayo, and Andrew Thomas. 1997. *New Englishes: A West African Perspective.* Trenton, NJ: Africa World Press.

Babalola, Emmanuel Taiwo. 2007. "Communicative Language Teaching and English Language Teaching in Nigeria". In Singh, A. k. *Teaching English as a Second Language.* New Delhi: Asoke K. Ghosh.

Baeta, C. G. 1962. *Prophetism in Ghana, a Study of Some "Spiritual" Churches.* World Mission Studies. London: SCM Press.

Barrett, David B. 1968. *Schism and Renewal in Africa; An Analysis of Six Thousand Contemporary Religious Movements.* Nairobi, Kenya: Oxford University Press.

Baur, John. 1998. *2000 Years of Christianity in Africa: An African History, 62–1992.* Nairobi, Kenya: Paulines.

Bloomfield, Leonard. 1966. *Language.* New York: Holt, Rinehart and Winston.

Burke, Lucy, Tony Crowley, and Alan Girvin. 2000. *The Routledge Language and Cultural Theory Reader.* Politics of Language. London, New York: Routledge.

Catford, J. C. 1965. *A Linguistic Theory of Translation; an Essay in Applied Linguistics Language and Language Learning.* London: Oxford University Press.

Christopher, I. Ejizu. The Influence of African Indigenous Religions on Roman Catholicism, the Igbo Example. http//www.afrikaworld.net/afrel/ejizu-atrcath.htm (accessed on September 22, 2013).

Crystal, David. 2004. *The Language Revolution. Themes for the 21st Century.* Cambridge ; Malden, MA: Polity.

Dollerup, Cay, and Annette Lindegaard. 1994. *Teaching Translation and Interpreting 2: Insights, Aims, Visions: Papers from the Second Language International Conference, Elsinore, Denmark, 4-6 June 1993.* Benjamins Translation Library; V. 5; Variation: Amsterdam ; Philadelphia: J. Benjamins.

Ebegbulem, Simon. 2013. "Rebellion in the Church: Binis at Daggars Drawn with Catholic Archbishops". In *Vanguard* Newspaper http://www.vanguardngr.com/2013/07/rebellion-in-the-church-binis-at-daggers-drawn-with-catholic-archbishop/ posted on July 27, 2013 (accessed on November 31, 2013).

Fatokun, Samson. 2006. "Women and Leadership in Pentecostal Churches". *Studia Historiae Ecclesiasticae* 32(3): 193–205.

Graham, Linda J. and David R. Cole. 2012. *The Power in/of Language.* Educational Philosophy and Theory Special Issues. Chichester, West Sussex; Malden, MA: Wiley-Blackwell.

Hackett, Rosalind I. J. 1987. *New Religious Movements in Nigeria.* African Studies; V. 5; Lewiston, NY: E. Mellen Press.

Halliday, M. A. K. 1964. "The Users and Uses of Languages". In J. Fishman (Ed.). *Readings in the Sociology of Language.* Mouton: The Hagu, pp. 139–169.

Isichei, Elizabeth Allo. 2004. *The Religious Traditions of Africa: A History.* Westport, CT: Praeger.

Kinge'I, Kitula. 1999. Language Development Research in 21st Century Africa. *African Studies Quarterly,* 3(3): 3. http://web.africa.ufl.edu/asq/v3/v3i3a3.htm.

Langacker, Ronald W. 1972. *Fundamentals of Linguistic Analysis*. New York: Harcourt Brace Jovanovich.

Robert Cameron, Mitchell and Turner, Harold W.. 1966. *A Comprehensive Bibliography of Modern African Religious Movements*. Evanston, IL: Northwestern University Press.

Oduro, Thomas. 2004. "Christ Holy Church International (1947–2002): The Challenges of Christian Proclamation in a Nigerian Context". (Unpublished PhD dissertation, St. Paul: Luther Seminary Library).

Oduro, Asante Thomas. 2006. "Theological Education and Training: Challenges of African Independent Churches in Ghana." In Journal of African Institued Churches Theology. Vol. II(I) (September); 1–15.

Ogungbile, O. David. 2001. "The Dynamics of Language in Cultural Revolution and African Spirituality". *Nordic Journal of African Studies*, 10(1): 66–79.

Omoyajowo, J. Akinyele. 1982. *Cherubim and Seraphim: The History of an African Independent Church*. New York: NOK Publishers International.

Payne, Thomas Edward. 2006. *Exploring Language Structure: A Student's Guide*. Cambridge; New York: Cambridge University Press.

Quirk, Randolph. 1962. *The Use of English*. New York: St Martin's Press.

Sanneh, Lamin O. 2009. *Translating the Message: The Missionary Impact on Culture*. 2nd ed., rev. and expanded. American Society of Missiology Series ; No. 42. Maryknoll, NY: Orbis Books.

Shopen, Timothy. 2007. *Language Typology and Syntactic Description*. Cambridge; New York: Cambridge University Press.

Simon, Ebegbulem 2013. "Rebellion in the Church: Binis at Daggers Drawn with Catholic Archbishop". In *Vanguard Online*, July 27, 2013. http//www. allafrica. com/stories/201307291478.htm (accessed on September 22, 2013).

Simpson, Paul. 1993. *Language, Ideology, and Point of View*. Interface Series; London; New York: Routledge.

Turner, H. W. 1963. "Chart of Modern African Religious Groups". In V. E. Hayward (Ed.). *African Independent Church Movements*. London: Edinburgh House Press.

Verburg, Pieter A. 1998. *Language and its Functions: A Historico-critical Study of Views Concerning the Functions of Language from the Pre-humanistic Philology of Orleans to the Rationalistic Philology of Bopp*. Amsterdam Studies in the Theory and History of Linguistic Science. Series III, Studies in the History of the Language Sciences; V. 84. Amsterdam: Benjamins.

Vyas, Manish A, and Yogesh L Patesh. 2009. *Teaching English as a Second Language: A New Pedagogy for a New Century*. New Delhi: Asoke K. Ghosh.

Gerald J. Pilay 2002. "World Christianity and the New Historiography: History and Global Interconnections". In Wilbert, R. Shenk *Enlarging the Story: Perspectives on Writing World Christian History*. Maryknoll, NY: Orbis Books.

10
Poverty, Prophets and Politics: 'Marxist' Discourses in Malawi Music, 1994–2012

John Lwanda

Introduction

Malawi: The geography and the socio-political environment

Malawi, a British protectorate from 1891, achieved independence in 1964. Then, under Dr Hastings Kamuzu Banda, Malawi quickly became a one-party state, which was highly intolerant of dissent, both written and oral (Short, 1974; Lwanda, 1993 and 2009; Ross, 2009). It had a 'feudal' political and economic climate, with an economy exploiting low wages (LESOMA, 1981, pp. 82–85; Pryor, 1990; Mhone, 1992, pp. 1–33), in which expression of socio-economic dissatisfaction was contained by political repression (Africa Watch, 1990).

A number of factors and events that shaped the role of music in social protest in Malawi include: culture; colonialism; the two World Wars; poverty; gender inequality (Gilman, 2001, pp. 43–64); post-colonial dictatorship; and a limited educational system, leading to low national literacy rates between 1891 and 2009, which perpetuates Malawi's oral culture. Given the repressive colonial and post-colonial governance and government control of the electronic and print media between 1964 and 1994, protests about social conditions and poverty, for example, could only be subtle and oral (Rotberg, 1966; Ranger, 1975; Lwanda, 2008b, pp. 26–40; Lwanda, 2008b, pp. 71–101; Lwanda, 2011, pp. 347–351).

It is significant that, in the context of race and class history, one of the first nationalist uprisings in the African British Empire occurred in Malawi, led by John Chilembwe in 1915. These protests were provoked by land, race and socio-economic issues (Shepperson and Price, 1958). Between 1915 and the establishment of the Nyasaland African Congress in 1944, partly due to weak leadership and state control, protests tended to be diffuse and localised at community or area levels, often using music, both traditional and popular (cf. Kaspin, 1993, pp. 34–57). Orality, in the form of music (cf. Kamlongera et al., 1992), gave an equality of protest, however muted, to most Malawi societies and groups.

Dr Banda's regime used women (*mbumba*) praise singers as part of his legitimating construct (Lwanda, 1993; Chirwa, 2001, pp. 1–27; Semu, 2002, pp. 43–64). These *mbumba* praise singers were part of the Malawi Congress Party Women's League-led party activists, volunteers and those who felt obliged or 'forced' to sing for the party in the context of a one-party state. Dr Banda often claimed to be the *Nkhoswe* (traditional male guardian for women) Number One for all women in Malawi. Some men did feel that the *mbumba* movement had a slight emasculating effect on men in general. For example the poet Jack Mapanje has an old man observing the youth dance and feels impotent to correct their mistakes (cf. Mapanje, 1981, p. 12). We can deduce that this fear arises from the prevailing political atmosphere.

Although his dictatorship constrained both written and oral media from the late 1960s, men, particularly, the young, who were marginalised from his patronage system, attempted to develop a counter voice to the Malawi Congress Party *mbumba* 'praise' music. Politically marginalised, usually with only primary education and unemployed and poor, the youth found a voice through the creation of a '*jazz*' band tradition. Jazz was a syncretic musical form, combining rural, traditional, regional and Western elements, mostly played on home-made instruments. They used this music in a coded subtle manner that evaded the censors to critique Banda's governance and to air grievances. Live, unrecorded performances, high syncopation, free-form lyrics and the use of metaphors, jokes and duplicate lyrics to suit the occasion provided a 'voice'. Songs like '*Mitala*' (Polygamy) by Mikoko Band, for example, critiqued the neglect of the rural people by Dr Banda's regime: 'I have two wives [yet] I earn nothing!' (Mikoko Band, c.1977). Yet they could be played on the national radio. This was achieved by the musicians using the comedic pretence of being polygamous just so that they could declare their poverty.

Jazz bands also spearheaded an alternative social movement to the hegemony of the one-party Youth League. From the early 1970s, musicians played in bottle stores, bars and canteens, and public entertainment places exploited radio cassettes. These places became centres where, with some due difference to the censors, all kinds of available music could be played, breaking the monopoly of the Malawi

Broadcasting Corporation (MBC) (cf. Chirambo, 2006, pp. 109–126). They also became centres of increased social interaction and communication – both oral and musical – a significant alternative in a dictatorship (Lwanda, 2008c).

The language landscape

Malawi uses English (understood, to a varying extent, by over 50 per cent of the population) as its primary official language and Chewa (understood by over 70 per cent of the population) as its 'secondary but national language' language (cf. Kayambazinthu, 1998a, pp. 369–439). After independence, Dr Banda leveraged Chewa over the other languages in an attempt at creating a national language and identity; in this regard, the language previously termed Nyanja in Malawi (and also spoken in Zambia, Zimbabwe and Mozambique) during the colonial era became Chewa (cf. Kishindo, 2001, pp. 261–283). There are eight ethnic groupings of various sizes, with the Chewa/Nyanja/Man'ganja group being the largest. In terms of music lyrics, the most *popular* singers use mostly Chewa, then Yao, Tumbuka/Tonga, English or Lomwe, in that order. Market forces determine that Chewa is the language used most commonly. Because most Malawi languages are of Bantu origin, it is fairly easy for the majority of listeners to follow what is being sung (except in the case of a few languages like Lomwe). Code switching is common (cf. Kayambazinthu, 1998b), pp. 19–43).

Theory I: The public sphere

The chapter builds on (my) previous work, summarised here, exploring the nature and role of 'Habermas's notion of the public sphere' (Habermas, 1981) in a developing nation like Malawi, which has a multiplicity of languages (Lwanda, 2008a). Given the English/urban language, on the one hand, versus the urban/vernacular and rural, on the other hand, does one argue for two or more public spheres or various compartments of the main one, each accessible to a particular grouping? This is particularly critical given the dominance of English, which colonialism bequeathed to Malawi (Matiki, 2001, pp. 201–218). An immediate question is how, if at all, these spheres communicate and compare in the import with each other and with external public spheres. Because of the nature of Malawi society, with its minority literate, English-speaking elite and majority poor, illiterate, vernacular-speaking peasantry, a comparison of inputs from literature versus orality can be seen to be unequal. Although most inputs into the public sphere are oral and vernacular – a daily discourse that reflects basic socio-economic realities as well as moral and higher concerns – the official and 'ruling' public sphere is in English (Lwanda, 2003, pp. 113–126).

Habermas's original public sphere had a large element of orality – he specified debate, discussion and associations (Habermas, 1991). In Malawi these would include anything from the modern internet chat room down to the village *bwalo* (open air meeting under a mango or baobab tree). Exploiting Habermas's concern about issues of representation and power, we can examine issues of a public sphere 'made up of private people gathered together as a public and articulating the *needs of society* to/with the state' (Habermas, 1991, p. 176). This concept of 'private people gathered together' has the communal ring to it that is characteristic of Malawi rural life. Habermas's distinction between the 'life world' (a person's immediate environment) and the 'system' (the state apparatus and the economy) is also highly relevant in an atmosphere where the state and other 'powerful systems are extremely strong compared to the average peasant'.

Rutherford, in his examination of the advertising industry, which exploits Habermas's work, argued that the success of a public sphere depends on four factors: 'access; the degree of autonomy ensuring that citizens are free from coercion; participation on an equal footing; and a quality of participation' (Rutherford, 2000, p. 18). In the Malawi context, English is leveraged higher than the vernacular languages, creating inequality in the official public sphere.

A second problematic factor in Malawi's public sphere dynamics is the role of powerful 'systems' and 'system' groups like media owners, government and government agencies, religious organisations and non-governmental organisations (NGOs), particularly those involved in advocacy; the English language gives them power to command the global and local media. I have elsewhere exploited Ekeh's argument to explain the creation of two major public spheres in Malawi, the English and the vernacular (Lwanda, 2008a, pp. 71–101). Mustapha expands on this to argue about 'a multiplicity' of public spheres (Mustapha, 2012, pp. 27–41).

Between 1964 and 1994 the state certainly attempted to fill the public sphere with its state occasions and state-sponsored and sanctioned theatre, *mbumba* music, traditional dances, numerous rallies and repeated presidential 'oral' speeches. This 'manipulative publicity' (Habermas 1991, pp. 178–245) has continued even after Dr Banda's death. The musician Nkasa posited his '*Anamva*' (They Heard) into the public sphere, a song alluding to the 'lies of a chief', to highlight, and counteract, the then President Bakili Muluzi's use of 'manipulative publicity'.

It will be argued that the 'class' struggles between 'bourgeois' capitalism and the labouring classes in post-Banda Malawi, as reflected in popular music lyrics, have features that suggest that musicians see the class and economic struggles in Malawi in terms that are reminiscent of Marxist discourses seen elsewhere.

Theory II: The Marxist discourse

To talk about Marxist discourse (cf. Marx, 1867) in a country where, less than 20 years previously, the mere mention of the word 'Karl Marx' was tempting 'detention without trial' may be surprising. Some academics and scholars argue that Malawi has only ever had one Marxist theorist, Dr Attati Mpakati, who was killed by Dr Banda's agents in 1983 (cf. Searle, 1980, pp. 389–401). Mpakati argued that, after independence, Malawi turned into a neo-colonial state with a corrupt, privileged elite exploiting the masses (Mpakati, 1973, pp. 33–68).

This chapter exploits Lefebvre's arguments in *Everyday Life in the Modern World* (1984) and his *Critiques of Everyday Life I* (1991), *II* (2002) and *III* (2005), a work based on his experience of a France that was 'urbanising' and developing, as Malawi is currently doing, a consumer capitalism in the post-war years. In *Everyday Life in the Modern World*, Lefebvre discusses the everyday conditions of people whose lives are affected by decisions in which they have no say and by dominant groups that have an interest in keeping things that way (Lefebvre, 1984, pp. 57). This analysis resonates with Malawi, a country that is undergoing significant urbanisation and also shows a feudal pattern of income distribution, power relationships and working conditions. The gap between Malawi's minority acquisitive, dominant elite and its majority 'wretchedly' poor, and how the ruling elite attempts to contain the status quo, are relevant to Lefebvre's arguments:

> The state is now built upon daily life; its base is the everyday. The traditional Marxist thesis makes the relations of production and the productive forces the 'base' of the ideological and political superstructures. Today – that is to say, now that the state ensures the administration of society, as opposed to letting social relations, the market and blind forces take their course – this thesis is reductionist and inadequate. In the course of major conflicts and events, the relations of domination and reproduction of these relations have wrested priority over the relations of production that they involve and contain. (Lefebvre, 2005, p. 123).

A further attraction of Lefebvre's work is its arguments that language and linguistics have a role to play in peoples' attempts to address their problems (1984, p. 20). In relation to music, Lefebvre notes:

> Does music express the secret nature of everyday life, or compensate, on the contrary, for its triviality and superficiality? Does it serve as a link between 'inner' and outer life, and, once such a link has been established, can it be forceful and meaningful, given the ever increasing split – now practically structural – dividing the quotidian and non-quotidian, the growing pettiness of everyday life? (1984, p. 20).

The significance of Malawi music, and I argue that lyrics here are part of the 'music', is part of the attraction of Lefebvre's argument.

Interestingly, Lefebvre also noted that the consumer society, unchecked, eventually evolves into a terrorist society.

> A terrorist society is the logical and structural outcome of an over repressive society (Lefebvre, 1971, p. 147, 1984 reprint).

Repression, in one form or another and to a greater and lesser extent, has been a feature of Malawi since independence in 1964.

Chirambo, in examining Dr Banda's (and his successors), used Gramsci's 'concept of hegemony' as a balance between using force and popular 'cultural acquiescence' and complicity in building and sustaining hegemonic dictatorship (Chirambo, 2006, pp. 109–126; Chirambo, 2009, pp. 77–94). Post-one-party-state rulers have tried to emulate this formula within a 'transitional democracy'. This work can be viewed as describing the attempts of musicians, using music, to reclaim part of the cultural role to critique and protest (Lwanda, 2011, pp. 347–351).

Music lyrics during the transition to 'democracy'

Between 1991 and 1994, popular music groups were used by both Dr Banda and the opposition groups. Musicians reworked their songs and traditional and historical songs and chants to either criticise the opposing side or to support their own side's argument. Opposition groups, then claiming to represent workers' interests, for example, criticised the *Chitukuko Cha Amai m'Malawi* (CCAM) (the Malawi Congress Party's women's movement), of which more elsewhere (Lwanda, 1996), by comparing it to *Thangatha* (the colonial indentured labour system). They sang

Kodi CCAM nchiani? (What is CCAM?)
Thangatha! ([If not] exploitative cheap labour!)
(UDF party workers, 1993)

In reply, Dr Banda's supporters, claiming Dr Banda's 'God-given right to rule for life', denounced those on the multi-party side as 'opposing the will of God'.

After the 1994 multi-party elections, musicians were quick to realise that promises made by largely middle-class politicians had been politic. Even as the multi-party dispensation, under the new President, Bakili Muluzi, was still being celebrated by writers, a number of musicians had already found alternative voices and were warning of disappointments already evident. Saleta Phiri had, as early as 1995, noted, in song, *'zinthu zasintha, malamulo sanasinthe'* (things have changed but the laws remain the same). These sentiments were echoed in the following year by Overton Chimombo in *'Zasintha'* (Things Have Changed).

As the new rulers accumulated wealth – mostly 'extraverted' from government coffers, at 'selfish speeds and levels' – and corruption accelerated, hospitals deteriorated, school standards fell and prices rose, musicians, some of whom had reappropriated traditional titles like *alangizi* (counsellors) and *aphungu* (prophets) as self-legitimation for their societal roles, started to sing more openly about social issues. Lucius Banda appointed himself the 'people's soldier' (Chirambo, 2002, pp. 103–122); Dennis Phiri, Overton Chimombo, Malume Bokosi, Charles Nsaku, Lawrence Mbenjere and others became *alangizi*; and Joseph Nkasa took the mantle of *phungu* (messenger or prophet). These personae harked back to 'griots' (oral historians and communal wisdom carriers), *imbongi* (the praise singers) and communal counsellors. Traditionally, these roles, like court jesters, ensure a degree of immunity from rulers. That the point of the music was sometimes in the lyrics can be gauged from one of the younger *alangizi*, Malume Bokosi. He stated:

Musatanganidwe ndi zing'wenyeng'wenye ayi, koma mvetsetsani uthenga wanga ndi chidwi (Don't be distracted by the instrumentation, but listen to my message critically) (Bokosi, 2006).

Passing messages was his main aim.

By the end of 1995, the Bakili Muluzi regime, like the one-party regime before it, came to be seen by musicians as government by *mabwana* (governors) *achikulire* (big men). The same thing was to happen to the Mutharika regime in 2005. In the context of a weak 'compromised' opposition and 'timid' print and broadcast media, musicians became powerful oral voices protesting at the economic, social and political injustices of the poor. Interestingly, musicians often used code switching (cf. Kayambazinthu, 1998b, pp. 19–43), using English for harmless or comedic phrases and 'deep' vernacular, proverbs, metaphors and other invented modes of social discourse for problematic subjects. Code switching is common in the Malawi public sphere. It is found in the political arena where politicians may choose to address an audience of 'donors' and recipients at the same time. President Muluzi was given to thanking the donors in English and then in the next breath, in the vernacular and much to his audience's delight, proclaiming that he would not tire of asking for aid from them. Code switching is also seen in intergenerational contexts where the youth do not want their elders to hear their 'talk'. Kayambazinthu has also noted that code switching is seen in gender-related contexts (ibid).

After the multi-party hangover

This chapter concentrates on the 1994–2012 period for two main reasons: prior to 1994 there was a strict censorship of musical lyrics and in 2011 the nearest to a post-Banda workers' revolt occurred.

Significantly, after elite Malawians had 'chanted themselves hoarse', 'lit another fire' (Mapanje, 1981, p. 18) and sank into 'multiparty complacency', the first song to be banned was '*Zilikudula*' ([Commodities] are Getting Expensive) by a female singer, Ethel Kamwendo:

> Before elections you said problems will be reduced
> Poverty will be reduced, now what is this?
> Everything is now expensive, no jobs
> Money is in short supply, corruption is increasing.
> (Kamwendo, 1994)

The song was not gazetted as banned; an order was simply given to MBC staff to stop playing it. And, as the new elite accelerated their acquisitive consumption between 1994 and 1999, instead of 'improving the lot of Malawians', as promised, Billy Kaunda sang:

> *Agalatia mwataya chipangano* (Mr Galatia, you have
> broken your promises). (Kaunda, 1999)

Class

There was an underlying peasantry discourse about the 'false' economic promises of multi-party politicians using phrases like '*sungadye demoka-lase*' (you cannot eat democracy) (Lwanda, 1996, p. 8). And song lyrics were not necessarily polemical; there were clear distinctions in the lyrics between the elite (*mabwana*) and peasants or the working class (*azimwale*) (cf. Mbenjere, 2007). Some of the methods of critique involved pointing out the inadequacies of service provision by attacking those agents of government who were making inflated claims. For example, while doctors and Malawi health authorities congratulated themselves on providing 'one of the best organized HIV prevention services in Africa', Joe Gwaladi, seeing the actuality in the misery of the community and overcrowded hospital wards, pointed out the inadequacies, not by criticising the government directly, but the doctors:

> *Tengani ochenjera onse* (Take all the clever people)
> *Kuwaunjika pamodzi* (Lump them together)
> *Tengani madokotala onse* (Take all doctors)
> *Mwaunjike* (Lump them together)
> *Akuchepera kaba* (They are not fit for purpose)
> *Edzi ndi dolo* (AIDS is mighty). (Joe Gwaladi, 2006)

Charles Nsaku's '*Kuchipatala*' (At the Hospital) uncannily chastises medical and nursing staff for their differential treatment of rich and poor patients, specifically on the grounds of 'class'. Nsaku deliberately starts his song by describing the interminable 'waiting' imposed on poor and working-class Malawians at shops, hospitals, food distribution centres and utility providers. In the case of clinics and hospitals it is often while clerks or clinicians chat on the phone, attending to private business.

> *Tsiku lina nditadwala* (One day after falling ill)
> *Ndinapita kuchipatala* (I went to the hospital)
> *Nditafika kumeneko* (When I got there)
> *Ndinapeza odwala ena* (I found some patients)
> *Ataima pakhomo* (Waiting by the door)
> *Kukanizidwa kulowa* (Forbidden to enter)
> *Ndinafunsa ndichiani* (I asked what it was about)
> *Akuti nthawi sinakwane* (They said it was not time yet)...
> (Nsaku,1999).

He emphasises the point of waiting further, before bringing in the issue of class:

> *Patapita nthawi pang'ono* (After a short while)
> *Mkulu wina anabwela* (Some gent arrived)

Atavala suti yache (Wearing his suit)
Alonda ananjenjemela (The guard shook with deference)
Abwana inu lowani (Sir, you can enter)
Kukodola mkulu uja (Pointing at the gent)
Tonsefe tinyangananana (We just looked at each other)
Tati   dziko lathu lokondedwa (Wondering about our beloved nation)
Kukhala tidzikhala chonchi? (Is this to be our lot?)
Pakuti tilibe maina (Because we are nobodies). (ibid)

Nsaku goes on to identify two descriptors that often confer the same advantages as higher class in Malawi: beauty and grooming. In Malawi, fame can be equated with power because most famous people tend to be politicians.

Kukongola ndikudziwika (Beauty and fame/power)
Ndiziwili zosiyana (are two differentiating factors). (ibid)

Finally, Nsaku blames poor and indifferent service delivery on unnecessary deaths that occur in hospital:

Komabe mudziyesetsa poti tilibe kopita (But please try to be fair as we have nowhere else to go).
Matenda oyenera kuchila (Diseases that should be cured)
Akufera kuchipatala (Are causing deaths in hospital).
(Nsaku, 1999).

Much earlier, in 1999, Lucius Banda, towards the end of his 'radical phase', had declared in '*Mzimu wa Soldier*' (The Soldiers' Spirit) (1999):

Mzimu wanga udzakondwa poona kuti (My spirit will be happy to see)
Odwala akuthandizidwa mwachangu ndi chikondi (The sick treated with haste and love)
Ndinali soldier wa amphwawi (I was a soldier of the poor).
(Lucius Banda, 1999)

A few years earlier, fed up with the corruption of the multi-party politicians most of them re-treads from the one-party era, he had observed in '*Ali Ndi Njira Zawo*' (They Have Their Sly Ways):

Dzana ndi dzulo takhalira kuphedwa (In the past they killed us)
Lero takhalira kunamizidwa (Today they lie to us)

Nanga titani poti anthu ndi omwewa? (But what do we do: they are the same people?) (Lucius Banda, 1995)

Lucius Banda's frustration boiled over, a year later, in 'Cease Fire', a no-holds-barred rap track in English:

Take a bus on the M1 tarmac
You'll be delayed and searched at over six roadblocks
But when white people, Indians, rich people and politicians
Are passing with their Mercedes, BMW
Full of drugs and guns in their boots
All they get is a heavy salute from the polite policeman.
(Lucius Banda, 1996)

But even if the working class had a job that could be considered 'good', the working conditions were often appalling. Charles Nsaku's *'Ndiphike Nyemba'* (Let Me Cook Some Beans) gives voice to a driver long abused by a boss with a 'feudal mentality' towards workers. When the driver decides to stop by the roadside and air his grievances, the class issues become clear:

Bwana ndi nkhanza zanji (Sir, what kind of cruelty is this)
Mukundizunza chonchi ine dalaiva wanu? (That you torture me, your driver, like this?)
Tanyamuka dzana kuchoka ku Lilongwe (We left Lilongwe the day before yesterday)
Kubwela kuno kudzagwira nchito ... (To come here to work ...)
Chakudya mungodya nokha (You are the only one eating)
Pamene dalaivala wanu chidyere cha dzana. (When your driver's last meal was two days ago.)
Sindingathe kugwira nchito (I can no longer work)
Sindingathe kusintha gear bwana (I cannot even change gears)
Njala iku wawa (The hunger is biting)
Ndiphike nyemba; (I will have to cook some beans;)
Zikapsya ndiphike nsima. (After that, some *nsima* [maize porridge].)
Kaya mundichotsa nchito (Whether you sack me or not)
Bola ndipeze moyo! (It is better for me to live!) (Charles Nsaku, 1999)

Similarly, Billy Kachepa sang about class:

Anthu olemera, (Rich folk,)
Musatinyoze (Do not disrespect us). (Kachepa, 2007).

The lack of social justice and equity before the law for rich and poor motivated Anthony Makondetsa to write *'Tidachimwanji?'* (What Did We Do Wrong?) after he noted the differential justice given to charcoal vendors and elite business people also trading in charcoal:

> *Walira! Walira!* (He cries! He cries!)
> *Mdziko lache lomwelo mwanayu.* (In his very land, this child.)
> *Nkhanza zamu Nyasalande amayo!* (The cruelty in Nyasaland,
> *mama mia!*)
> *Tidalakwanji ifeyo?* (What wrong did we do?)
> *Mtundu wanga sukukondana ndi chilungamo;* (My people have no
> love or justice;)
> *Kuthetsa mitengo,* (Cutting trees)
> *Osauka okha* (Only [punish] the poor). (Makondetsa, 2006)

The human element is, of course, present. Lawrence Mbenjere admitted as much in *'Ndimasilira'*(I Do Envy):

> *Ndimasilira* (I do envy)
> *Ndimasilira ine nditakhala wochita bwino* (I wish I was rich)
> *Magalimoto kumangosintha sintha* (Changing cars often)
> *Tsoka ilo a Mbenjere kubadwa osauka* (Poor Mr Mbenjere, you
> were born poor). (Mbenjere, 2005)

Patronage

Given their critical voices, it is not surprisingly that some musicians experience both politically induced persecution and inducements. Evison Matafale, an outspoken Rastafarian musician, whose music criticised corruption, was allegedly tortured while in police custody (Tenthani, 2001). The 'people's champion', Lucius Banda, later succumbed to political patronage and by 2004 he was an opposition United Democratic Party MP, a big music promoter and one of the *mabwana* (big men). However, his sung criticisms of the incumbent Democratic Progressive Party and state President Bingu wa Mutharika earned him a prison sentence in 2006 after being found guilty of 'forging a school leaving certificate to qualify as an MP'.

It is this forceful, vengeful (as some would say) and poverty-driven patronage that binds poor Malawians to poor governance, as Joseph Nkasa observed in *'Nkhope'*, where he suggests

> *Kale kalero ...* (Long long ago ...)
> *Anasankha molakwika.* (They made the wrong leadership choice.)

Mwaumphawi, ndi umbuli (Due to poverty and ignorance)
Anasankha molakwika! (They made the wrong choices!) (Nkasa, 2003)

Nkasa was at his height during the second term of Bakili Muluzi and the first term of Bingu wa Mutharika. Like the first multi-party president, Bakili Muluzi, the second, Bingu wa Mutharika, had used patronage and some economic and physical repression to keep the opposition weak and divided. While Muluzi had been particularly adept at guiding the resurgence of the small middle-class elite at the expense of the peasantry, Mutharika was awkward and lacked the presentational skills to 'hoodwink' the peasantry. As the media was slowly muzzled and writers and journalists began to censor themselves, musicians took on more political stances. Joseph Nkasa, having blazed the trail as a major musical political critic, succumbed to the then President Bingu wa Mutharika's patronage in 2008. He wrote a praise song declaring Mutharika *'Mose Wa Lero'* (Today's [Biblical] Moses).

Anger

Like Lucius Banda, and before he became a millionaire from music and became partisan, Nkasa had, with irony and humour, reflected ordinary people's anger at their social conditions. In *'Ukali'* (Anger) he cheekily suggested that God, rather than poor governance, had brought the problems:

Nakulenga chepetsani ukali! (God, please reduce your anger!)
Ukaliwanu wabweletsa miliri muno! (Your anger has brought suffering!)
Ukali wanu watseketsa makampani! (Your anger has closed companies!)
Ukali wanu mafumu akudana! (Your anger causes chiefs to argue!)
Ukali wanu ndalama zikusowa! (Your anger has made money scarce!)
Ukali wanu watekenyesa edzi! (Your anger has spread AIDS!)
Ukali wanu kundende kukudzadza! (Your anger has filled prisons!)
(Joseph Nkasa, 2005)

And anger had from 1995 increasingly filled the working-class end of the musical public sphere, reflecting the patronage inspired 'hate speech' of politicians (Kayambazinthu and Moyo, 2002, pp. 87–102).

In *'Phungu Wanga'* (My Member of Parliament), Malume Bokosi chastises his, now corrupt, MP for forgetting the ideals that got him elected:

Phungu wanji wosalimbana ndichitukuko, (What kind of MP avoids tackling economic development,)
Koma kulimbana ndi makamisolo? (But instead spends time fighting ladies' undergarments?)

Malinga ndi sitailo mukugwira masiku ano (As for your political style nowadays)
Mwati chitukuko basi ndi chikho cha mpira! (You think football trophies are development!)
Bvuto latigwera pa Malawi lero (The problem with Malawi today is)
ndale tazisandutsa ngati mgode. (We have turned politics into personal goldmines.)
(Malume Bokosi, 2006)

Bokosi's reference to 'football trophies' is a riposte to the common ruse by politicians to form 'foundations' or 'trusts', often foreign- or local donor-funded. These trusts and foundations seek to promote development. In practice however, giving 'football trophies' and supporting football teams gives the politicians maximum exposure for very little return and infrastructural development. Surprisingly, a significant section of the youth appears to be impressed by these football trophy *phungus* (members of parliament).

Bokosi's anger is nothing compared to Lawrence Mbenjere's in '*Liyanja Achuma*' (Suits the Rich), where he complains

Kubadwa kosaukaku, (When you are born poor,)
M'mawa fwefwe kuseteka bwemba. (Smelly unwashed
body in morning.)
Akamakudutsa anthu akumayenda atatseka mphuno
(When people pass you they pinch their noses)
Kuopa kafwifwinono konunkha! (To avoid your body odour!)
Kamba kosowa sopo (Because we lack soap)
Tidzisamalira bwanji poti (How can we care for ourselves when)
Tikhalira tikusambira mchere? (We have to wash ourselves with salt [sweat]?)
Pamene anamafweteke (Meanwhile the filthy rich)
Akungoponda maGeisha! (Waste *Geisha* soap!)[1] ...
Umoyo wadziko lino unawayanja olemelawa! (Life on this earth suits these rich folk!) (Mbenjere, 2006)

Having made the complaint, he states that he sees the status quo as putting 'them' in a state of servility. It is a state of servility more akin to feudalism:

Chafera kwa ampichawa (The way things are)
Tidzingokhalira maganyu. (We should just depend on casual labour.)
Olo titatitipume (Even if we wanted to rest)

Atikoleka chingwe mkhosi (They would chain us)
Atikhikha chamkholingo (And kick us)
Ngati akuzinga kabado (As if chasing trash). (ibid)

It is a state in which they survive by hard work and a poor rough diet:

Nabola mukudya (As long as you eat)
Nsima yachigaiwa aNamgetso (Rough maize meal, Namagetso dear)
Toto ine! (Wife groans: Mama mia!)
Mamawa ulendo kukacha (At dawn, on daybreak go)
Kukatibula kumphanje! (Straight to till the hard soil). (ibid)

Mbenjere is not, however, accepting this state of affairs to last indefinitely:

Ndalama zimalamula (Money rules)
Koma lidzafika lachigumula; (But revolution day will come;)
Sitalaka ya a zimwale (The workers strike)
Pambali idzapha mashasha. (As a side effect it will kill the rich/elite's system.)
Tikhala ogodomala (We are being patient)
Pofuna kuona maso a nkhono. (Hoping to see the snail's eyes.)
(Mbenjere, 2006)

Mbenjere's 2006 song is notable for its 'Marxist' elements and the prediction that the workers' strike will, one day, 'kill' or 'bring down' the elite system'.

Mbenjere is not alone. One of the CD compilations, '*Defao Collection: Tidzatuluka M'munda*', has a title that translates as 'We Shall Come Out of the Field'. Students of Afro-American studies will recognise the 'coming out of the [cotton] fields' analogy. In another track, '*Bwanji Ndisowe*' (Let Me Commit Suicide), Nduna McLondon wants to escape from the 'poverty which has denied him food and clothes for his family' and from his 'unvalued' proletarian life. His violence, for now, is aimed at the self.

Singing the capitalist dream

In the title track of the *Defao Collection*, Evans Meleka reflects the 'feudalism' painted in Mbenjere's song:

Malawi ooh! (Malawi ooh!)[2]
Dziko langa! (My country!)

Mwadzinalako (Just like your name) *Tilipamalawi amoto!* (We are on flames of fire!)
Mulungu sanalenge munthu kuti akhale wopempha. (God did not create man to be a beggar.)
Tsiku lina (One day)
Tidzatuluka m'munda, (We will walk out of the fields,)
Tidzakolola tidzaimba lokoma. (We shall reap and sing a good song.)
(Evans Meleka, 2006)

And lest the listener blame a lack of education on their plight, we are told that they are educated:

Kusukulu tinapitako, tilinazo zoyeneretsa (We went to school and have qualifications)
Koma taonani lelo tingo tambalala pansi. (But see how unemployed we are.) (ibid)

However, educated or not, the bosses treat them with harshness:

Olo tigwire nchito tili ndi mabwana oopsya mtima, (And even when we work we have cruel bosses,)
Zowerenga za moto wathu angotiyesa akapolo ... (Counting our hell, they treat us as slaves ...)
Kuchita kusowa choti timeze! (We can't even find a mouthful to eat!)
Kuchita kusowa choti tivale! (We can't even find a thread to wear!)
Kumangolira ine. (I just cry.) (ibid)

Even those who choose to go a little beyond the subsistence level and follow the smallholder farming route find that, in the context of Malawi, nothing is like the promise:

Chuma chili munthaka koma lero sizikusonya. (Riches are in the soil, but today nothing is promising.)
Mlimi kupita kumsika pobwera akungolira. (Farmers take produce to markets and come back crying.)
Chabwino tigwire nchito malipilo akewo pepani. (Even when we work the salaries are miserable.) (ibid)

And finally Meleka asks the question that many Malawians have asked over the decades; a question that has seen Malawi, like Nyasaland before it, become a nation of migrant workers and migrants:

Kodi zoipa zoterezi zikuchitika kwathu kokhakuno? (Do these bad
things only happen in our land of Malawi?)
Kapenanso ku Amerika amaona zoterezi, ndakaika (Maybe in the
USA they experience similar things – I doubt it!)
(Evans Meleka, 2006)

This general dream is given focus by Charles Nsaku in *'Zelo-Zelo
Tambala'* (Net Payment to You Zero *Tambala*). In this song. Nsaku sings
about the exploitative capitalist tobacco-growing agri-business in which
smallholder tobacco farmers sometimes end up with negative payments
after loans and other input costs are deducted:

Nchito yoyambira kunasare kuja (Hard work dating from the nursery)
Lero kukolola zelo-zelo tambala (Now we reap zero *tambala*).
ONajere kubvutika kuthilila, (Najere struggled to water the seedlings)
October dzuwa lonse pathupi (In the scorching October sun),
Achita chiani aNajere ndiwana? (What will Najere feed the children?)
Kaselo shiti zelo-zelo tambala. (Sell sheet payout zero zero *tambala.*)
(Nsaku, 2007)

Nsaku then proceeds to list the way smallholder farmers get a shock at
the tobacco sales, as various deductions are made:

Kodi tinalakwa chiani eh paMalawi pano? (What sin did we commit
here in Malawi?)
Ndimvere chisoni (Give me a break)
Andidula ka one percenti (I have been deducted one per cent)
Sopo pomwepo (And soap expenses)
Auctioni pompo (And auction floor fees)
Oh transipoti (And transport fees)
Kubwela wotapa. (And the loan I took.) (ibid)

And then while praising the *bwana* (president) for opening a market for
smallholder farmers, he asks that he reduce the sales tax levied on the
small farmers 'next year'. He further records the toll on families, both
physical and emotional:

Oh thukutha lonse lija zelo-zelo tambala! (All that toil for zero zero
tambala)
Nanga Jemusi mumuuza chiani (What will we tell our son James?)
Mwana wolimbika (Our hardworking son)

Nchito yoyambira kunasare kuja (Hard work dating from the nursery)
Lero kukolola zelo-zelo tambala (Today we reap zero zero *tambala*)
ONajere kubvutika ndi khasu (Najere breaking her back hoeing)
Kusota fodya msana kuchita kupindika (Back bent sorting tobacco)
Ndikanena chiani kwa a Najere ndi wana (What will I tell wife Najere and the kids?)
Kaseloshiti zelo-zelo tambala. (Sell sheet reads: zero zero *tambala.*)
(Nsaku, 2007)

Some musicians suggested that, even if one survived the poor working conditions, it does not end there. Malume Bokosi spelled out the further problems in *Peshoni* (Pension), or rather the lack of it, in rural contexts:

Kuyambira nthawi ya Welensky[3] (Since Welensky's time)
Mpakana lero (Till now)
Ndikanagwirabe nchito ya ulimi (I am still a [subsistence farmer)
Ndikukalamba mphamvu zatha With age my strength is gone)
Lero kugwila mpini ungondipulumuka (Now when I hold a hoe it just slips through my fingers)
Umphawi walasa (Poverty bites)
Ukadya kukhuta thupi limabwela mphamvu (If you eat well the body regains strength)
Koma kudya kwalero (But today's diet)
Chikhala kuti kulima amapatsidwa peshoni (If subsistence farming was a pensionable occupation)
Ndikana pempha peshoni (I would have asked for a pension)
Kuti nanenso ndipume (So that I too can rest)
Peshoni! Ah! Peshoni! ([If only I had] a pension! Oh! Pension!)
(Bokosi, 2006)

The writing of this song coincided with Mutharika's first open moves towards favouring big business. Civil society activists, who were regarded by the peasantry as part of the elite, had helped to stop Bakili Muluzi's third term attempt and helped Mutharika during his first term. Mutharika's first term (2004–2009), given his small majority, was characterised by how religious and secular civil society activists came to his government's rescue, forcing a numerically strong but weak and disgruntled opposition to pass various bills. This dynamic helped Mutharika deliver 'significant developmental gains' in his first term for the peasantry. But these 'developmental gains' were temporary and merely consolidated a new elite-accelerated accumulation, rather than expand and diversify the economy in a 'pro-poor' manner. Even as he 'delivered', Mutharika was building a patronage system of Banda-esque strong-man power politics, including muzzling the press and academics, unwitting encouragement of tribalism by privileging one ethnic group (the Lomwe), authoritarianism and intolerance of dissent. This became overt during his second term, beginning in 2009. The success of the first term was, as in Mpakati's time in the 1980s, based on low wages.

By 2010, a convergence of global and internal economic and political factors, including human rights repression and worsening poverty, led donors to cut, suspend or withdraw aid, leading to significant hardships (foreign currency, commodities, fertiliser and energy shortages). These economic problems, in the face of a weak and inarticulate opposition, and now affecting the elite as well, brought together a disparate group of civil society, religious leaders, workers and their leaders, activists and vendors into a loose movement. By the beginning of 2011, matters were such that civil society organisations were spearheading opposition to the government, articulating the very concerns that musicians had been singing about two to ten years earlier. An agreed list of demands was put to President Mutharika with the proviso that if he did not respond positively there would be a mass protest on 20th July. Such was the 'arrogance' or confidence of the government that, the day before the demonstrations, Democratic Progressive Party 'Young Democrats' were sent out on to the streets to intimidate potential demonstrators.

Despite last minute injunctions, the demonstrations went ahead on 20th July 2011. Most of the demonstrators were *azimwale* from the peri-urban areas. The Malawi police over-reacted and 19 people were killed before the army was called out to restore order (Thom, 2011; BBC News, 2011).

Despite a change in government, occasioned by the sudden death of Bingu wa Mutharika in April 2012, little appears to have changed in the political economy of Malawi. The new administration, led by Joyce Banda, followed its own chosen path: that of power politics. The building of her People's Party at the expense of the people's expectations took precedence. The manner in which vast public resources were garnered to fund this exercise is still unravelling in 'Cashgate', a process that diverted funds from public sectors and that involved and politicised the Army, Police and parts of the Civil Service (Baker Tilley and the Malawi National Audit Office, 2014). Throughout her two year period, like Bakili Muluzi and Bingu wa Mutharika before her, she spent most of her time campaigning.

After a short honeymoon period with new President Joyce Banda's administration, the rising cost of living led to another mass demonstration, organised by the Consumer Association of Malawi (CAMA) with more support from *azimwale* than from the middle-class elite, which was planned for 17th January 2013. However, this demonstration was a limited success because 'elite' leaders, mostly belonging to non-governmental organisations, pulled out at the last minute citing security reasons. This move by the 'middle-classes' was seen as a betrayal by the *azimwale* some of whom accused the non-governmental organisations' leaders of having been fed 'scones' (being bought) by the government. Indeed Joyce Banda had co-opted critical journalists like Brian Banda of Capital Radio, as well as some NGO activists. And there was a sense of palpable expectation by elements of the NGO cadre and other middle classes that they would be co-opted.

Conclusion

Discourses, as we have briefly examined, are rarely if ever found in written reports, studies or other literature, despite these reports being about Malawi's 'dire poverty'. While writers, largely but not exclusively from the elite, tend to concern themselves more with human rights issues (Chimombo and Chimombo, 1996) and are intermittently and reactively active, most orature practitioners tend to be continuously active.

Orature addresses issues across the spectrums of religion, politics, economy, health and social concerns. Oral practitioners were, and are, arguably much more adventurous and brave than the writers in their composing, lyrics and ability to disseminate their product. Class separates most writers from most oral practitioners. There is an increasing resort to anonymity by writers so they can both criticise and continue to be part of the elite patronage network –that way they will not become economically marginalised.

Anger about neglect, marginalisation and repression, rather than despair, was characteristic of much of the post-1995 orature that I examined. And there was an almost palpable 'Marxist nature' to some of it. Schoffeleers and Roscoe (1985, p. 9) argued that [orature], if properly examined, 'provides a penetrating picture of a society's whole way of life'. This prediction, made when the façade of Dr Banda's autocracy obscured some of the underlying cultural dynamics, has proved accurate. This 'penetrating picture', in the case of Malawi, is often presented in a social vein with subtle, if at times shocking, humour in the lyrics (Lwanda, 2003). In 2003, I posited:

> It is often tempting to judge African popular music, due to the multiplicity of languages and its dance orientation, by its form or style

rather than its content. The meaning may thus often be ignored. (Lwanda, 2003, pp. 113–126)

In the case of Malawi, the content is both potent and portent, despite its often ambiguous nature (cf. Lwanda, 2003). Malawi musicians had been predicting:

> *Koma lidzafika lachigumula* (But revolution day will come)
> *Sitalaka ya a zimwale pambali* (The workers strike will)
> *Idzapha mashasha* (Kill the elite's system.) (Mbenjere, 2006)

On 20th July 2011, when some *azimwale* (peasants) took to the streets, it nearly did.

The current state of power political patronage, the relative passivity of the opposition (waiting their turn to 'eat'), the complicity of sections of the civil service and business as they seek to prolong a particular regime, all against a background of a gendered and stratified state and a civil society that is class oriented in the context of a Malawi afflicted with poverty, means that musicians will, for the foreseeable future, continue with similar discourses.

Notes

An earlier version of this work was first presented at the International Association for the Study of Popular Music (IASPM) Conference held at the Institute of Popular Music (IPM) at the University of Liverpool, 13–17 July 2009 and appeared in the conference proceedings edited by Geoff Stahl and Alex Gyde. See http://www.iaspm.net/proceedings/index.php/iaspm2009/iaspm2009/paper/viewFile/782/77. I would like to thank many colleagues for their helpful comments.

1. A luxury soap.
2. Malawi means 'flames of fire'.
3. Welensky was the Federal Prime Minister from 1956 to 1958.

References

Africa Watch (1990) *Where Silence Rules: The Suppression of Dissent in Malawi.* London: Africa Watch.

Baker Tilley and the Malawi National Audit Office, (2014). 'Report on Fraud and Mismanagement of Malawi Government Finances Covering transactions and controls in the six month period 1 April 2013 - 30 September 2013'. Report dated 21 February 2014, London: Baker Tilley business Services.

BBC News (2011) 'Malawi riots erupt in Lilongwe and Mzuzu' http://www.bbc.co.uk/news/world-africa-14217148 (Accessed: 23 July 2012).

Chimombo, S. and Chimombo, M. (1996) *The Culture of Democracy: Language, Literature, the Arts and Politics in Malawi, 1992–94*. Zomba: WASI.

Chirambo, R. M. (2002) 'Mzimu wa soldier: Contemporary popular music and politics in Malawi', in H. Englund (ed.) *Democracy of Chameleons: Politics and Culture in the New Malawi*. Uppsala: Nordic Africa Institute, pp. 103–122.

Chirambo, R. M. (2006) 'Traditional and popular music, hegemonic power and censorship in Malawi: 1964–1994', in M. Cloonan and M. Drewitt, M. (eds) *Popular Music Censorship in Africa*. Aldershot: Ashgate Publishing Limited, pp. 109–126. Chirambo, Reuben Makayiko (2009), Democracy as a Limiting Factor for Politicised Cultural Populism in Malawi, in: Africa Spectrum, 44, 2, 77–94.

Chirwa, W. J. (2001) 'Dancing towards dictatorship: Political songs and popular culture in Malawi' Uppsala: *Nordic Journal of African Studies*, 10, 1, pp. 1–27.

Gilman, L. (2001.) 'Purchasing Praise: Women, Dancing, and Patronage in Malawi Party Politics'. *Africa Today*, 48, 3, pp. 43–64.

Habermas, J. (1981) *The Theory of Communicative Action*. London: Beacon Press.

Habermas, J. (1991) *The Structural Transformation of the Public Sphere*. Cambridge MA: MIT Press.

Kamlongera, C., Nambote, M., Soko, B. and Timpunza-Mvula, E. (1992) *Kubvina: An Introduction to Malawian Dance and Theatre*. Zomba: Centre for Social Research.

Kaspin, D. (1993) 'Chewa visions and revisions of power: Transformation of the Nyau dance in Central Malawi', in J. Comaroff and J. Comaroff (eds) *Modernity and its malcontents*. Chicago: University of Chicago Press, pp 34–57.

Kayambazinthu, E. (1998a) 'The Language Planning Situation in Malawi', pp. 369–439 http://citeseerx.ist.psu.edu/viewdoc/download?doi=10.1.1.125.18 03&rep=rep1&type=pdf (Accessed: 21 November 2013).

Kayambazinthu, E. (1998b) 'I just mix: Code switching and code mixing among bilingual Malawians'. *Journal of Humanities* (Malawi), 12, pp. 19–43.

Kayambazinthu, E and Moyo, F. (2002) 'Hate Speech in the New Malawi', in H. Englund (ed.) *A Democracy of Chameleons: Politics and Culture in the New Malawi*. Blantyre: CLAIM, pp. 87–102.

Kishindo. P J. (2001) 'Authority in language: The role of the Chichewa Board (1972–1995) in prescription and standardisation of Chichewa'. *Journal of Asian and African Studies*, 62, pp. 261–283.

Lefebvre, H. (1971) (1984 version used) *Everyday Life in the Modern World*, translated by Sacha Rabinovitch. New York: Harper and Row.

Lefebvre, H. (1991) *Critique of Everyday Life, Volume I*, translated by John Moore. London: Verso.

Lefebvre, H. (2002) *Critique of Everyday Life: Foundations for a Sociology of the Everyday, Volume II*, translated by John Moore. London: Verso.

Lefebvre, H. (2005) *The Critique of Everyday Life, Volume III: From Modernity to Modernism (Towards a Metaphilosophy of Everyday Life)*, translated by Gregory Elliott with a preface by Michel Trebitsch. London: Verso.

LESOMA (The Socialist League of Malawi) (1981) 'Briefing: Malawi and SADCC'. *ROAPE*, 8(22), pp. 82–85.

Lwanda, J. (1993) *Kamuzu Banda of Malawi*. Glasgow: Dudu Nsomba.

Lwanda, J. (1996) *Promises, Power Politics and Poverty*. Glasgow: Dudu Nsomba Publications.

Lwanda, J. (2003) 'The [in]visibility of HIV/AIDS in the Malawi public sphere'. *African Journal of AIDS Research*, 2(2), pp. 113–126.

Lwanda, J. (2008a) 'Poets, culture and orature: A reappraisal of the Malawi political public sphere, 1953–2006'. *Journal of Contemporary African Studies*, 26(1), pp. 71–101.

Lwanda, J. (2008b) 'The history of music in Malawi'. *Society of Malawi Journal*, 61(1), pp. 26–40.

Lwanda, J. (2008c) *Music, Culture and Orature: Reading the Malawi Public Sphere, 1949–2006*. Zomba: Kachere.

Lwanda, J. (2009). *Kamuzu Banda of Malawi: a study in Promise, Power and Legacy*. Zomba: Kachere.

Lwanda, J. (2011) 'Music and social protest in Malawi', in D. H. Downey (ed.) *Encyclopedia of Social Movement Media*. London: Sage Publications, pp. 347–351.

Mapanje, J. (1981) *Of Chameleons and Gods*. London: Heinemann.

Marx, Karl. (1867) (Translation by Ben Fowkes, 1990) *Capital, Volume I*. London: Penguin Books.

Matiki, A. (2001) 'The social significance of English in Malawi', *World Englishes*, 20(2), pp. 201–218.

Mhone, G. Z. (1992) 'The political economy of Malawi – an overview', in G. Mhone (ed.) *Malawi at the Crossroads: The Post-colonial Political Economy*. Harare: Sapes Trust, pp 1–33.

Mpakati, A. (1973) 'Malawi: The birth of a neo-colonial state'. *The African Review*, 3(1), pp. 33–68.

Mustapha, A. F. (2012) 'The public sphere in 21st century Africa: Broadening the horizons of democratisation'. *Africa Development*, XXXVII(1), pp. 27–41.

Pryor, F. L. (1990) *Malawi and Madagascar: The Political Economy of Poverty, Equity and Growth*. New York: Oxford University Press.

Ranger, T. O. (1975) *Dance and Society in Eastern Africa 1890–1970*. London: Heinemann.

Rotberg, R. (1966) *The Rise of Nationalism in Central Africa: The Making of Malawi and Zambia*. Harvard: Harvard University Press.

Ross, A. C. (2009) *Colonialism to Cabinet Crisis*. Zomba: Kachere.

Rutherford, P. (2000) *Endless Propaganda: The Advertising of Public Goods*. Toronto: University of Toronto Press.

Schoffeleers, J. M. and Roscoe, A. A. (1985) *Land of Fire: Oral Literature from Malawi*. Blanytre: Popular Publications.

Searle, C. (1980) 'Struggling against the "Bandastan": An interview with Attati Mpakati'. *Race and Class*, April 1980, 21, pp. 389–401.

Semu, L. (2002) 'Kamuzu's Mbumba: Malawi women's embeddedness to culture in the face of international political pressure and internal lecal Change'. *Africa Today*, 49(2), pp. 77–99.

Shepperson, G. and Price, T. (1958) *Independent African*. Edinburgh: Edinburgh University Press.

Short, P. (1974) *Banda*. London: Keegan Paul.

Tenthani, R. (2001) 'Malawian farewell to "the prophet"' http://news.bbc.co.uk/1/hi/world/africa/1682708.stm (Accessed: 20 August 2006).

Thom, M. (2011) 'Exposed: 15 die of gunshots, MHRC reveal'. *Daily Times*, 16 August 2012.

Discographical references

Banda, Lucius. *'Ali Ndinjira Zawo'* On the CD *Cease Fire*. 1996. Balaka: IY Productions.

Banda, Lucius. *Cease Fire*. CD. 1996. Balaka: IY Productions.

Banda, Lucius. *Unity*. CD. 1999. Balaka: IY Productions

Banda, Lucius. *'Yahwe'* On the CD *Unity*. 1999 Balaka: IY Productions

Bokosi, Malume. *'Peshoni'* on MC *Malaulo Samapemphedwa*. 2006. Blantyre: OG.

Bokosi, Malume. *'Phungu wanga'* on the MC *Malaulo Samapemphedwa*. 2006 Blantyre: OG.

Chimombo, O. *'Zasintha'*. 1996 Blantyre: MC.

Defao Music. *Defao Collection: Tidzatuluka M'munda*. 2006. Blantyre: OG

Gwaladi, Joe. *Zakanika*. CD. 2006. Blantyre: Tempest.

Kachepa, Billy. *Anthu Olemera*. MC 2007. Kachepa cassette in my archives.

Kamwendo, Ethel and the Ravers. *'Zilikudula'*. 1994. Blantyre: Ravers.

Kaunda Billy. 1999. *'Agalatia Mwataya Chipangano'*. Balaka: IY Productions.

Makondetsa, Anthony. *Tidachimwanji*. MC 2006. Blantyre: Makondetsa.

Mbenjere, Lawrence. *Ndimasilira*. MC. 2005. Lilongwe: Mbenjere.

Mbenjere, L. *'Liyanja Achuma'* on *Biliwita*. CD. 2006. Lilongwe: Mbenjere.

Mbenjere, Lawrence. *'Amati Azimwale'* on *Udzaleka*. MC. 2009. Lilongwe: Mbenjere.

Meleka, Evans. *'*Tidzatuluka M'munda' on *Defao Collection: Tidzatuluka M'munda*. 2006. Blantyre: OG.

Michael B. *'Tilire'*. MC 2001. High Density Records HDBM5010.

Mikoko Banda. *'Mitala'*. c.1977. MBC recording in my archives.

Nkasa, Joseph. *'Nkhope'*. On .*Tigwilane Manja*. CD 2003. Blantyre: OG.

Nkasa, Joseph. *'Ukali'*. On the *Defao Collection*. CD. 2005. Blantyre: OG

Nkasa, Joseph. *Mose Wa Lero*. CD. 2008 Blantyre: OG

Nsaku, Charles. *'Ndiphike Nyemba'*. On *COSOMA 10th Anniversary*. CD. Lilongwe: COSOMA.

Nsaku, Charles. *'Kuchipatala'*. On *Charles Nsaku*. CD 1999 Balaka: IY.

Nsaku, Charles. *'Zelo-zelo Tambala'* On the MC *Tiwana Kundende*. 2007. Blantyre: OG

Phiri, Saleta. *'Zinthu Zasintha'*. On *Ndirande Blues*. CD PAM 025 1995. Glasgow: Pamtondo.

UDF Party Workers. 1993. *'Kodi CCAM Nchiani?'* Song on the video *UDF Rally at Chiradzulo*, February 1993. Copy in my archives.

Index

Printed and bound by CPI Group (UK) Ltd, Croydon, CR0 4YY